Mountaineer Jamboree

JACK   GEORGIA SLIM

SMILEY

BETTY LEE   LEE MOORE   BUDDY

BUDDY STARCHER
— AND HIS —
MOUNTAINEERS

MAGGARD
STUDIO
CHARLESTON W VA
1938

Mountaineer Jamboree

Country Music in West Virginia

Ivan M. Tribe

Foreword by Senator Robert C. Byrd

THE UNIVERSITY PRESS OF KENTUCKY

Frontispiece: Buddy Starcher and his Mountaineers, 1938.
Standing, l-r, Jack Carter, Robert (Georgia Slim) Rutland, and Smiley
Sutter. Seated, l-r, Betty Lee, Lee Moore, and Buddy Starcher.
Photo from the author's collection.

Scholarly publisher for the Commonwealth,
serving Bellarmine College, Berea College, Centre
College of Kentucky, Eastern Kentucky University,
The Filson Club, Georgetown College, Kentucky
Historical Society, Kentucky State University,
Morehead State University, Murray State University,
Northern Kentucky University, Transylvania University,
University of Kentucky, University of Louisville,
and Western Kentucky University.

Editorial and Sales Offices: The University Press of Kentucky
663 South Limestone Street, Lexington, Kentucky 40508-4008

00 99 98 97 96   5 4 3 2 1

Library of Congress Cataloging-in-Publication Data

Tribe, Ivan M.
    Mountaineer jamboree : country music in West Virginia / Ivan M.
 Tribe.
        p.   cm.
    Republication of the 1984 ed. with an afterword.
    Includes bibliographical references, discography, and index.
    ISBN 0-8131-0878-0 (pbk. : alk. paper)
    1. Country music—West Virginia—History and criticism. I. Title.
ML3524.T74   1996
781.642'09754—dc20   96-28809

To Deanna

We love to hear those Hill Billys
With guitar or string band
Because they play old-fashioned tunes
Us folks can understand.

—Louvada Caplinger

Contents

Illustrations follow page 114

Foreword

People often ask me, "What is folk music?" "What is country music?" "What is bluegrass?" "What kind of music do you have in West Virginia?" These are not easy questions to answer, and they will perhaps never be answered to everyone's satisfaction. But Ivan Tribe's meticulous study, *Mountaineer Jamboree*, is a welcome contribution in showing what a many-splendored thing country music in West Virginia has been.

At the base of it all stands the folk music—that rich repository of song and tune expressed and shared by people for their own enjoyment and satisfaction. Whether sung or played, whether performed at home or away, whether in private or in public or in communal gatherings ranging from homecomings to church services, folk music in West Virginia has provided the cultural reservoir out of which all other forms of regional music have sprung. There is music from the early pioneers but also music from a variety of ethnic groups and from Afro-American West Virginians. And while this music is an integral part of West Virginia's history, I am happy to say that it remains a part of our present as well.

What we call country music in West Virginia is rooted in the folk music, yet it also shows influences from the popular music of America. People today think of country music as a national style emanating from Nashville and other central locations. But Ivan Tribe's history shows us how much more complicated the development of country music has been, and—in West Virginia, at least— how strongly it is rooted in local and regional tastes and values. We may be proud of how many West Virginians made records in the history of country music, but those records also remind us that country music styles have varied in different regions. There is not, and should not be, a single country music style. Rather, we can all take pride as Americans in the regional diversity that exists throughout our great country.

One of Professor Tribe's most interesting contributions is his history of country music on radio in West Virginia. Perhaps because radio broadcasts have been less well preserved than commercial recordings, we sometimes forget the importance of radio as a medium in the development of country music. Certainly this volume indicates how important radio and television have been in West Virginia—from the nationally famous Wheeling Jamboree to a kaleidoscope of local and regional programs.

Bluegrass occupies a special niche in West Virginia's history, as it does in other states of the Upper South. It developed in the years after World War II as an alternative to the emerging standard country sound. West Virginians participated in the development of bluegrass in its early years, and it continues to be a popular grassroots style throughout the state.

As one reads *Mountaineer Jamboree*, one is struck not only by the famous names associated with West Virginia, but also by the hundreds of other singers and instrumentalists who have made their unique contributions. This is a history not simply of famous personages but of those who have worked and shared and contributed their creative spirit to give musical expression to West Virginia's values and heritage.

Robert C. Byrd

Preface

Some years ago a country music novice suggested that Bill Malone's fine book *Country Music U.S.A.* covered everything that anyone might possibly wish to know about the subject. Although Malone did indeed produce an excellent piece of scholarship, it soon became apparent to numerous scholars, collectors, and fans that the soft-spoken gentleman from Texas had barely scratched the surface. In the fifteen years since *Country Music U.S.A.* first appeared, several top-flight monographs have examined various aspects of this cultural form by means of biographies, stylistic analyses, and intense looks at particular geographic regions. The present work fits into the last category, making a special effort to examine the role played by radio stations and musicians in disseminating the music to their fans. Since West Virginia is a relatively small state with a population distributed in many working-class industrial towns over a rough and broken topography, it offers a good opportunity to study the impact of regionally popular entertainment.

Numerous persons have earned my gratitude for a variety of assistance—in fact, far too many to mention all of them here. Many musicians and their kinfolk gave generously of their time through interviews and answering letters; most of them are listed in my citations. Those who gave repeatedly of their time and deserve special mention include John, Kyle, and Walter Bailes; John Bava; Slim Clere; Wilma Lee Cooper; Jimmy Dickens; Ernest Ferguson; Melvin Goins; Garland Hess; Lee Moore; Charles Satterfield; Margie Shannon; Buddy Starcher; Doc, Chickie, and Peeper Williams; and the Boys from Kentucky.

In Washington, I appreciated the support of Senator Robert C. Byrd, Carl Fleischhauer, and Alan Jabbour, the latter two of the American Folklife Center. Other country music scholars and collectors such as Joe Bussard, Norm Cohen, Bob Coltman, Steve Davis, Eugene Earle, Dave Freeman, Linnell Gentry, Archie Greene, Bob Hyland, Fred Isenor, Bill Jaker, Pete Kuykendall, Bill Malone, Frank

Mare, Guthrie Meade, John Morris, Don Nelson, Eddie Nesbitt, Robert Nobley, Earl Northrup, Bob Olson, the late Reuben Powell, Steve Tucker, D.K. Wilgus, and Charles K. Wolfe came to my aid more than once. So too did Bob Pinson and Ron Pugh of the Country Music Foundation, Linda Painter of the John Edwards Memorial Foundation, Bill Schurk of the Music Library and Sound Recordings Archive at Bowling Green State University, Ken Sullivan of the West Virginia Department of History and Culture, and the staff of the West Virginia Collection at Morgantown. John Newbraugh of Berkeley Springs and Ed McDonald formerly of Burlington helped with their data on the geographically remote—from me—eastern panhandle. Patsy and Donna Stoneman proved helpful as friends in Nashville.

Although this field of scholarship may seem somewhat distant from my studies with premier urban historian Charles N. Glaab, his influence and mature judgment are nevertheless reflected here. At Rio Grande my colleagues Marcella Barton, Linda Bauer, James Doubleday, Jack Hart, Jerry Jones, Bob Pfeifer, Merlyn Ross, Leonard Seyfarth, Gloria Wood, and Sharon Yates offered bits of aid and encouragement, as did administrators David Black, Clyde Evans, Paul Hayes, Clodus Smith and Wade Underwood. Two students, Lori Meadows and Donna Pasquale, helped sustain my spirit with their heart and humor. Local friends who have helped in various ways include Neil and Marie Dickson, Meryl Houdasheldt, the Ralph Jetts, Ron Nelson, the Grady Newman family, and the William Ratliffs.

The National Endowment for the Humanities provided Summer Seminars for college teachers at opportune times to allow me to study at the JEMF and with folk-culture historian Lawrence LeVine, southern historian George B. Tindall, and two dozen stimulating young scholars including West Virginia native Marie Tyler-McGraw. The Berea College Appalachian Studies Fellowships through Appalachian Center Director Loyal Jones also provided some funds that helped subsidize my research. Darlene Stuchell typed the final manuscript. Rio Grande College provided timely financial support. Finally, my wife Deanna spent many hours at the typewriter, endured more than a few headaches, and accompanied me on numerous trips into the West Virginia hills. All of these persons and institutions have earned my gratitude.

Lastly, a personal note seems to be in order. My original interest in West Virginia country music dawned back in 1950 when I first heard the voice and deejay work of Cherokee Sue at WPDX radio in Clarksburg. Unlike the country stations nearer my home in southeastern Ohio, Sue played records by the likes of Molly O'Day, the Bailes Brothers, the Coopers, and Buddy Starcher. She also sang on live programs, as did people like Cindy Coy and the Mayse Brothers. On Saturday nights, distant favorites on the "Grand Ole Opry" included Little Jimmy Dickens and Hawkshaw Hawkins. Later I had ample television exposure to Buddy Starcher, Ralph Shannon, Sleepy Jeffers, the Davis Twins, Lori Lee Bowles, and the comedy of Herman Yarbrough. Although my interests, schooling, and work sometimes took me far afield, an appreciation for their sound never left me. Some ten years ago I became interested in country music scholarship. Being geographically remote from Nashville my inclinations most often led me in the direction of such unheralded Mountain State practitioners of the art as the Lonesome Pine Fiddlers, the Goins Brothers, the Lilly Brothers, the Bailes Brothers, Molly O'Day, and Lee Moore—in essence, those who came from, moved to, or lived in West Virginia. Finally, with a little prodding, first from *Goldenseal*'s Tom Screven and then from the University Press of Kentucky the book has become a reality. I hope that I have done justice to an important part of the heritage of West Virginia, the Appalachian region, and indeed America and even beyond.

1. The Mountaineer Folk Music Heritage

Back in 1918 a lady named Anna Davis Richardson accidentally encountered two elderly women in Clarksburg, West Virginia. The first, Rachel Fogg, had migrated to the city from the rural county of Upshur some decades earlier with her blacksmith husband. Mrs. Fogg had a daughter named Viney who played the mouth-harp. The other lady, Nancy McAtee, some years older, had grown up in more distant Randolph County but had lived for some fifty years in a tiny shack between the railroad track and the Monongahela River in Clarksburg. Both women lived in relative poverty in different—albeit equally unfavorable—neighborhoods and did not know one another. Yet to Mrs. Richardson's amazement, both knew many old songs and ballads. These included such lyrics as "The Ship's Carpenter," "Jesse James," "The Little Rosewood Castel [*sic*]," "A Pretty Fair Maid in a Garden," "My Name is Bill Staffato," and a gospel song called "The Raising of Lazareth." "Old Nance" McAtee recalled that she had "heered the soldiers singin'" when the war wuz goin' on and pickin' their banjos and fiddles." In all, she contributed some twenty-four song texts to Mrs. Richardson, while Rachel Fogg supplied twenty-two. Mrs. Fogg, uneasy about her meager education, later sent a note telling Mrs. Richardson to "plese tipe rite them before you send them to the office."[1]

Anna Davis Richardson, a middle-class urban lady much interested in mountain folklore, had become increasingly aware of a musical culture that persisted among rural and rural-derived white people especially, but not exclusively, in the Appalachian and southern piedmont areas. In 1918 the commercial phenomenon that later came to be termed first hillbilly and then country music did not yet exist. Yet elements that went into that music had been around in one form or another for quite some time. In fact, representatives of the scholarly world and modern technology both discovered these various components within a few years of one another. Their responses to the sounds they heard, however, moved in diverging directions. The scholars sought to preserve the tunes and texts of the mountaineers before modernization could change their vanishing way of life. The technicians, propelled by the American capitalistic spirit and scientific innovation, sought to reproduce and distribute the music via phonograph recordings and radio to a larger audience, and to augment not only their own income but perhaps that of the musicians as well.

In earlier days the native populace of western Virginia and surrounding areas played instruments and sang songs primarily for their own amusement. From the planting of the first settlements, this situation seemed to hold true whether the pioneer residents came from English, Scotch-Irish, or German forebears. One of the most notable types of music was that of the fiddlers who accompanied country dances. These frolics provided some of the rare diversions from the backbreaking labor that went hand in hand with turning virgin forest lands into farms. In 1824 Joseph Doddridge wrote of the significance of weddings in his youthful days a half-century earlier. "After dinner the dancing commenced, and generally lasted till the next morning. The figures of the dances were three and four-handed reels, or square sets and jigs. . . . Toward the latter part of the night, if any of the company, through weariness attempted to conceal themselves for the purpose of sleeping, they were hunted up, paraded on the floor, and the fiddler ordered to play 'Hang on till to-morrow morning.'"[2] One reason for the immense popularity of weddings, according to Doddridge, was that, unlike other frontier social activities such as barn raisings or corn huskings, the marriage celebration contained no labor obligations. This left more time for fiddling and dancing.

As one can easily surmise, the fiddle constituted the one essential instrument that provided a little fun and pleasure for those living in the backwoods. That other Scottish musical instrument, the bagpipe, never gained a foothold on the American frontier, and the fiddle alone could, if needed, furnish sufficient dance music. Eventually other instruments played background rhythm and added to the fullness of the sound. These included the banjo, apparently of African descent; the guitar, which seemingly arrived later on the scene, making its way into the mountains sometime after 1900; and the piano, which provided good backing but had the disadvantage of being both expensive and relatively immobile.

With the passing of time, the mountain people attained sufficient leisure to hold country dances for more than just special occasions.

In his autobiography William MacCorkle, a prominent West Virginia political figure, described life as he had known it in the remote mountain counties of Nicholas and Webster as a young lawyer in the late 1870s. Calling the dance "the chief joy in the lives of these people," MacCorkle recalled that dances usually lasted "all through the holidays and continued for a month thereafter." The dancers favored the "square-dance and the Virginia Reel" and frequently arranged a night in advance which neighbor would host the next evening's festivities. The dance would go on until midnight and then break up, only to resume again the following evening. According to MacCorkle, "certain people who were great dancers," together with musicians and dance callers, gained the status of being "pre-eminent in their community."[3]

Some West Virginians acquired a love of country dancing that became almost legendary. One Captain John Slack told how he and a noted dancer named Safe Jones once piloted a raft of logs down the Elk River. Someone on shore invited Jones to stop and he "danced two whole nights and then came back to the raft taking it on to Charleston." An old fiddler once told MacCorkle that he and his caller Steve Weeks had played all over Clay, Webster, and Nicholas counties for years until the caller "got religion" and decided to quit working dances. The fiddler began worrying about ruining the social life of a three-county area, and after he and Weeks consulted the scriptures the latter concluded that "there was no harm to play on the fiddle," but not for dancing. Weeks went on to become a successful preacher, and the fiddler played for his own amusement only, while other musicians and callers appeared who filled the musical needs of the local populace.[4]

The country dance remained popular in rural West Virginia and other Appalachian states into the twentieth century. Many of the older country musicians who became professionals, including such diverse figures as Chickie Williams, Buddy Starcher, James (Carson) Roberts, and Harry Tweedy, all received their first impressions of music through the dance. Williams, Starcher, and Roberts were influenced by their old-time fiddling fathers, and Tweedy learned dance music from neighbors and through his own activity as a pre-adolescent old-time fiddler.[5]

By the same token, strictly traditional musicians of a similar generation, such as John Johnson of Braxton County, Blackie Cool of Randolph County, and Mose Coffman, had similar early musical experiences, although their parents had less musical background, and they never gained wide fame as professionals. But both Johnson and

Cool had brief flirtations with careers as radio "hillbillies." One early twentieth-century fiddler, Harvey VanGoshen of Morgan County, gained sufficient local fame that President Woodrow Wilson invited him to the White House. According to one anecdote, VanGoshen asked the president if he could get the slick train that transported him home—the Capitol Limited—to stop at the tiny station nearest his home, and Wilson obliged. An eastern panhandle fiddle band, the Morgan County Ridge Runners, retained sufficient popularity in their locality to endure for some forty years from 1906.

The country dance generally featured many old hoedowns for the faster reels and square dances, including "Devil's Dream," "Billy in the Lowground," and "Soldier's Joy," and used slower tunes like "Over the Waves" and "Midnight Serenade" for waltzes. They also included hornpipes of popular origin that had entered tradition, such as "Durang's Hornpipe," originally written to commemorate the talents of the early nineteenth-century professional dancer John Durang of Philadelphia, or "Rickett's Hornpipe," which honored one John Bell Ricketts, an antebellum entertainer who delighted his audiences by dancing hornpipes on the backs of galloping horses.[6]

The fiddle and the country dance, while of prime significance, comprised only one portion of the entire folk music heritage. Ballad singing held an almost equally important position. The ancestors of the pioneer settlers had brought with them a wide variety of old lyrics which had already passed through several generations of oral tradition in the British Isles and would continue to be handed on by parents to their offspring. These ballads told of love, crime, human foibles, and experiences with the supernatural encountered by both commoners and noblemen in Britain's bygone days. By the late nineteenth century the scenes their words painted must have seemed strange to the Appalachian mountaineers who had little with which to identify in the words they continued to sing. Nonetheless, ballads such as "Barbara Allen," "Lady Alice," "Henry Lee," and "The Farmer's Curst Wife" persisted through oral tradition from the late middle ages into the era of the automobile.

In 1824, Joseph Doddridge wrote: "Singing was another . . . amusement among our early settlers. . . . Robin Hood furnished a number of our songs, the balance were mostly tragical. These last were denominated 'love songs about murder.' " Doddridge suggests that native American ballads had already begun to compete with those of British origin. This is further substantiated by the 1830 diary of Luther Haymond, who traveled eastward from Clarksburg and apparently heard songs dealing with the exploits of pioneer adventures and heroes not yet totally vanished from the contemporary scene and memory.[7] It is not surprising, given this heritage of translating memorable events and myths into song, that West Virginians would continue the tradition in coming decades. They supplemented their oral transmission with printed songsheets and eventually made use of technological innovations such as the radio, phonograph record, or television to further this goal.

While the West Virginia mountaineer retained much of his British ballad heritage and sometimes supplemented it with lyrics of his own creation, he also enriched his musical knowledge with songs of commercial origin. Minstrel shows attained popularity from the 1840s and some of their folk-derived and folklike material found its way into the hearts and heads of rural and hill people. So too did songs from the Broadway stage and New York music publishers. Sentimental numbers that told of tragic love or nostalgia for mother and home in particular retained a popularity in the backwoods long after they had been forgotten by their professional and urban creators. The professional folklorist in later years might draw a great distinction between the sad, romantic tales of unfortunate love found in such antiquated ballads as "Barbara Allen" or "Fair Ellen and Lord Thomas," and the lyrics of Tin Pan Alley origin like "The Little Rosewood Casket" or "Two Little Girls in Blue," but the rural Appalachian did not. The true "folk" music lover had no use for academic criteria in his choice of favorites. He could-and did-incorporate both types of songs into his heritage without seeing any inconsistency.[8]

A song of particular importance to the West Virginia tradition came into existence in 1886 when H.E. Engle, a Braxton County singing school teacher, obtained a copy of a poem written some time earlier by Ellen Ruddell King, a former Glenville resident then living in Pennsylvania. Engle composed music to fit Mrs. King's lyrics, entitled "The West Virginia Hills," and eventually it became the state song. The first verse and chorus of the lyrics read:

Oh the West Virginia Hills how majestic and how grand,
With their summits bathed in glory like our Prince Emmanuel's Land,
Is it any wonder then that my heart with rapture thrills,
When I stand once more with loved ones in the West Virginia Hills.

Oh those hills, beautiful hills,
How I love those West Virginia Hills
Whether o'er land or sea I roam, still I dream once more of home
A-nd my friends among the West Virginia Hills.

Most Mountain Staters have apparently found both words and tune to their liking. Although not a true folksong, its lasting popularity with the folk can be demonstrated by citing the numerous parodies it has inspired on subjects ranging from farm life to labor protest.[9] Especially after the advent of Prohibition, "The West Virginia Hills" inspired songs about West Virginia moonshine, as John and Emery McClung did in the couplet "Bright lights on Broadway; the sun shines down in Dixie, / But we'll have moonshine in the West Virginia Hills" or Billy Cox in his verse:

> Oh the West Virginia Hills, and it's how I do love you,
> For I've got the sweetest girlie and she makes the best home brew,
> And when I rise up in the morn I go out and get my corn
> From my friends among the West Virginia Hills.

Around the beginning of the twentieth century American scholars began to discover that the Appalachian Mountains extending from Pennsylvania to Alabama contained a vast repository of story and song that represented a fast vanishing way of life, indeed even a disappearing civilization, that of the Anglo-Saxon. Old-stock intellectuals such as Henry and Brooks Adams thought they saw America being overrun by a wide variety of inferior immigrant groups who were diluting if not outright corrupting Anglo-Saxon blood and civilization. The southern mountain dwellers—virtually forgotten since their Union loyalties were exploited during the Civil War—suddenly began to receive new attention. Home missionaries sought to uplift Appalachians into the American mainstream while ballad scholars rushed into the hills to obtain texts of medieval British lyrics before it was too late.[10] Although civilization both within and without the mountains failed to collapse, the academics did arrive in time to convey to later generations some idea of what songs circulated in oral tradition before the impact of the radio and the phonograph.

The most renowned of all these collectors, the Englishman Cecil Sharp, came to America at the urging of Olive Dame Campbell, whose husband presided over the Pine Mountain Settlement School. From 1916 through 1918, Sharp spent some forty-six weeks in the five mountain states of West Virginia, Virginia, Kentucky, North Carolina, and Tennessee. He concentrated his efforts in the two latter states and spent relatively little time in West Virginia, where he collected only three ballad texts, all in Greenbriar County. At that time the Mountain State seemed more under the impact of industrialization than the upland portions of those states farther south (the number of coal miners in the state had indeed more than tripled—to 92,132—between 1900 and 1918) and therefore less fertile ground for the preservation of old British ballads.[11] Yet the contacts between this new industrial society and mountain culture in West Virginia had already resulted in the creation of some of the most memorable and enduring native American folksongs, including "John Henry," "John Hardy," "The New River Train," and "The Wreck on the C. & O." But Sharp interested himself primarily in British balladry, only secondarily in American originals, and not at all in religious lyrics, which he dismissed as not being "folk" no matter how persistent they might be in oral tradition.

That West Virginia proved fertile ground for the kind of folklore that produces good ballads should be demonstrated by the aforementioned songs. Although no historian or folklorist has come up with any more evidence than oral tradition can substantiate, it seems likely that a Negro steel driver named John Henry worked on the Big Bend Tunnel construction crew in the early 1870s. His feats of strength and endurance subsequently resulted in songs about him by both blacks and whites. The songs' theme of man challenging the machine has appealed to men of all races and Henry has become perhaps Afro-Americans' all-time leading folk hero. The former slave and steel-driving man taking on the white man's technology in the form of the steam drill and defeating it with fatal consequences transcends the West Virginia locale of the original.

> John Henry was standing on my right hand side,
> The steel hammers on my left, Lord! Lord!
> "Before I'd let the steamer beat me down,
> I'd die with my hammer in my hand, by God!
> I'd die with my hammer in my hand."

Some seventeen years after the Chesapeake and Ohio Railway's completion, a brave young locomotive engineer named George Alley met his death within a few miles of the tunnel where John Henry achieved folk immortality. On October 23, 1890, Alley's train, the F.F.V., ran into a landslide three miles from Hinton. According to some stories, a Negro who worked in the Hinton roundhouse put together the essentials of a ballad that has become known by such titles as "The Wreck on the C. & O.," "George Alley," and "Engine 143."

> Along came the F.F.V., the fastest on the line,
> Came running o'er the C. & O. Road, just twenty minutes behind;

Came running into Sewell, lies quartered on the line,
And then received strict orders for Hinton, away behind.

When she got to Hinton, her engineer was there,
Georgie Allen was his name, with blue eyes and curly hair;
His fireman, Jack Dickinson, was standing by his side,
Waiting for his orders, and in his cab to ride.

Georgie's mother came to him with a basket on her arm,
Saying, "Now, my darling son, be careful how you run;
For many a man has lost his life trying to gain lost time,
And if you run your engine right, you'll get there yet on time."

"Mother, I know your advice is good; to your letter I'll take heed;
I know my engine is all right and I know that she will speed;
And o'er this road I mean to fly with a speed unknown to all,
And when I blow for the Big Bend Tunnel, they will surely hear
   my call."

Georgie said to his pal, "Jack, just a little more steam;
I mean to pull old No. 4 the fastest ever seen;
And o'er this road I mean to fly with a speed unknown to all,
And when I blow for the Stock Yard Gate, they will surely hear
   my call."

Georgie said to his pal, "Jack, a rock ahead I see;
I know that death is waiting to grasp both you and me;
So from this cab you must fly, your darling life to save,
For I want you to be an engineer when I am sleeping in my grave."

"O no!" said Jack, "that will not do; I want to die with you."
"O no!" said Georgie, "that will not do; I'll die for me and you."
So from the cab, poor Jack did fly; the river it was high,
And as he kissed his hand to George, old No. 4 flew by.

Up the road she darted; against the rock she crashed;
Upside down the engine turned, upon his breast it crashed;
His head upon the firebox door, the burning flames rolled o'er;
"I'm glad I was born an engineer to die on the C. & O. Road."

Georgie's mother came to him, "My son what have you done?"
"Too late, too late my doom is almost run."
The doctor said to Georgie, "My son, you must lie still;
Your precious life may yet be saved, if it be God's holy will."

"O no, doctor, O no! I want to die so free;
I want to die with my engine, old 143."
His last words were, "Nearer, my God, to Thee, nearer to Thee,
Nearer, my God, to Thee, nearer to Thee."

A third West Virginia incident that produced a major folksong hero took place in 1893 and 1894 in McDowell County, where a petty black outlaw named John Hardy received a death sentence for killing a man during a card game argument. Hanged on January 19, 1894, Hardy in real life seemingly had few of the qualities to become a folk hero:

John Hardy was a desperate boy,
He carried a gun and a razor every day;
He killed him a man for a rowdy young girl,
And you ought to have seen Johnny get away, poor boy.

The similarity of the names Hardy and Henry, together with some confusion among singers, led some scholars (including John Harrington Cox) to believe that John Hardy and John Henry were the same man. Although some doubt still exists as to whether they were in fact one person or two, there can be no question that there are two distinct songs.

Other folksongs also came out of the Mountain State. "A West Virginia Feud Song" related the details of personal quarrels in Lincoln County that involved a man named Ale Brumfield. Although the composer of the ballad borrowed rather heavily from a Kentucky ballad about "The Rowan County Crew," his parodied composition managed to be orally transmitted over a hundred miles to Pocahontas County on the state's eastern edge where a communicant sent it to Cox. "The Logan County Jail" related a youth's descent into a life of crime and an eventual prison sentence. Another widespread folksong of possible West Virginia origins is "The New River Train," in which only the chorus alludes to either the railroad or the stream, but the close relationship between the Chesapeake and Ohio and its line through the narrow New River gorge leaves the impression that when one is "Ridin' on that New River Train," one may well be somewhere between Montgomery and Hinton, West Virginia.[12]

The formal collection of West Virginia folksongs began in 1913 when a student from Lewis County named E.C. Smith gave West Virginia University (WVU) English Professor John Harrington Cox a copy of "John Hardy." Cox promptly sent the text to *The Journal of American Folk-Lore* and also initiated the West Virginia Folk-Lore Collection. Two years later a WVU summer school lecturer, C. Alfonso Smith, suggested that the state's public school teachers could provide a noteworthy service by collecting old ballad texts from their individual, scattered locations throughout West Virginia. Cox, together with WVU Vice President Robert Armstrong and Walter Barnes of Fairmont Normal School, organized the West Virginia Folk-Lore Society. Smith left a copy of an article he had previously written entitled "A Great Movement in which Every One can Help" suggesting methodology in ballad gathering. Over the next several years—especially in the next two—a great amount of material was accumulated, sent to Cox by teachers, students, and other interested persons. Most of this material found its way into Cox's doctoral dissertation, "Folk Songs from West Virginia" at Harvard in 1923, and two years later appeared in book form as *Folk-Songs of the South*, containing 398 texts of 185 ballads.[13]

In retrospect, John H. Cox seems an unlikely person to have led the folklore movement in West Virginia. A native of Madison County, Illinois, he came to Morgantown and WVU in 1903 at the age of forty with a background that included public school teaching, YMCA directing, and a year of teaching English at the University of North Dakota. Although previously unacquainted with mountain culture, he evidently adjusted well to life in the state, for he remained in Morgantown not only for the rest of his academic career but for his entire life. (He lived until 1945.) Prior to 1913 his scholarly pursuits consisted primarily of translating and adapting tales of medieval knighthood and chivalry for children and upgrading the quality of English instruction in public schools.[14]

While Cox and his volunteers conducted their search for West Virginia folksongs, they came into contact with some interesting singers of these old-time numbers. In Clarksburg, as mentioned earlier, Anna Davis Richardson located a pair of elderly lady "minstrels" with "cracked old voices," Rachel Fogg and Nancy McAtee, who proved so interesting that Cox visited them himself in 1921.

Cox received direct communications of ballad texts and also did some of his own field collecting. From former Governor MacCorkle, for instance, he gathered a text of "John Hardy" and some information that contributed to the confusion of the individual's identity. From John Adkins, a crippled printer living in Lincoln County, Cox obtained thirteen texts and an account of how Adkins had learned the songs as a boy at "log-rollings, house raisings, parties, dances, etc.," where "some singer" would "be called upon to render one or more selections of these old-time songs." Burwell Luther, a Wayne County farmer and sometime state political appointee, contributed numerous texts to Cox before his death in 1920. Luther had learned his material while calling square dances at work-related social events such as corn-huskings in his younger days. In the summer of 1918, Cox visited the southern counties where he found such interesting characters as Sam Turman, an unlicensed pension attorney who lived near Williamson. The old gentleman stayed up late into the night relating ballad texts until the excitement caused by a train wreck in front of Turman's home terminated their labors. The local school administrator Charles Ellis contributed an account of the Hatfield-McCoy feud and sang a ballad about Kentucky's Martin-Tolliver feud. He planned to take the university professor to see the already legendary Devil Anse Hatfield, but they were unable to rent horses and had to cancel their trip. In McDowell County, Cox located a sixty-seven-year-old fiddler and singer, A.C. Payne, who had been on the jury at the trial of John Hardy. Payne entertained the learned man for an entire day with his fiddling, singing, and story telling. Last and most interesting of all, Cox visited James Knox Smith, a Negro lawyer, who not only sang "The Vance Song" for Cox but also furnished him with an account of the crime, trial, and execution of John Hardy and even presented a photograph of the hanging to the West Virginia Folk-Lore Society.[15]

Although Cox's *Folk-Songs of the South* proved to be the premier collection of West Virginia ballads, both he and other scholars supplemented this work. In 1939, Cox authored a follow-up study entitled *Traditional Ballads and Folk-Songs Mainly from West Virginia.* Another folklorist, Josiah H. Combs, concentrated his efforts on Kentucky texts, but about a third of his collection came from West Virginia. This situation derived from the two years Combs served on the WVU faculty and also from his relationship with Carey Woofter of Glenville State College. Combs once described Woofter as "an eccentric West Virginia Mountaineer, as eccentric as his name sounds" and "an avid student and collector of folksongs and Highland dialect." Woofter contributed much of the West Virginia material to the Combs Collection, although suspicion exists that he sometimes altered the texts of the material he gathered. The Combs book, containing only about 14 percent of his entire collection, appeared as *Folk-Songs du Midi des Etats-Unis* in a 1925 French edition. An English version containing a chapter omitted from the original was not published until 1960, some seven years after Combs's death. Although the published part of the song collection is not a large one, it and the entire Combs Collection remain useful. Furthermore, his lengthy introduction on the Appalachian mountaineer and his music is quite perceptive. As the academically trained son of an Eastern Kentucky highland family (his father had served as a county sheriff during the infamous

French-Eversole feud), Combs could describe the upland dwellers from an almost unique viewpoint.[16]

The accomplishments of Cox and Combs in ballad collecting was complemented by the later work of Louis Watson Chappell in field recording. Chappell, a North Carolinian and an English Professor at WVU, purchased a disc recording machine in 1937 and spent more than a decade gathering material from West Virginia instrumentalists and singers. Those recorded by Chappell included fiddler Edden Hammons and at least one person who had some experience as a radio performer, John F. Johnson, who played several times in Charleston and then at WRVA in Richmond, Virginia. Scott Phillips, as a member of the St. Leo Puddle jumpers string band, had played often at WMMN Fairmont in the early years of that station.

A third factor influencing the West Virginia folk music heritage, supplementing the traditional fiddle-dance tunes and ballads, derived from the gospel singing of the backwoods camp meetings. The great wave of religious enthusiasm on the Appalachian and Ohio Valley frontiers dates from the Cane Ridge Revival of Bourbon County, Kentucky, in 1801. From that beginning the Second Great Awakening spread throughout the region. Some evidence exists that the revival phenomenon in western Virginia may have at least partially manifested itself earlier and somewhat independently of the well-known excitement in Kentucky. At any rate, denominations like the Baptists and the then relatively new Methodists who "sang the rousing Wesleyan hymns" established themselves as the most widespread sects in the area. In those early days both groups relied heavily on emotional preaching and fervent hymns to bring their spiritual messages home. By 1845 traveler Henry Howe could sketch and describe the presence of a Methodist "Religious Encampment in the Mountains." Unfortunately no meetings took place during Howe's visitation. After 1830 another new sect, the Campbellites or Disciples of Christ, led by Alexander Campbell of Bethany in the nonhem panhandle, exerted wide influence, especially in the nonhem counties. Like some Baptist groups, the Disciples frowned upon instruments in the churches and stressed a cappella, or unaccompanied, hymn-singing.[17]

Although strongest in Kentucky, certain Baptist groups such as the Primitive and Old Regular Baptists (sometimes called "Hard-Shell" Baptists) also had some strength in southem West Virginia. These denominations often followed such antiquated practices as having some leader "line-off" or chant a line of a hymn which the rest of the congregation would then sing. Like Alexander Campbell's followers, these groups opposed musical instruments in the churches, preferring to "make a joyful noise unto the Lord" with their voices only.[18]

These sacred folksongs derived from a variety of oral traditions and printed matter. Many seem to have been written by local composers during or shortly after the great periods of religious fervor. Some likely developed from slaves' spirituals. Others came from the pens of English hymn-writers of the earlier Great Awakening, such as Isaac Watts, Charles Wesley, and John Newton. By the second decade of the nineteenth century local compilers arranged them into book form and area printers serviced their regional markets. These compilers often included songs of their own composition and arranged the music in shape-note form for use in the singing schools. Ananias Davidson's *Kentucky Harmony*, published at Harrisonburg, Virginia, in 1817, was probably one of the first to make its way into the western counties. Two hymnals printed in Winchester—James M. Boyd's *The Virginia Sacred Musical Repository* in 1818 and James P. Carrell's and David S. Clayton's *The Virginia Harmony* in 1831—likely had some impact in the mountain areas. Hymnals published in river cities, such as William Moore's *Columbian Harmony* in Cincinnati (1825) or Samuel Wakefield's *Western Harp* at Pittsburgh (1844), undoubtedly influenced those areas serviced by Ohio River transport. By the middle of the century, denominational printing houses began to issue standard hymnals which eventually displaced the older and folksier harmony and harp books. By 1870 the newer books began to displace the older ones in the northern two-thirds of West Virginia and by 1900 they were becoming dominant also in the southern third. The influence of the older styles remained, however, in oral tradition.

As decades passed and numerous Methodist and some Baptist congregations became more sedate and sophisticated in their religious practices, many mountain people began to seek spiritual comfort and emotional release in the newer and more fundamentalist Protestant bodies. These denominations included the Church of God, Church of the Nazarene, Assembly of God, and groups whose names included such words as Apostolic, Holiness, and Pentecostal. Highbrow Christians often termed these sects "Holy-Rollers" because their services were characterized by fervent preaching, enthusiastic singing, and emotion-filled experiences of confession and conversion. Such practices had become an almost necessary folk ritual to thousands of marginally educated churchgoers, particularly in the rural South and mountain areas. Although the more affluent, schooled, and urban Christians—both black and white—heaped scorn upon their less fortunate country kin, the practitioners of the "old-time religion" defiantly continued to shout and sing in the manner to which they were accustomed. In so doing they not only maintained their right of religious freedom but also helped to preserve another aspect of their folk music culture. As commercial country music began to develop in later decades it owed a great debt to gospel music traditions. Nationally this can be demonstrated through examining the careers of performers as wide-ranging in style as Andrew Jenkins and Elvis Presley, or through such West Virginia groups as the Bailes Brothers or Wilma Lee and Stoney Cooper.

A few other factors influenced the West Virginia mountaineer's folk music heritage—and indeed that of other Appalachian dwellers—in addition to the long-established traditions of country dances, ballads (British, American, and sentimental), and songs of the camp meeting and rural church. The music of Afro-Americans looms as an important contribution to the tradition although it tended to be felt less in West Virginia than in other southern states because of the lower black population. Still it had considerable impact, especially in the southern part of the state. Instrumental stylings, bluesy lyrics, and songs like "John Henry," "John Hardy," "Stacklee," and a variety of couplets that appear to float from one song to another, all illustrate Negro influence. And in northern West Virginia the music of East European immigrants made its presence felt and led to some fusing of polka sounds into country dance music and to an interest in and some appreciation for such an instrument as the accordion among Mountain State dwellers.

In the earlier days the various strands of this West Virginia musical tradition displayed only a slight tendency to mingle. Church people frowned on country dances as sinful and strongly opposed the fiddle because of its association with dancing—hence the nickname "devil's box." The back-up instrument, the banjo, fared little better, drawing the wrath of many preachers and churchmen. Ballad singing had little in common with dance music although some fiddlers might on occasion sing short nonsense rhymes or phrases associated with certain tunes. If ballads were sung at country dances, it was usually as entertainment while the dancers and musicians took rest breaks. Banjo pickers eventually became the instrumentalists most likely also to sing ballads. "Follow the boy with the banjo," came to be the advice given by some folklorists to young collectors, although Josiah Combs scoffed at this because he contended that banjo pickers' "songs are hardly to be recognized." He held that banjo players who sang excessively readapted material to make word phrasings more compatible with instrumental accompaniment or to assimilate new songs. Thus he argued that the banjoist may indeed perform an old ballad like "The Gosport Tragedy" or "Pretty Polly," but he may also pick and sing something like the once popular Will S. Hays love song, "I'll Remember You Love in My Prayers."[19] Although Combs might not have agreed at the time, in retrospect one can say that what the scholar saw as poor taste was simply the way the folk process worked. The folk do not pick and choose their material according to any set academic standard.

Eventually other instruments and songs found their way slowly into merging musical traditions. Some fiddlers finally sang now and then although seldom at the same time they played. A fiddle player who held his instrument under his chin, for instance, found it quite difficult to sing while playing. One who held the fiddle against his breast could—at least in theory—do both simultaneously. At one time in the mountains it was said that a fiddle and a banjo played together comprised a band, and if any instrument accompanied singing it tended to be the dulcimer. But by the time of World War I the primitive dulcimer had become increasingly rare and string bands of three or more members more common. Guitars and mandolins, once scarce in the mountains, came into wider use after the 1890s as they gained in accessibility through the Sears, Roebuck and Montgomery Ward mail order catalogs.[20]

Folklorists and historians in the last decade and a half have increasingly realized that the musical form called by such names as old-time tunes, hillbilly, and most recently country, evolved directly from the Appalachian and southern folk heritage. One finds this assumption in the work of a broad sampling of academic writing. Cultural historian Russel Blaine Nye, for instance, argues that country music developed from three major "strands"—the ballad tradition, the Protestant evangelical hymn, and the sentimental popular songs of the nineteenth century. English Professor Charles K. Wolfe views it as having been, like jazz, "a regional folk art" in the beginning that helped the rural southern populace "come to grips with the traumatic changes of the modern age," and as originating from such diverse sources as ballads, fiddle, church, and black music. Folklorist-anthropologist John Greenway calls it "a folk music supported by the folk" which "to the White south is the equivalent of Negro 'soul'" and "a rallying point of a defeated but fighting culture." Historian Bill C. Malone writes: "Hillbilly music developed out of the reservoir of folksongs and ballads brought to North America by the Anglo-Celtic immigrants and gradually absorbed influences from other musical sources until it emerged as a force strong enough to survive, and even thrive, in an urban-industrial oriented society."[21]

These ideas have not always been current in academic circles, however, and are not yet universally accepted. For many years most of the scholarly world viewed country music as commercial trash "unworthy of serious attention." Numerous trained folklorists and song scholars disliked its crass and openly commercial character. Malone writes that "hillbilly music," although "the creation of the folk," failed to "conform to the romantic conception of folk music so prevalent in the twenties." It also did not meet that self-image which many middle-class mountain and southern people had of themselves and their region.[22]

In West Virginia this negative viewpoint remained current in the 1960s. Writing for a state centennial folksong book in 1963, one ballad scholar wrote: "With the advent of radio and the public juke-box, . . . a new kind of music called 'hillbilly' was first heard by the American public. It was supposed to have come from the hills, but no real hill-dweller had ever before heard it. Actually, much of it came from the pens of those who sang it, with a good part of it coming from the confines of Tin Pan Alley."[23]

Why did "hillbilly music, the creation of the folk," face such rejection from the same scholars who so idealized the folksongs of the mountain people of West Virginia and other Appalachian states? As this book and others demonstrate, most of the early "hillbilly" performers heard on phonograph records came from rural southern backgrounds, including many from the uplands. Even the Tin Pan Alley figures, sometimes dubbed "citybilly" writers and singers, such as Vernon Dalhart, Carson Robison, Bob Miller, and Bobby Gregory, have been shown to have possessed strong rural or southern roots and turned to hillbilly music only when its commercial success seemed likely. As Nye correctly stated, many of the early country songs had originally been of sentimental popular (or Tin Pan Alley) background, but in most instances they had long been forgotten in cities and survived mostly in the oral traditions of backwoods America. In many cases the old popular lyrics outlasted the original Tin Pan Alley tunes, for the hill-country singers frequently sang them to tunes quite different from those composed by their creators. Within West Virginia all of the early recording artists and the vast majority of radio performers were authentic rural and mountain people who spent most of their lives in the state or in adjacent Appalachian areas.

The first problem faced by mountain musicians in gaining acceptance came from the label "hillbilly," which bore strong negative connotations that soon carried over to the music as well. Although mountain people do not seem to have applied this label to their music, the name once applied became forever fixed as a stereotype. One early recording group took the name Hillbillies and have been styled "the band that named the music." Early professionals accepted this sobriquet for their material in innocence, and their successors have since fought to overcome it and gain acceptance.[24]

One suspects also that within hill-country culture some prejudice had arisen against professional musicians rather than their music. Melvin Artley, in his dissertation on West Virginia country (meaning "folk") fiddlers, tried to distinguish the "hillbilly fiddler" from the "true country fiddler." Through all this explanation of the amateur versus the professional and the one who learned through tradition versus the one who learned from radio or records to supplement the old master's teaching, Artley suspected that "jealousy" on the part of the non-pro toward the pro had a lot to do with this attitude. Josiah Combs stated that by 1925 the notion had developed that fiddlers who went from dance to dance trying to make a full-time occupation of their musical skill were often regarded as lazy and a threat to the work ethic. As emerging show business people, their morals were suspect. Combs cites one old mountaineer who said that whenever he heard there was a fiddler in town, he went home and hid his daughter. While people could still claim a love for fiddle music, the term "thick as fiddlers in hell" conveys a great deal about the declining image of the man who wielded the bow. Finally, Molly O'Day, a successful hillbilly performer for a decade, contends that her community had an ambivalent attitude toward musicians. While the majority apparently enjoyed, appreciated, and identified with the music, they thought that anyone who played for a living, including radio entertainers, were too lazy to perform manual labor.[25]

So while the academic and scholarly world looked down on hillbilly music and those who played it, the hill and country folk, whose culture and romantic past these learned persons so zealously studied, took it to their hearts and saw it as their own, despite some continuing doubts about professional entertainers. Louvada Caplinger, wife of one of the early West Virginia artists who embraced musicianship as an occupation, probably stated the attitude of the listener better than anyone:

We love to hear those Hill Billys
With guitar or string band
Because they play old-fashioned tunes
Us folks can understand.[26]

It would be wrong to argue that country music as it developed was pure folk music, but in the beginning there existed within it a great deal of folk music. When the early country artists first began to step in front of a radio or phonograph microphone, they did not suddenly create a new type of music but rather performed the music they had already been playing for some time, in a new setting. Even as the music became ever more commercialized and encompassed other cultural influences within it, much of the old remained. Country music was—and continues to be—very much a folk-derived art form.

2. Pioneer Recording Artists

The formal recording of what we now call country music began in June 1922 when the Victor Talking Machine Company received the duo of Alexander Campbell "Eck" Robertson and Henry C. Gilliland—both old-time fiddlers—into their New York studios. The pair had recently performed at a Civil War Veterans' Reunion and then decided on their own initiative to see if they could make phonograph records. Victor engineers allegedly recorded the young Texas cowboy Robertson and the elderly ex-Confederate Gilliland to get rid of them. They subsequently released two fiddle solos by Robertson and two twin fiddling pieces without much fanfare.

Quite independently the real boom in recording such musical material took place the following March in Atlanta. At that time Ralph Peer of the General Phonograph Company (Okeh Records) went to the Georgia city to seek material for the firm's prospering new line of "race" records, or Negro music for black audiences. While he was there a local distributor named Polk Brockman persuaded Peer to record two numbers by Fiddlin' John Carson, a local entertainer of some renown among the white working-class populace. Carson's renditions of "The Old Hen Cackled and the Rooster's Going to Crow" and "The Little Old Log Cabin in the Lane" sold surprisingly well. Peer scheduled another session for Carson and also recorded an Atlanta group, the Jenkins Family, led by the blind evangelist, songwriter, and singing newsboy Andrew Jenkins.

Okeh also released a pair of vocals made in New York by a young Virginia textile worker, Henry Whitter, who like the Texas fiddlers made the journey north in hope of cutting records. Like Carson's records, Whitter's vocals of "Lonesome Road Blues" and "Wreck of the Southern Old 97," accompanied by his own guitar and harmonica, sold well. In 1923 phonograph record sales had begun to decline because of public infatuation with the new medium of radio, and executives sought new markets for their products. Having recently found one promising outlet for expanding sales in race records, they now saw similar possibilities in what Okeh began to label "old-time tunes."

In 1924 three rival companies entered the new field in rapid succession. Columbia found the team of Riley Puckett and Gid Tanner, a blind vocalist-banjoist and a fiddler, in the Atlanta area, a lady fiddle-banjo duo from North Carolina named Samantha Bumgarner and Eva Davis and in Winston-Salem they located Ernest Thompson, a blind ballad singer with a high (almost squeaky) tenor voice who played a wide variety of instruments. The Aeolean Company (Vocalion Records) tapped Tennessee talent, recording the fiddling of one Uncle Am Stuart, the harmonica and guitar of Blind George Reneau (a young studio vocalist named Gene Austin did the singing on Reneau's earliest recordings), and, most significant of all, a banjo player and vocalist of some years' experience on southern vaudeville circuits, Uncle Dave Macon.[1]

The third firm, the Starr Piano Company of Richmond, Indiana, makers of Gennett and Champion Records who also leased material to Sears, Roebuck and Company, recorded West Virginia (and also Kentucky) performers. On June 14, 1924, a fiddle band composed of two brothers, Charles and Harry Tweedy, made five masters in the Richmond studio. Three numbers consisted wholly of traditional fiddle tunes, "Rickett's Hornpipe," "Wild Horse," and "Chicken Reel." "Turkey in the Straw Medley" and "Repaz Band" featured Charles "Big Red" Tweedy playing piano. The fiddle tunes boasted the talents of the not quite eighteen-year-old Harry "Little Red" Tweedy.

Recording constituted a new experience for the Tweedys that June day in Indiana, but performing did not. Sons of an Ohio County country doctor, the Tweedy Brothers learned their community's music as children in the environs of the family home four miles north of Wheeling. Harry recalls that although an older sister read music he did not, and while she originally taught him the basics of fiddling he soon surpassed his teacher. He picked up techniques from older area musicians, especially an old fiddler named Bill Rausch. Charles Tweedy, four years older, began to play piano and spent a lot of time listening to recordings of everything from ragtime to light classics. The oldest brother George also fiddled, but apparently never with the dexterity of young Harry, who began playing at square dances when he reached the tender age of seven. By the late teens Charles and Harry had become established musicians in their locality. About 1921 or 1922 the Tweedy Brothers took to the road as professional musicians under the guidance of their father. They soon found themselves entertaining in a wide variety of locales, including Ohio riverboats, small town theaters, county fairs, medicine shows, and even burlesque houses. They first played on radio in 1922 at the then new and relatively weak station of WLW in Cincinnati.

After their initial recording session (they would subsequently do four more between 1925 and 1930) the Tweedys adopted a format that while perhaps crude by urban standards proved lucrative to them for several years in rural parts of the Upper South and Midwest. They traveled from town to town performing shows from the rear of a flatbed truck. Their record firm furnished a piano bearing a sign "Donated by the Starr Piano Company, Richmond, Indiana," while Harry and sometimes George performed a variety of fiddle tunes. Sometimes they had advance bookings but at other times they might just drive in, set up their show, and when a crowd had gathered pass the hat. Although in the beginning the Tweedys performed mostly old traditional hoedown numbers and waltzes, they eventually played some popular songs as well. Much of their crowd appeal apparently derived from Harry's use of a variety of substitutes for a fiddle bow, including a rolling pin, a large wooden spoon, and even a large piece of wood painted yellow and carved to look like a giant banana. They also tried singing at times—mostly comedy numbers—but Harry contends that none of the brothers had much vocal talent. In the mid-1930s Harry obtained a girl vocalist (and wife) known on stage as "Cindy, the Singing Cowgirl," who filled their needs for a singer.

By the 1930s the Tweedys usually worked regularly on some radio station, where they built up a reputation in order to draw bigger crowds at their live appearances. They performed throughout much of the United States, even going as far west as Reno, Nevada, and California. At times they worked shows with cowboy actors such as Hoot Gibson. Frequently they returned to West Virginia, working at WWVA Wheeling two or three times, and also at WCHS Charleston. Charles Tweedy remained a bachelor his entire life, but after Harry and Cindy had children in school, traveling became more difficult and in the mid-1940s the Tweedys began to ease their way out of the business. Settling in Columbus, Ohio, Harry became a city bus driver but continued to play here and there on a part-time basis. Bars, local dances, and shows at Hillbilly Park near Newark, Ohio, furnished him plenty of opportunity to keep his fiddle active. Charles died in 1970 and Harry plays but little today—mostly to amuse himself or close friends. George Tweedy lives in Pittsburgh, but he and Harry seldom have a chance to see one another. Nonetheless, the Tweedy Brothers played a highly significant role in the 1920s, not only because they were talented musicians and the first West Virginians to record, but because they were one of the first professional hillbilly bands in the country and among the few to successfully use a piano in their act. Furthermore, their recordings of such tunes as "Cripple Creek," "Birdie," "Sugar in the Gourd," and "Ida Red" received wide distribution through Sears, Roebuck and Company catalog sales.[2]

Based on the pattern established elsewhere by other companies, one would expect Starr's and West Virginia's second recording artist to be a ballad singer, preferably blind. Whether by accident or design, this did indeed prove to be the case. On December 16, 1924, David Miller recorded "Lonesome Valley" and "Little Old Log Cabin in the Lane" in a Cincinnati studio. Apparently only the latter song, an obvious cover of the Carson and Puckett renditions already available on Okeh and Columbia respectively, was ever released although a later re-recording of "Lonesome Valley" by Miller eventually appeared on Gennett. W.R. Callaway, a sometime Huntington resident and talent scout, wielded a guiding hand in the career of Miller and other recording artists from that area.

In a technical sense Miller was not a West Virginian, but he had lived in the Mountain State for several years. Born in the small Ohio River community of Miller in Lawrence County, Ohio, on March 7, 1893, David Miller worked primarily as a laborer on a local fruit farm before entering military service in World War I. Soon after joining the army he developed granulated eyelids which caused eventual blindness, but the government turned down his pension request. He had earlier moved across the river to the Huntington suburb of Guyandotte and taken up music seriously to sustain himself and his family. Known as "the Blind Soldier," Miller developed a unique guitar style and possessed an adequate, albeit archaic and perhaps erratic, tenor vocal style. Much of his recorded work remains unreleased, leading one to question the evenness of its quality.

Miller placed a number of fine old ballads, hymns, and especially antiquated popular songs on record over the next seven years but never attained much fame outside the Huntington area and relatively little even there. He did play extensively on WSAZ, the local radio station, but often as part of a group. The Gennett record label was the only one to use his real name and they sold fewer copies than Champion, on which label he was known as Oran Campbell, or as Dan Kutter or Frank Wilkins on the Sears, Roebuck releases. All of Miller's 1929 Paramount recordings used the pseudonym Owen Mills, and on his 1931 work for the American Record Corporation sometimes only the nickname "the Blind Soldier" appeared on the labels. Although Miller remained active in music until just a few years before his death on November 1, 1959, he remains little known even to many of that small fraternity of dedicated old-time record collectors. This is unfortunate because Miller constituted one of the most traditional singers and guitar players ever to record, even in the earliest years. His repertoire, for instance, included such material as an early white version of the Negro ballad "That Badman Stacklee," the old sentimental Civil War song "Faded Coat of Blue," "It's Hard to Be Shut Up in Prison" (a variant of the traditional "Logan County Jail" [Laws E 17]), and the guitar instrumentals "Jailhouse Rag" and "Cannonball Rag."[3]

The Tweedy Brothers recorded again in January 1925 and thrice afterwards. David Miller had five more sessions beginning in 1927. Meanwhile Ernest Stoneman, a Virginian working in Bluefield, heard Whitter's records and, believing he could do better, proceeded to prove his point by initiating a long career as a recording artist.

Becoming a country recording artist in the early days seems sometimes to have been a relatively simple process if one had such an inclination. Local record distributors or retailers might suggest hometown musicians whose popularity seemed marketable, as Polk Brockman had done with Carson. In other instances figures such as Eck Robertson, Whitter, Stoneman, and later Blind Alfred Reed would contact the record firms and work out their own arrangements. Here and there an enterprising individual such as Dennis Taylor of central Kentucky or the Huntington area's W.R. Callaway would become middlemen in the process by recruiting, auditioning, and managing musicians and in return would receive all or part of their royalties. Eventually Callaway went to work for the American Record Corporation, concentrating his efforts on such major figures as Gene Autry, Cliff Carlisle, and the threesome of Asa Martin, Doc and James Roberts (who had been among Taylor's early discoveries). Along with Ralph Peer, first of Okeh and then of Victor, Frank Walker of Columbia, and Callaway, the company-hired "A. & R. men" (artist and repertoire) emerged as the key figures who auditioned talent, chose songs, and made decisions concerning releases. Men working for the largest company, Victor, such as Peer, Eli Oberstein, and Steve Sholes, and for its chief rival, Columbia, led by Walker and, perhaps most significant of all, Art Satherly and his successor Don Law, directed record sessions from the earliest days into the era of the Nashville sound.

After the pioneering efforts of the Tweedys and David Miller, no new West Virginia musicians entered recording studios until the fall of 1926. The first of these to do solo performances, Frank Hutchison, who became known as the Pride of West Virginia, attained a degree of individuality in his stylings that marks him as one of the most unusual old-time musicians in the entire spectrum of the 1920s. A native of Raleigh County, where he had been born March 20, 1897, Hutchison grew up in Logan County and became one of the few white guitarists who displayed sufficient black blues influence to play in the bottleneck style, in which the guitarist slides a bottleneck across the strings rather than fretting with the fingers. Hutchison probably used a penknife, however. He also recorded unique songs that in one form or another would endure in the developing commercial country music tradition—"Coney Isle," which would reappear as a top hit in 1961 as "Alabam" and would revitalize the sagging career of Cowboy Copas, and "The Train that Carried My Girl from Town," which brings wild applause from modern folk festival fans when performed by Doc Watson. Between 1926 and 1929 Hutchison waxed thirty-two numbers on the Okeh label, of which twenty-nine would be released. His songs also included "Johnny and Jane," an unusual variation of the old British broadside "Will the Weaver," the black badman ballad "Railroad Bill," and novelties like "C. & O. Excursion" and "K.C. Blues," both of which afforded Hutchison the opportunity to display his instrumental talents on both guitar and harmonica.

During the 1920s Hutchison pretty much made his living as a musician, putting on shows in coal-camp theaters which often included not only his music but such features as black-face comedy and even motion picture showings. At a 1927 Okeh session he took to the studios with him three local associates who recorded six sides as the Williamson Brothers and Curry. Led by twenty-three-year-old fiddler Arnold Williamson, the band cut an early version of "John Henry" entitled "Gonna Die with My Hammer in My Hand." Although they never did another session, Arnold and Irving Williamson continued to play in Logan County for many years.

The Depression hit hard in Logan County and by 1932 Frank Hutchison moved to Chesapeake, Ohio, where he worked and entertained on steamboats. For a time he resettled in West Virginia, operating a small grocery/post office in the hamlet of Lake. A fire in April 1942 destroyed his combination business and home and he went to Ohio again in search of work. He died in Dayton of cancer on November 9, 1945, virtually a forgotten man.[4]

The other West Virginian to first record in 1926, Roy Harvey of Beckley, alternated between playing guitar in a well-known group, Charlie Poole's North Carolina Ramblers, and leading his own band.

More often than not Harvey used the same name for his aggregation as Poole did, although fellow West Virginians comprised most of the membership. Harvey had been born in Monroe County in 1892 and went to work for the Virginian Railway. He eventually became an engineer but lost his job as a result of a labor dispute in 1923 (which he later immortalized in his song "The Virginian Strike of '23"). He then went to work in a Beckley music store and joined the Poole band as guitar player in time for their 1926 Columbia session. In the late 1920s the North Carolina Ramblers probably constituted the best rural string band in the country and—next to the Skillet Lickers, a Georgia group that included Tanner and Puckett—the best known. The North Carolina Ramblers played a variety of traditional breakdowns mixed with old minstrel songs and sentimental popular material of Tin Pan Alley origin. They even recorded a couple of old British ballads found in the Child Collections.

In addition to his Columbia recordings with the North Carolina Ramblers, Harvey recorded some solo songs on that label, duets with Poole, duets with the band's first fiddler, Posey Rorer (the band's second fiddler, Lonnie Austin, lived in Charleston, which then made the North Carolina Ramblers two-thirds West Virginian), and duets with at least three fellow Mountain Staters. The latter included vocals with Earl Shirkey (1900-1951), a native of the village of Freeport in Wirt County. Shirkey, the son of a local physician, had allegedly been schooled in Switzerland where he learned yodeling techniques. Combining this new talent with the vocal music of his mountain heritage made Shirkey a welcome addition to the North Carolina Ramblers' touring unit.

Since Poole disliked it, Shirkey never yodeled on the Rambler recordings, but he displayed his skills on a series of sixteen duets with Harvey released under the names Roy Harper and Earl Shirkey. Several of these songs parodied older ballads and enlarged upon the myth of the mountaineer as a maker of corn liquor—"When the Roses Bloom Again for the Bootlegger," "The Bootlegger's Dream of Home," and "Moonshine in the West Virginia Hills." Others such as "Kitty Waltz Yodel," spotlighted Shirkey's specialty or dealt with more serious topics like the Virginian railroad strike. "When the Roses Bloom Again for the Bootlegger" proved to be one of Columbia's better selling discs of 1928, with sales of 72,545. Harvey also waxed six guitar duets for Columbia in 1930 with another Beckley resident, Leonard Copeland. Experts consider these numbers to be among the best old-time guitar instrumentals ever recorded.

Harvey also recorded with his own North Carolina Ramblers band on both the Brunswick and the Paramount label. Those for Brunswick apparently all stem from a 1928 session held in Ashland, Kentucky, and include a fine version of "George Collins" (Child 85) and such old sentimental favorites as "Mary Dear" (in which the soldier survives the war but returns to find the grave of his true love at their prearranged meeting place), together with a newly composed event song, "The Bluefield Murder." In June 1931 Harvey did a session with Gennett which included more guitar duets, this time with a Wolf Pen, West Virginia, fiddler named Jess Johnston (1898-1952). "Guitar Rag," apparently learned from blues guitarist Sylvester Weaver's recording, featured Johnston on slide guitar. Newer fans would recognize it as "Steel Guitar Rag," made famous some years later by Bob Wills and his Texas Playboys with Leon McAuliffe on steel in the western-swing style. The Harvey band, which finally took the name West Virginia Ramblers, also included two Princeton musicians, Bernice Coleman and Ernest Branch. They recorded some interesting material, including "John Hardy Blues," "You're Bound to Look Like a Monkey When You Grow Old," and a new train wreck ballad composed by Coleman entitled "The Wreck of the C. & O. Sportsman." Unfortunately in the depth of the Depression even good records sold poorly. The latter song, for instance, released only on the Superior label under a pseudonym, sold a mere 58 copies in a three-month period, and the best selling items from the session sold only 235 copies in the same span of time. By this time Harvey's recording career had begun to fade, not only because of the Depression but because his friend Poole had died after a drinking spree. Harvey moved to Florida and again resumed his old trade, becoming an engineer for the Florida East Coast Railway and remaining on the job until his death in 1958.[5]

By 1927 the largest of the recording companies, Victor, had contracted the services of a traditional West Virginia performer, Blind Alfred Reed. Possession of a rich baritone voice and an archaic fiddle style made Reed one of the most appealing of old-time artists, especially when combined with his special talent as a true folk composer. Born at Floyd, Virginia, on June 15, 1880, and blind from birth, Reed spent most of his life in the area of Princeton, West Virginia. He managed to maintain a wife and six children on his meager earnings as a musician. Reed and other neighborhood pickers played for dances and political rallies and gave shows in country schoolhouses. In between these more formal engagements he also played on street corners with a tin cup. Reed learned songs through oral tradition and later from the radio and phonograph records. He had a special knack for composing, and friends, neighbors, and local politicians sometimes got him to write songs for special events. He also printed his songs on small cardboard sheets and sold them for ten cents each.

Reed's recording career began in August 1927, when Ralph Peer asked him to come to Bristol and wax a local train wreck ballad he had written some weeks earlier entitled "The Wreck of the Virginian." The sessions Victor held in Bristol proved to be highly significant because they led to the discovery of several important artists, including not only Reed but the decade's two hillbilly superstars, the Carter Family and Jimmie Rodgers.

As a recording artist Blind Alfred Reed's career lasted only a little over two years, but every one of his twenty-one songs has significance. He composed every number, although at least one, "Explosion in the Fairmont Mines," is a recomposition of "Dream of the Miner's Child." Most Reed songs contain valuable social commentary which helps in understanding the philosophy of mountaineers like the composer and his neighbors who purchased and treasured his records and songsheets. They included local disaster ballads such as "The Fate of Chris Lively and Wife," who met death when a train struck their horse and buggy at a crossing, and protests against economic injustice such as "How Can a Poor Man Stand Such Times and Live?" and "Money Cravin' Folks." Perhaps more than anything else, however, Reed's songs complained about social change. "Why Do You Bob Your Hair Girls?" attacked new feminine hairstyles and cautioned young ladies that they could not hope to "reach the Gloryland" unless they maintained the traditional long hair. In songs like "Woman's Been After Man Ever Since" and "Black and Blue Blues," Reed took a stand against the rising independence of women, although he conceded their necessity in "We've Just Got to Have Them, That's All." A deeply religious man and a lay Methodist minister, Reed could still criticize the materialism of the clergy in songs like "I Mean to Live for Jesus." While most of his lyric messages are apparently serious, a strong trace of cynical humor also intrudes into many of them, except for those dwelling on tragedy.

At Reed's second recording session in November 1927 he brought along a string band known as the West Virginia Night Owls comprised of his son Arville (mistakenly identified as Orville on record labels) on guitar and Fred Pendleton on fiddle. Arville recorded one of his father's songs, "The Telephone Girl," which provides an excellent example of mountaineer reaction to a new technology—the young male narrator falls in love with the female voice that keeps saying "hello." The Night Owls recorded four numbers but only two were ever released, "Sweet Bird" and "I'm Goin' to Walk on the Streets of Glory." Unfortunately the unreleased songs sound more interesting—"The Fate of Rose Sarlo" and "Give the Flapper a Chaw" have the intriguing sound of Alfred Reed songs that document local tragedy and humorously criticize modern woman, respectively.

Reed's last session in November 1929, which had Arville assisting on guitar and choral vocals, included two of his most memorable numbers. "There'll Be No Distinction There," with its line "We'll all be white in that heavenly light," reminds us of the equality before God of all men, including Negroes and Jews. His inclusion of the latter perhaps expressed more toleration than the assumption of black equality, Jews being non-Christian. "Beware" warned young ladies against the possibility of seduction by fast-talking, false-tongued men, which suggests that despite his criticisms of women in other songs Reed still viewed young maidens as symbols of purity and virtue.

Although Reed's recording career ended with the deepening of the Depression, he continued his local playing until about 1937, when local municipal authorities insisted on enforcing statutes prohibiting blind musicians from playing on the streets. New Deal social legislation presumably made such "begging" obsolete. The aging Blind Alfred continued to perform at home for neighbors who still loved his artistry until his death in 1956.[6]

In addition to Alfred Reed, the August 1927 Bristol sessions put another Mercer County group on record. On August 5 a string band called the West Virginia Coon Hunters waxed a pair of sides entitled "Greasy String" and "Your Blue Eyes Run Me Crazy," the latter a variant of the better-known "Fly Around My Pretty Little Miss." Their instrumentation featured two banjos, fiddler W.A. Boyles, a guitarist, and W.A. Meadows on vocal. Although they performed very good mountain fiddle band music, they never recorded again and little information on their identity has been uncovered.[7]

The Brunswick-Balke Collendar Company, another major record firm, initiated their "Songs from Dixie" series early in 1927 and that March added a West Virginia duo to their talent roster. John and Emery McClung were born in 1906 and 1910 in Mt. Hope and Beckley respectively. By 1918 the failing health of the boys' watch-repairman father led them to start making music on Beckley street corners to help raise grocery money. As their skills at playing fiddle and guitar together with singing increased, they were asked to perform at local social events ranging from gatherings at the Miner's Convention Hall to the Shriners'. Their most requested song, an original and a parody of the state anthem, quickly brought them acclaim in the Beckley area. By the early 1920s the McClungs formed a string band called the West Virginia Trail Blazers which included fellow Beckley residents George Ward and John Lanchester. Traveling in a Studebaker, the band took their music over a goodly part of the country, even going as far as California on one occasion. Generally, however, they played much nearer their home base. The McClungs kept this band together until about 1934.

The McClung Brothers participated in only two recording sessions. The first was with Brunswick in March 1927, when they journeyed to New York and cut eight numbers. This small recorded repertoire included everything from sacred songs to a fiddle tune, with some popular and minstrel lyrics in between. Carson Robison, the New York songwriter, even added whistling to two of their masters. Oddly enough, they never recorded the crowd-pleasing favorite about West Virginia moonshine, although their friend Roy Harvey did it as one of his duets with Earl Shirkey on Columbia Records. Working without their entire band, the McClungs came up with a new nickname, dubbing themselves the West Virginia Snake Hunters. Two years later the McClungs recorded again, a Chicago session for the Wisconsin Chair Company's Paramount label. Cleve Chafin (1885-1959), a Wayne County carnival musician, accompanied them. Chafin had something of a career in his own right, doing a solo session for Gennett in 1927 (none ever issued) and possibly one for Paramount in 1928 with two men named Stevens and Bolar under the name Fruit Jar Guzzlers. After the four songs of the 1929 session, none of the three ever recorded again, although the McClungs and Chafin both continued the professional music careers they had previously followed. In their later days the McClungs had a gospel quartet on radio station WJLS Beckley, and John won an old-time fiddlers' contest there in August 1950 in which Emery took second place. Emery died in 1960, but John eventually retired to a quiet life in Alexandria, Virginia.[8]

Another duo who first entered the studio in 1927 turned out to be the most recorded of all early West Virginia performers. Between November 1927 and 1933 Frank Welling and John McGhee waxed over 300 masters for four different companies, making them among the most frequently recorded old-time musicians in the entire country in that early era. But they never became major best sellers, probably because much of their repertoire consisted of gospel material, many of their recordings were released under pseudonyms during the darker days of the Depression, and their music tended to have less appeal than that of major artists like the Carter Family, Jimmie

Rodgers, Uncle Dave Macon, and the Skillet Lickers. Nonetheless, Welling and McGhee deserve considerably more fame than they have attained to date.

Frank Welling was born in Lawrence County, Ohio, on February 16, 1900. His father, Harvey Welling, a farmer and old-time fiddler of local renown, actively played at numerous square dances in the southern tip of the Buckeye State. In 1913 the Wellings moved across the Ohio River to Huntington, and about that time Frank began to play the guitar. About 1919 he worked in a vaudeville act known as Domingo's Filipino Serenaders, where he learned the Hawaiian steel guitar. In the next few years Welling traveled with different vaudeville groups including one known as Rose's Wintergarden Girls, played in a variety of skits and shows in Huntington area theaters, and did radio work on local station WSAZ. About 1917 he met John McGhee, born in Griffithsville in 1882, and they performed in minstrel shows and Huntington churches. They did their first recording session for Gennett in November 1927 and subsequently did eight more for that company. In January 1928 they had their first of eight Paramount sessions in Chicago, and in February of that same year recorded for Brunswick-Vocalion in Ashland, Kentucky. They had sessions in 1930 and 1931 for the American Record Corporation. In addition, they assisted David Miller on some of his work. At one point, in late 1928, Bill Shannon recorded with Welling while McGhee did a session with Tom Cogar. They also did some sessions with Elbert Miller Wikel, a Summers County native. In some instances McGhee's daughter Alma or Welling's wife Thelma joined them, creating the Welling and McGhee Trio. Each man also waxed solo numbers at various times. Some of their material was released even on original labels under such names as Red Brush Rowdies (which included Wikel on fiddle), the Martin Brothers, and Frankie and Johnnie. Material released on subsidiary labels carried such pseudonyms as Wilkins and Sharon, Wilkins and Moore, Joe Summers, Roy Deal, Harkins and Moran (a pseudonym also used by the Tennessee duet of Harkreader and Moore), and John Moore.

Much of the Welling and McGhee repertoire consisted of sacred material and several of their best-known songs were recorded two or three times for the different companies. Numbers like "Whosoever Meaneth Me," "In the Garden," and "Picture on the Wall," for instance, received three different versions each on varying labels. On the other hand, some of their most interesting secular numbers were only recorded once—such topical songs as "The Crime at Quiet Dell," "The Marion Massacre," and "North Carolina Textile Strike." The first of these numbers dealt with the highly publicized West Virginia "Bluebeard" murders of Harry Powers in 1931, while the latter two concerned the same 1929 labor violence in the Carolinas which made the martyred worker-songwriter Ella May Wiggins famous. The duo also waxed comic parodies like "Sweet Adeline at the Still" and "Old Kentucky Dew," which offered commentary on prohibition, and sang about the Depression in "Bank Bustin' Blues" and "Money Can't Make Everybody Happy." Welling and McGhee also sang the praises of W.K. Henderson, the Louisiana radio orator and enemy of chain stores, in "Hello World Dog Gone You" and chronicled Kentucky's and West Virginia's famous "Hatfield-McCoy Feud." They sang a number of old popular sentimental songs and even a few old country dance tunes like "Beech Fork Special," "Birdie," and "Red Wing" which featured McGhee's harmonica. In 1928 Welling apparently introduced the recitation to country music with his Paramount version of "Too Many Parties and Too Many Pals." In all, Frank Welling and John McGhee performed an extremely varied type of old-time music.

John and Alma McGhee lived in Huntington until their respective deaths in 1945 and 1973. William Shannon, briefly Welling's recording partner, moved to Toledo, Ohio, where he worked as a house painter and part-time entertainer until he died in 1962 at age sixty-two. Miller Wikel lived in Maryland until his death in 1967. Welling himself moved to Charleston and became an announcer at radio station WCHS for some twenty years. Oddly enough, many of his later radio associates seem not to have known that he had once been much recorded, more so in fact than any other West Virginia artist of his era. In 1955 Welling left WCHS and moved to a station in Chattanooga. He soon fell victim to peritonitis and returned to Charleston, where he died January 23, 1957. He was buried at Spring Hill Cemetery in Huntington.[9]

By 1928 the Columbia Phonograph Corporation, the biggest rival to Victor and producers of the highly successful 15,000 D series of hillbilly recordings, belatedly began issuing material by West Virginia artists. (Of course Roy Harvey as a North Carolina Rambler had been recording on that label for some two years.) Back in 1924 or 1925 Columbia had planned some sessions for a northern panhandle fiddler named Fred Crupe, but his unexpected death ended the venture. In October, Columbia set up a studio in Johnson City, Tennessee, perhaps hoping to emulate Victor's phenomenal discoveries at Bristol the previous year. Columbia's initial Mountain State solo artist, Richard Harold (1884-1947), experienced a life somewhat similar to that of his friend and contemporary Alfred Reed. Born in Carroll

County, Virginia, Harold moved with his family to the Princeton area in 1888 and subsequently worked in the coal mines until an accident in 1904 left him sightless. Thereafter he supported himself and his growing family through broom-making and music.

Harold often played in the Princeton area with Blind Alfred Reed and his son Arville. Although he played a wide variety of instruments, he did only guitar work on his recordings. Harold had a "distinctive, commanding baritone singing style" which makes it unfortunate that he made only four sides. These included a coupling of two old sentimental ballads, "Sweet Bird" (which the Carter Family erroneously titled "Sweet Fern") and "Mary Dear" along with the comedy song about the Spanish-American War, "The Battleship Maine," and another number called "The Fisher's Maid." A couple of years later Harold recorded again with Fred Pendleton and the West Virginia Melody Boys on Gennett, but did no singing. He lived in Princeton until his death.

In October 1929 a pair of new West Virginia groups, in addition to the established duo of Harvey and Shirkey, appeared at the makeshift Columbia studio in Johnson City. The first constituted a unique sounding string band called the Moatsville String Ticklers, named for their home community in Barbour County. Led by fiddler Cecil Frye and banjoist Brooks Ritter, the aggregation cut four masters of which only the instrumental "Moatsville Blues" and a rousing version of "The West Virginia Hills" were released. A second group consisting of Vance and Wiley Weaver hailed from Beckley and came to the studios at the urging of Roy Harvey. They too saw only half the material from their session released. "Prison Sorrows" proved to be a fine duet version of the song David Miller called "It's Hard to Be Shut Up in Prison," while "You Came Back to Me" featured Wiley on a sentimental vocal solo. Vance played an excellent fiddle accompaniment on both numbers. Both the Moatsville band and the Weavers displayed a high quality in their music and had it not been for the Great Depression it seems probable that Columbia's Frank Walker would have wanted to record them again.[10]

In February 1928 Brunswick-Vocalion set up a temporary studio in Ashland, Kentucky, from which their engineers recorded a number of outstanding old-time artists including several West Virginians. The Roy Harvey band did several outstanding sides, as did Welling and McGhee. But from the Mountain State viewpoint the most significant development came in two recording debuts—of a duo who later became two of West Virginia's leading country radio personalities, and of the state's most renowned fiddler of all time.

The duo traced its beginnings to the birth of Samuel Warren Caplinger at Kanawha Station, Wood County, in 1889. Caplinger's original family name had been Pritchard, but after his father died in a coal mine accident young Warren used his stepfather's surname. In 1920 he moved to Tennessee where he, like a number of other West Virginia musicians, began working in the mines. He soon met a young fiddler from Oliver Springs named Andy Patterson (1893-1950). The two called themselves the Cumberland Mountain Entertainers and on their Ashland recordings they had assistance from another east Tennessee group, the Rainey Family. With Patterson's spirited fiddling the high point of their music, the Cumberland Mountain Entertainers picked their way through "Old McDonald's Farm," "Nobody's Business," "Big Ball in Town," and "Saro." The following year Caplinger and Patterson left Tennessee and made their way to the booming industrial city populated with West Virginia hillbillies, Akron, Ohio, where they formed another string band, the Dixie Harmonizers, and had three recording sessions for Gennett in Richmond, Indiana. They cut twenty-three masters, but Starr released only eight sides. Their unreleased material included such gems as the earliest recording of the Tennessee ballad "Willis Mabery" or "Hills of Roane County" as well as a new tragedy ballad, "Cleveland Hospital Disaster." Starr did choose to release such interesting songs as "The Music Man," a clever rewrite of "The Roving Gambler," which may have been somewhat autobiographical, and a pair of intriguing novelties entitled "Advice to Wife Seekers" and "Advice to Husband Seekers."

During their brief stay in Akron, the Dixie Harmonizers furnished the music for what later became a national institution in network radio, the "Lum and Abner Show," using the name Pine Ridge String Band. They also had the then-youthful Grandpa Jones in their act for a time. Jones, in fact, later married Patterson's niece. In 1931 Caplinger returned to West Virginia, taking Patterson and a young Alabama musician named William Strickland with him. This began another phase of their careers which will be discussed in detail later.[11]

The second new West Virginia group to record at Brunswick's Ashland, Kentucky, sessions consisted of a thirty-two-year-old fiddler and his rhythm-guitar picking younger nephew. They called themselves the Kessinger Brothers—Clark and Luches. Clark Kessinger, born in 1896, lived most of his life in the Kanawha County towns of St. Albans and South Charleston where he learned to play the fiddle at an early age. French Mitchell, a noted Putnam County fiddler, contends that Clark Kessinger had gained considerable renown throughout the Kanawha Valley by the beginning of the 1920s. When only a child Mitchell met the noted fiddler at a contest in Point Pleasant, and he recalled that many contestants dropped out of competition rather than lose to Clark. Although this incident preceded Clark Kessinger's recording career by at least four years, it indicates that he already possessed a wide reputation.

Although he fiddled for dances and on the early Charleston radio station WOBU, Kessinger also worked as a chauffeur for a wealthy Charlestonian, which afforded him the opportunity to hear and meet such famed concert violinists as Fritz Kreisler, with whom the young mountaineer reportedly exchanged techniques. In the two years following the Ashland sessions, the Kessinger Brothers easily ranked as the instrumental stars of the Brunswick "Songs from Dixie" Series, having some twenty-nine releases (fifty-eight sides) on that label. Additional tunes on Vocalion brought Clark's number of released sides to seventy. Clark fiddled not only such well-known pieces as "Wednesday Night Waltz," "Sally Goodin," "Turkey in the Straw," and "Arkansas Traveler," but also local rarities like "Kanawha March," "Going Up Brushy Fork," "Old Jake Gillie," and "Chinky Pin." Although an outstanding breakdown fiddler, Clark Kessinger was probably unexcelled in his ability to play the slower and more difficult waltzes and marches with almost equal dexterity. As with many other recording artists of the early era, the Depression ended the career of the Kessinger Brothers on the broader scene although they continued to be active in the Charleston area until Luches died in 1944 at age thirty-eight. Clark continued playing locally for several years and found himself "rediscovered" in 1964, after which he again became a national figure.

A final West Virginia performer, John B. Evans (1902-1955), did his only session at Ashland. Blind and a native of North Carolina, Evans lived in Charleston from an early age and attended the State School at Romney. His Brunswick offerings included the traditional "Whoa Mule," "Three Nights Experiences" (Child 274), and a pair of hymns. Later Evans worked in the Union Mission Blind Quartet, sang on Charleston streets, and sold newspapers until his death.[12]

The Starr Piano Company added another Mountain State act to their talent roster in 1928. That October their engineers cut matrixes of the songs "Old Wooden Leg," "Lost John," and "Bald-Headed End of a Broom" by an obscure team (who possibly had some connections with Welling and McGhee) known as Blevins and Blair. Unfortunately, the firm never released any of this material and neither they nor any other manufacturer ever again recorded the duo. A similar fate befell the trio of Midkiff, Spencer, and Blake, who did a session somewhat later.

But in 1929 Starr brought what would become a major West Virginia performer into their Richmond studio, a Charleston radio singer known as Bill Cox, the Dixie Songbird. Born William Jennings Cox at Eagle, West Virginia, in 1897, Billy was the son of a section foreman for the Kanawha and Michigan Railroad. Somewhere along the way he learned to play the harmonica and later the guitar. When he grew to adulthood Bill went to work for the Kelley Axe Factory in Charleston and later became a stationary engineer at the Ruffner Hotel, where in 1927 Walter Fredericks established a fifty-watt radio station, WOBU. By this time Billy possessed some reputation as an entertainer at local parties, and Fredericks induced the young boiler-room worker to do a short daily show since he could easily combine it with his regular job without leaving the confines of the Ruffner. By his own account only one or two other Charleston residents could play a guitar at that time (one must have been Luches Kessinger, who did not sing) and the Dixie Songbird's show became popular.

By all accounts Billy Cox in his younger days had a reputation as a free spirit and rounder. He himself later said that he absented himself from the show frequently, so Fredericks suggested that he make some records that could be played when he failed to appear. Bill consented and went to Richmond, Indiana, in July 1929, where he began a long recording career. Many of his early offerings were covers of Jimmie Rodgers's songs, but he increasingly performed a variety of older sentimental songs and original compositions. In the latter he had a special flair for comedy songs, some of which, such as "Rollin' Pin Woman," "Alimony Woman," and "The Jailor's Daughter," were allegedly inspired by his own hectic domestic life. He also composed his own white blues songs in the manner of Jimmie Rodgers and numerous contemporary black performers. Some of the best of these include "East Cairo Street Blues" and a fine piece of labor protest from the early New Deal days called "NRA Blues," whose lyrics are essentially those of an exploited sweatshop worker whose owner has not yet affiliated with the Blue Eagle. Bill also performed tragedy songs, many of them by the New York writer Bob Miller. One which he apparently wrote himself was the extremely rare and widely sought "Death of Frank Bowen," which described the killing of a local service station owner.

Although the Depression curtailed the recording activities of virtually all other West Virginia artists, Cox simply switched companies, going to the American Record Corporation in 1933, and continued recording. In the early 1930s he suffered a temporary hand injury, and employed a teenage boy named Cliff Hobbs (1916-1961) to play guitar on his radio shows. In 1936 Cox's record manager, Art Satherly, responding to the increasing popularity of duet acts, suggested that Bill get a tenor singer, so the young Hobbs went to New York and joined in on the chorus of the Dixie Songbird's vocals. Through the next four years this duo waxed some sixty sides to go with the eighty-eight solos of Bill's already released. This era resulted in many of his best-known songs, including two especially humorous and clever commentaries on the 1936 national election, "Franklin D. Roosevelt's Back Again" backed with "The Democratic Donkey (Is in His Stall)." In "The Whole Dam Family" he displayed a remarkable flair for double entendre. In 1937, he recorded two songs that have become national country standards, "Filipino Baby" and "Sparkling Brown Eyes." Although Bill contended that he had written the former song about his Uncle Fred's taking a Filipino wife while on a navy stint during the Philippine Insurrection, the lyrics apparently derived almost word for word from an 1899 popular song, "Mah Filippino Baby," copyrighted in that year by Charles K. Harris. "Sparkling Brown Eyes" was also recorded by numerous other artists and sung by Tex Ritter in a movie, and has remained a perennial country hit. Although no doubt exists as to Cox's authorship, he made little from it.

In addition to writing many of his own songs, Bill Cox also managed to record some unusual and archaic material. In 1939 he and Hobbs recorded two old traditional British ballads. The first was an excellent version of "The Farmer's Curst Wife" (Child 278), which he called "The Battle Axe and the Devil." The other is usually known as "One Morning in May" or "The Soldier and the Lady"; Cox and Hobbs called it "The Fiddling Soldier." At his last session in 1940 Cox rendered the first hillbilly recording of the nineteenth-century temperance ballad "Licensed to Sell" which he titled "Little Blossom," the name by which it too has become a standard in the bluegrass genre.

Bill Cox's last years saw a slow drift into obscurity. Although his records apparently sold moderately well all over the country, he never really had a major hit except for "Sparkling Brown Eyes." He spent all of his radio career in Charleston with the possible exception of brief stints in Ohio. Worst of all, he never worked extensively on live shows, and his own erratic behavior caused numerous additional problems. The axe factory closed and his job at the hotel was eventually phased out. He subsisted on odd jobs until he became eligible for minimal social security. In 1965 an amateur folklorist found him living in dire poverty in a tiny converted chickenhouse shack in a slummy part of Charleston, more subdued than earlier but still congenial. He then received some financial help and made a new album before he died on December 10, 1968. In those later years he sang at an area rescue mission and talked with a few scholars and song collectors who sought his story. Oddly enough, when asked about his New Deal songs, he almost seemed to be lacking in political philosophy. Although presumably a Roosevelt supporter, he merely replied that the lyrics were "cute ideas" that just "came to me."[13]

Another West Virginia artist who recorded in 1929 had only one session but it proved to be a significant one. Dick Justice, a Logan County man, visited the Chicago Brunswick studio on May 20. He waxed two blues numbers, "Brown Skin Blues" and "Cocaine," which show that he had absorbed considerable black influence. But Justice also performed two traditional British ballads, "Henry Lee" (Child 68) and "One Cold December Day" (Child 85). He also did a pair of mountain songs, "Old Black Dog" and "Little Lulie"; the latter is usually performed as a banjo song although Justice did it with guitar. Reese Jarvis (1900-1967), a fiddler from Clendenin, West Virginia, also recorded in the Brunswick studio that day, and Justice backed him on guitar although Jarvis later claimed that the two had never worked together prior to the time of the session. All of the Jarvis tunes are relatively uncommon. He did two waltzes on his first disc, "The Guian [sic] Valley Waltz" and "Poor Girl's Waltz." His other offering consisted of two faster numbers, "Poca River Blues" and "Muskrat Rag."

Little information has surfaced on either Justice or Jarvis. Justice is believed to have been born about 1906. He worked in the coal mines and apparently knew and occasionally played with Frank Hutchison. He also teamed up at times with a black fiddler named Pete Hill. Aunt Jennie Wilson, an elderly but contemporary folk performer, recalls that "he could play anything" but mostly did "mountain ballads." He is believed to have died in the mid-1950s. Jarvis later sold insurance in Clendenin until he died at sixty-seven in 1967. A few scholars contacted him in his later days, but seemingly found him a difficult interviewee.[14]

The prosperous economy that sustained much of the recording activity during the 1920s took a strong downward turn at the end of the decade. Coal mining served as the mainstay of West Virginia's economic base, and as the demand for this mineral declined, the populace suffered accordingly. Although mine employment fluctuated from year to year and with the season, the rate of decline accelerated. Between 1926 and 1932 the number of working miners went from 120,638 to 86,829 and those remaining on payrolls toiled less often and for lower wages. New rounds of labor strife hit the coalfields as miners reacted with violence to their deteriorating conditions. Within a few years paid membership in the United Mine Workers of America—already proportionately low in West Virginia because of operator opposition in the southern counties—sank from 45,000 to barely over 1,000. The record industry, largely dependent on working-class consumers for hillbilly sales, experienced similar difficulties. Income from record sales in 1933 constituted only 7 percent of what it had been in 1929. Roy Harvey and Earl Shirkey, whose three releases following their original hit had averaged 10,592 copies, saw the sales of their three releases after October 1929 average only 4,723. The last Roy Harvey and Posey Rorer release in November 1931 sold only 625. Major stars like Jimmie Rodgers were not doing much better. Phonograph records that had once sold well at seventy-five cents each now sold poorly on budget labels at thirty-five cents.

With the onset of the Great Depression, most West Virginia recording artists (with the exception of Billy Cox) ceased these activities. Recording had never paid more than nominal fees although some musicians like Hutchison and Harvey managed to earn a living for a few years from live performances. The blind singers like Miller, Reed, and Harold turned to music from necessity prior to recording and continued their dependence on it, although the 1930s social legislation seemingly eased their burdens somewhat. A few musicians found they could continue their careers through the increasingly popular medium of radio. These included the Tweedys, Caplinger and Patterson, and Frank Welling, although the latter worked more as an announcer than as a musician. Others such as Hutchison, Harvey, Justice, Arville Reed, and the Kessingers returned to the working class which they had never fully left. The recording activities of the prosperous late 1920s proved to be—from the economic viewpoint of the musician—only an interesting but temporary and limited income supplement.

This is not to say that recording activity ceased in the early 1930s. On the contrary, several new West Virginia groups visited the studios during that period but none had much success, even though in many instances their music was as good as any ever recorded. A pair of young Jackson County schoolteachers and local entertainers, John O. Harpold and Elman W. McClain, traveled to Richmond in the spring of 1930 and did a session which resulted in four sides released under the name Jackson County Barn Owls. The duo accompanied themselves on guitar, banjo, and harmonica, cutting an interesting version of "I Wonder How the Old Folks Are at Home" and a rare local instrumental, "Letart Isle." McClain and Harpold split up shortly afterward, the former going to Wyoming County, where he died some years later, and the latter serving as an elementary school principal at Gay until his death in 1956.

Fred Pendleton, who had been part of Blind Alfred Reed's West Virginia Night Owls, organized a band in 1930 which he called the West Virginia Melody Boys. Then twenty-six years of age, he displayed skill on a wide variety of instruments but favored the fiddle. In August 1930 and April 1931 Fred took his Melody Boys, consisting of L. Vernal Vest on ukelele, Basil Selvy on mandolin, and Richard Harold on guitar, to Richmond, Indiana. They recorded a total of ten songs of which Starr eventually released four on their Champion label. (The premium-priced Gennett label had been discontinued by this time.) The most interesting song, "Wreck of the West Bound Air Liner," described the disaster that took the life of Notre Dame football coach Knute Rockne. On May 26, 1931, Pendleton returned with a new band comprised of Lundy Akers, banjo, Woody Leftwich and Roy Lilly, guitars, and himself on fiddle. They made three masters but their only release consisted of one side of a Champion record credited to Leftwich and Lilly. Pendleton worked during these years as a road laborer and played music part-time up into the 1970s.

Another Princeton area musical duet that made a go of recording was Joe Gore and Oliver Pettry. Gore was born in Morristown, Tennessee, but came to Princeton as a child. He often played guitar for his fiddling father. In 1929 he met twenty-six-year-old Oliver Pettry and the two worked together quite extensively playing in the southern West Virginia coal camps. Gore recalled in 1971 that on their best days they might earn up to fifteen dollars "in ten minutes of playing." They recorded five songs for Starr in April 1931 of which "I'll Not Be Your Sweetheart" and "Goodbye Sweetheart" were released on a single record. Pettry eventually went back to the mines, dying in 1963. Gore became a pipefitter and continued to play for dances in the Princeton area with other musicians for many years.

A final Princeton duo to record, Bernice "Si" Coleman and Ernest Branch, had helped Roy Harvey on some Gennett sessions in early 1931. In October of that year Branch and Coleman went to Atlanta and waxed eight sides for Okeh Records. Branch played banjo, Coleman the fiddle, and both sang while Harvey played guitar. At the time, Coleman was thirty-three years old and Branch, whose banjo work closely resembled that of the famed North Carolinian Charlie Poole, was about eighteen. Coleman still worked on the railroad and usually played music only on weekends. Having mastered the telegraph, he spent forty-four years in service with the Norfolk and Western Railway, working his way up to assistant train master by the time of his retirement. Branch returned to the mines but mashed his fingers in an accident, which hampered his banjo playing. Coleman in the 1970s proved to be an important resource person for folksong scholars and also helped to entertain the less fortunate elderly in the Princeton area.[15]

Two more West Virginians tried recording in 1932, one each from the central and northern tiers of counties. Huntington, the state's largest city, which had not produced a record artist since Dave Miller, John McGhee, and Frank Welling, came up with one that July in the unlikely person of Richard Cox. Born on April 26, 1915, the youngster started singing on the local station WSAZ in 1929. Despite his youth he organized and led bands in the Tri-State area (West Virginia and adjacent portions of Ohio and Kentucky). He apparently favored a mixture of older ballads and original compositions. Cox soon acquired such nicknames among his radio listeners as "The Singer of Sentimental Heart Throbbing Ballads" and "West Virginia's Master Mountaineer." On July 29, 1932, he took a string band, the National Fiddlers, to Richmond, Indiana, and a Starr session. This group featured Bernard Henson on fiddle. The duo of Cox and Henson cut a pair of fiddle tunes and the entire group made seven additional masters. They fared somewhat better with production officials than the Princeton groups—all but one number appeared on the Champion label. Following his one session Cox appeared on radio in such Great Lakes cities as Detroit, Windsor, and Gary. By 1936 he joined forces with two old pros from the Deep South, Bert Layne and Riley Puckett, and an Ashland youth, Slim Clere, as part of a group called the Mountaineer Fiddlers. This band played radio shows and personal appearances in the Gary, Indiana/Chicago area.[16]

From northern West Virginia, Frank Dudgeon came to the Starr studios on October 20, 1932. A native of Jackson County, Dudgeon moved to Perry County, Ohio (birthplace of Stephen M. Elkins, a longtime Mountain State political power), in 1919 at the age of eighteen. Calling himself "The West Virginia Mountain Boy" he played on radio at both Wheeling and Fairmont. Either he or the record company officials must have been extremely cautious on the day he recorded, for Dudgeon did only two songs—"I Hate to Be Called a Hobo" and "Atlanta Bound." They did release the numbers, however, and on

March 8, 1933, Dudgeon returned to cut six additional songs including a cover of the Vagabonds' popular hit "When It's Lamplighting Time in the Valley" and the old gold-rush favorite "Sweet Betsey from Pike." Keeping active as a radio artist, the West Virginia Mountain Boy lingered in Wheeling, Huntington, and Fairmont for a few years and then moved on to other stations and fresher territory. By 1946 Dudgeon based his activity at KLRA, a Little Rock, Arkansas, station, but then returned for brief periods to Wheeling and Fairmont and to recording again before settling down to industrial work in Cleveland.[17]

Although not positively identified as such, a few other early recording artists or acts seem likely to have been West Virginians. In 1929 Cecil Vaughn had one session each for Columbia and Gennett, but only two Columbia sides were released. An unissued version of a local topical ballad, "The Murder of Jay Legg," almost certainly marks him as a native of the Elk River country. Fiddler Jess Johnston recorded with Hoosier musicians Jess Hillard and Duke Clark, and Jim Smith and Ed Belcher appeared on Brunswick with H.M. Barnes's Blue Ridge Ramblers. Charles DeWitte, who called himself "The Vagabond Yodeler," was another probable West Virginian. He too had some Champion releases in 1931 and 1933, including a song entitled "The Girl I Met in Bluefield." At least two Mountain State musicians composed songs which they sent to Vernon Dalhart rather than try to record themselves. Cleburne C. Meeks of Fayette County wrote three railroad ballads, "Billy Richardson's Last Ride," "Wreck of the C. & O. Number Five," and "Wreck of the N. & W. Cannonball." John Unger, a blind street singer from Berkeley Springs, authored "The Miner's Doom," about a local accident in a sand mine. Blind Ed Haley (1883-1954), a legendary Logan County fiddler who eventually settled in Ashland, Kentucky, repeatedly refused to record, but did belatedly cut some home discs for his children in 1946. Last but not least, a group called the Kanawha Singers recorded several numbers for Brunswick between 1927 and 1930. This name was sometimes used as a pseudonym for the well-known "citybilly" team of Vernon Dalhart and Carson Robison. Although more a barbershop quartet than country, a real group called the Kanawha Singers existed, particularly on recordings of songs like "West Virginia Hills" and "Hail, West Virginia."[18]

From the mid-1930s on a few new West Virginia performers began to record, including Dick Hartman, Harry Blair, Don White, Big Slim Aliff (McAuliffe), Blaine and Cal Smith, Judie and Julie (Jones), and Cap, Andy, and Flip. But all of these individuals owed their primary success to radio, and in the cases of Hartman and White even this was gained largely in the Carolinas. Their careers will receive major attention in connection with their radio artistry. So too will those non-West Virginia artists who spent notable portions of their professional careers working on West Virginia radio stations.

In the first decade of hillbilly recordings, a surprisingly high number of West Virginia performers found their way into the studios. While it would be ridiculous to contend that the industry would not have succeeded without West Virginians' participation, it is no exaggeration to state that the state's musicians greatly enriched the quality of recordings in those early years. Only artists from Texas, Virginia, and Georgia enjoyed the advantages of getting into the business earlier. Musicians from West Virginia began recording at about the same time as North Carolinians, Kentuckians, and Tennesseans, and several months before performers from other Appalachian and southern states.

Perhaps unfortunately for the degree of personal fame attained, many Mountain State artists recorded for the Starr Piano Company, whose best sales came on those labels which often used pseudonyms rather than real names. Nonetheless, West Virginia people recorded with success on virtually every major label in the period and executed some outstanding performances. Certainly the Tweedys and David Miller deserve recognition as the first recorded instrumentalists and vocalist, respectively, from their state. Frank Hutchison created one of the most unusual styles. Blind Alfred Reed possessed one of the richest voices and wrote some of the most powerful lyrics ever to appear on discs. Billy Cox composed some of the cleverest lyrics ever written on subjects ranging from humor to romantic love. Roy Harvey together with his associates Jess Johnston and Leonard Copeland preserved some of the best old-time guitar stylings on early record, while Clark Kessinger ranks among the best fiddlers. Frank Welling and John McGhee probably recorded more than any other performers prior to 1934 except for Vernon Dalhart and his associates. These Mountain Staters all took the music of their folk heritage, adapted it to their purpose, and created new music from within the scope of their own traditions. It could hardly be termed music "no real hill-dweller had ever before heard." Quite to the contrary, the music created by these people could best be labeled music of, by, and for the rural highlanders—or hillbillies, if you prefer!

3. WWVA and the "World's Original Jamboree"

Although the phonograph recording industry discovered West Virginia musicians a bit earlier and carried their sounds a greater distance, the newer medium of radio reached a much larger audience. Listeners began to hear country music radio broadcasts as early as 1922. A few years elapsed before a significant number of Mountain State families had receiving sets, and in many rural communities neighbors gathered at the home or store of an owner to take their turns at listening with the earphones to the voices and sounds coming over the airwaves. By 1930 only 23.4 percent of the families in the state owned a radio. In Ohio County 46.7 percent of the households boasted sets in that year and the other northern panhandle counties ranked next highest in radio ownership. In fact, the northern panhandle as a whole, with only 10.21 percent of the state's families, had a disproportionately high 18.15 percent of West Virginia's radio sets.[1]

A higher degree of affluence, industrialization, and urbanization may be cited as reasons for this disproportion. Another reason could be found in this area's geographic closeness to Pittsburgh and pioneer station KDKA, and also to Wheeling, site of WWVA, "West Virginia's first broadcasting station." Granted a license on December 6, 1926, WWVA went on the air a week later with the initial program originating from a private residence via a fifty-watt transmitter. Over the next two years WWVA periodically increased its power until July 1, 1929, when it became a 5,000-watt station.[2]

Like many other radio stations that played a key role in the dissemination of country music, WWVA and its management moved somewhat slowly in the direction of hillbilly commercialization. Most of the earliest performers played or sang popular music. William Wallace Jones began to appear regularly on the station as part of a harmony foursome known as the Sparkling Four before his graduation from high school in 1927. In the fall of 1927 the station established a broadcast studio in the Fidelity Investment Building. By that time the boys were doing some Hawaiian numbers, since they featured a steel guitar. They especially played late on Saturday nights and took requests over the telephone, and this circumstance led to listener demand for what came to be country or hillbilly songs.

In 1928, as the recordings of Jimmie Rodgers began to attract attention, the Sparkling Four began getting requests for yodeling songs. Jones, who had experimented a bit with this vocal technique, made an effort to please his audiences by yodeling, while announcer Holland Engel sang "Red River Valley." As the demand for Rodgers-type songs increased, Bill sang them too. In 1929 Howard Donahoe, another announcer, dubbed him the Silver Voiced Yodeler, later shortened to Silver Yodelin' Bill Jones. The name stuck with him throughout his radio career.

In 1931 George Smith became program director at WWVA and undoubtedly played a key role in the station's development as a major country music station. According to Bill Jones, Smith looked seriously at country music and, more than any other management figure, "saw its potential." It seems likely that as a broad-minded businessman Smith realized that as radio became increasingly available to mass audiences a generous amount of down-home style music would enable a station to attract and retain a large number of listeners. No doubt this philosophy permeated his thoughts in 1936 when he wrote about the tendency of radio to "level all humanity" and that "it has been our privilege to enter the humble mountainside cabin." Smith also most certainly realized that the Wheeling station had more daytime listeners in eastern Ohio and western Pennsylvania than in its own Mountain State, and that the even broader evening audience tended to be located north and east of Wheeling.

Bill Jones remembered that WWVA had a late Saturday night studio program called the Jamboree for several years before inaugurating its live-audience theater performance on April 1, 1933, though later printed material contended that the Jamboree dated only from January 7, 1933. Whichever, there seems no doubt that the 3,266 persons who jammed the Capitol Theater in downtown Wheeling on April 1 at 11:00 PM witnessed the premiere of a stage show destined to rank second only to Nashville's "Grand Ole Opry" in longevity. The "World's Original WWVA Jamboree" continued to broadcast throughout the decade from a variety of locations after February 1934, usually the smaller Wheeling Market Auditorium, which held only 1,300. On three occasions, all associated with Ohio River floods, the show had to go on without a live audience. In one instance, September 22, 1936, the WWVA management held the Jamboree in a football stadium and attracted a crowd in excess of 5,000.

Meanwhile more authentic mountaineer musicians had begun to enter the WWVA studios on a regular basis. Fred Craddock (1890-1965), a resident of the Moundsville area, sang old ballads in a credible fashion and sometimes led a string band, Craddock's Happy Five. Elmer Crowe (1909-1978), who hailed from the same town, remained a regular on the station until 1940 and helped keep the WWVA sound tradition-oriented in those early years. By the time Craddock and Crowe had become established, the Sparkling Four had broken up and Bill Jones had helped form a new group, the Rhythm Rogues, which also included Fred Gardini on accordion, Blaine Heck on guitar, and Paul Myers on bass. Beginning in 1934, Jones worked both solo and with a group called the Peruna Panhandle Rangers. By 1935 his transition from a middle-of-the-road popular singer to country-western was complete as he began to play personal appearances and donned western clothes in the manner of Gene Autry, who was then making the singing cowboy a popular character on the Hollywood scene.[3]

By that time, however, more entertainers had appeared at the WWVA studios. In 1932, the trio of Cap, Andy, and Flip (Warren Caplinger, Andy Patterson, William Strickland) arrived on the scene and, according to Bill Jones, ushered in a degree of professionalism hitherto unknown to relative amateurs such as Craddock, Crowe, and himself, who played primarily to please their listeners. Caplinger had seen in his earlier experiences in Knoxville, Akron, and the recording studios that it was possible to earn a living as a musician. By using radio as a means of promotion, musicians could book shows in neighborhood schools and attract listeners who would pay to see and hear the artists in person. They could also sell songbooks. About this time the Tweedy Brothers, who had apparently played briefly at WWVA in its infancy, returned to Wheeling as a home base while continuing their round of county fair and carnival tours. Such acts also demonstrated the potential for hillbilly professionalism.[4]

Neither the Caplinger nor the Tweedy group seems to have made it quite as well with the WWVA audience in the mid-1930s as did a relative newcomer known as Cowboy Loye. Born Loye Donald Pack in Nashville, Tennessee, on June 3, 1900, the Cowboy apparently wandered around somewhat in his early adulthood and spent several years working on a ranch in Nebraska. He entered radio in January 1929, played in Columbus, Ohio, for a time, and began his career at WWVA on November 11, 1933. If his songbooks represent his repertoire correctly, Pack knew and performed a wide variety of material ranging from lyrics of likely New England origin such as "Nell of Narragansett Bay" to western ballads like "The Dying Cowboy." At Wheeling, Loye generally performed with another artist known as Just Plain John Oldham and became known for his salesmanship talents and ability to draw mail. In April 1934 Pack asked his listeners to help name his newborn son and subsequently received 11,255 letters in six days. Grandpa Jones, who knew him quite well, once remarked that even though he was not "flashy" Cowboy Loye "could sell anything." After nearly four years at WWVA, Pack returned to Nebraska briefly before moving on to Fairmont in 1937, where he repeated his earlier successes only to die tragically from a kidney ailment in March 1941.[5]

A variety of other performers also came to WWVA. These included Hank and Slim Newman, a brother duet of Georgia origin whose harmony stylings showed more of a Carson Robison-Frank Luther influence than their own rural background. Based generally in Columbus, Ohio, the Newmans eventually added a third brother to their act and became a slick sounding trio that divided its time between radio shows and Hollywood horse operas. Another duo, Chuck and Don, claimed a Tennessee heritage and featured a steel guitar accompaniment to their mountain ballads. The twosome of Handsome Bob (Bouch) and Happy Johnny (Zufall) in 1935 emphasized fiddle accompaniment to their vocal harmonies. The latter eventually became a popular country music figure on Baltimore radio. Slim Carter, a Pennsylvanian, achieved a strong following for a time and later recorded for MGM. Murrell Poor, an announcer from Illinois, joined the staff in March 1935. A veteran of the Chautauqua and vaudeville circuits, Poor played the tiple (a ten-string instrument the size of a baritone ukelele) and sometimes sang and did recitations.

Still other early artists endeavored to create a cowboy image. Mel "Slim" Cox and his Flyin' X Roundup consisting of Red Kidwell and Hal Harris came to Wheeling from earlier radio work in Columbus, Ohio, and Cox later became affiliated with the Texas-based Light Crust Doughboys. Tex Harrison's Texas Buckaroos featured a tenor-banjo-strumming leader along with the fiddling of French Mitchell, a Putnam County youth who favored the stylings of Clark Kessinger. On one of their show dates with poor attendance, Mitchell recalled that after taking out the expenses, profits amounted to three cents each! French's brother Auvil, who had been a member of the group, then decided to quit show business and go home. French, somewhat more patient, awaited better times. A third group, the Rhythm

Rangers, included Hoosier natives Loren Bledsoe and Harold (Pete) Rensler, together with a girl vocalist, Mary Ann Estes, among its members. The Rangers combined forces with Marshall "Grandpa" Jones when he came to WWVA in 1936. Grandpa stayed only a year, although he returned again for the 1941-42 season and briefly in 1945.[6]

In addition to Jones, who would enter the Country Music Hall of Fame in 1978, several other significant performers came to WWVA in the mid-1930s. Some had already carved out notable careers in the field while others made the Jamboree a milestone in their upward climb. One veteran of both radio and recording studios, Hugh Cross, came to WWVA in 1935 sponsored by Georgie Porgie Breakfast Foods. Born on October 19, 1904, in Oliver Springs, Tennessee—also the hometown of Andy Patterson—Cross grew up in a musical family and recorded extensively on the Columbia and Vocalion labels in the late 1920s. His waxings included the earliest version of the standard "Wabash Cannonball" and numerous duets with Riley Puckett. In 1930 he joined the WLS "National Barn Dance" in Chicago and remained there for three years. In 1935 he teamed up with George "Shug" Fisher, a stuttering comedian who had already been with the California-based Beverly Hillbillies and appeared in motion pictures. Their band, the Radio Pals, traveled to some of their showdates in their own private plane and must have seemed highly professional to the less experienced local hillbilly performers. Fisher, however, commended the WWVA audience, calling it "the best and most appreciative" he had "ever played" to. In addition to their daily shows and Jamboree appearances, Hugh and Shug's Radio Pals journeyed to New York and cut sixteen sides for Decca—a somewhat unusual feat for a WWVA act since the management did not encourage their radio talent to make phonograph records. In 1939 the Radio Pals moved to WLW Cincinnati although Cross returned to WWVA several years later.[7]

A new arrival in May 1937 subsequently developed into the most durable figure in the city's musical history. Doc Williams and his Border Riders came to WWVA from Pittsburgh and in 1938 won a loving cup as the station's most popular act. Williams possessed a unique background for a hillbilly musician in that his heritage included no southern roots and little that could be classed as either Appalachian or rural. Nonetheless he managed to become a major figure on the country music scene and a traditionalist as well.

Born Andrew J. Smik, Jr., of Slovak parents in Cleveland on June 26, 1914, Doc grew up largely in the small towns of western Pennsylvania listening to his father play the fiddle music both of Eastern Europe and of his adopted homeland. Doc and his brother Milo (Cy) played locally in the Kittaning area until Doc went to Cleveland in 1932. There he joined a group known as Doc McCaulley and his Kansas Clodhoppers. McCaulley, a West Virginia native, taught the young Slovak a great deal about Appalachian music. Soon Doc formed his own group which he called the Allegheny Ramblers. It included his brother Cy on fiddle and Curley Sims on mandolin in addition to Doc on guitar and harmonica. In 1935 the group left Cleveland, came to station KQV Pittsburgh, and changed their name to the Cherokee Hillbillies in the process.

After a few months, the Cherokee Hillbillies became partners with a girl singer named Billy Walker as the Texas Longhorns. When Walker went to WWL New Orleans early in 1937 the band members recovered their own identity, renaming themselves the Border Riders. About this time young Andy Smik—already known as Cowboy Doc—took the stage surname of Williams. In May 1937 Doc Williams and his Border Riders, consisting of Curley, Cy, a girl vocalist, Mary "Sunflower" Calvas, and comedian Hamilton "Rawhide" Fincher, became regulars on the Jamboree. Harry C. McAuliffe (Big Slim the Lone Cowboy) came into the band in December 1937 as a featured vocalist. Like most country groups of their day the Border Riders displayed considerable versatility. Doc, Slim, and Sunflower all did solo vocals while Doc and Cy had a solid duet and Cy did spirited fiddle tunes as well. Fincher and his replacement, James "Froggie" Cortez, took the lead in comedy, but the entire group participated in a variety of skits. Doc later added an accordion played by Marion Martin, which helped give him his distinct sound of straightforward country music with a strong dash of Eastern European influence. In regions like northern West Virginia, Pennsylvania, and eastern Ohio, which sustained a large immigrant populace, this blending of styles proved to be a definite asset. While the Border Riders were neither the first nor the only band to accomplish this musical amalgam, they probably did it best.[8]

One of the musicians who came to WWVA as a Border Rider soon branched out on his own. Big Slim McAuliffe had already experienced a wide degree of geographic and occupational variety. Born in Mercer County, West Virginia, on May 9, 1903 (or 1899, or 1904, or 1905), the facts of Slim's personal life have become somewhat clouded largely because of his own capacity for contradictory statements. For instance, in a 1939 autobiographical statement in one of his songbooks Slim claimed to have been born in the city of Bluefield and on a 750-acre farm. He also contended he had been orphaned at eight, left home at eleven, and become a radio trick rider that same year, while on another page he displayed a contemporary photo of his father. Slim also punched cows and railroaded according to his "Life Story" before entering radio work in 1929. He gained radio experience in Pittsburgh and on a border station at Eagle Pass, Texas. On December 17, 1936, he did a session for Decca under the name Big Slim Aliff which included the initial recording of the country standard "Footprints in the Snow" under that title. He came to WWVA late in 1937. At five feet eleven inches and 175 pounds he was neither very big nor very slim, but the nickname did seem to be in character with his other qualities.

Big Slim possessed a rich and deep voice and rendered good versions of both common and more obscure western songs such as "The Strawberry Roan" and "Patanio, the Pride of the Plains." He also sang mountain ballads like "Hills of Roane County" and copyrighted some good original material such as "On the Sunnyside of the Mountain" and "Moonlight on My Cabin" (although he reportedly wrote none of them). Slim had other talents which supplemented his stage shows, including whip and rope tricks along with a trained horse act. While the Lone Cowboy generally stayed close to WWVA, he went to other stations for brief stints and later helped younger artists such as Hank Snow and Hawkshaw Hawkins.[9]

Another artist who came to Wheeling with an established name, Frankie More, worked for Pinex Cough Syrup in the same manner that Hugh Cross had promoted Georgie Porgie products. Of Louisiana birth, More had a dozen years of radio experience behind him including stints at WLS Chicago and WHAS Louisville when he came to WWVA in 1936 at the age of thirty. He had also participated in recording sessions for both Decca and the American Record Corporation with one Freddie Owen as half of a duet called the Log Cabin Boys. The two had apparently split by the time More arrived in Wheeling, but he retained the term Log Cabin for his band, calling it at various times the Log Cabin Boys, Gang, or Girls, with the latter aggregations being the most memorable.

Cousin Emmy (Cynthia) Carver, one of the original banjo pickin' girls who initially popularized such songs as "Ruby Are You Mad at Your Man" and "Lost John Dean from Bowling Green," along with teaching Grandpa Jones to play the banjo, was the most significant girl to work in More's group although her stay at WWVA was relatively brief. Emmy's niece, Alma Crosby, known professionally as Little Shoe, served the longest stint with the Log Cabin Gang in Wheeling, putting in at least five full years. Like her more famous aunt, Little Shoe sang and did spirited banjo tunes. Other Log Cabin Girls included fiddler Rhoda Jones, accordionist Penny Woodford, Celia "Cricket" Mauri, and a variety of others who served for briefer periods. More selected some members of the Log Cabin Girls as a result of widely publicized contests which focused considerable attention not only on the band but on the ever popular Pinex Products. Notable Log Cabin Boys included Dale Cole, who also fiddled with Charlie Monroe, and Dolph Hewitt, who subsequently spent many years as a star on the "National Barn Dance." After 1941 More, always at least as much a promoter as a musician, moved to Nashville and worked as manager for several acts before his death, although he returned to WWVA briefly in 1948.[10]

The WWVA Jamboree gave more attention to female performers than the industry did as a whole. Whether the activities of More's Log Cabin Girls sparked this focus is unclear, but female vocalists got a strong share of the attention at the "World's Original Jamboree." Gertrude Miller (1915-1967), later the wife of Jack Dunigan, was an early featured singer. In the Doc Williams group Mary "Sunflower" Calvas, daughter of an Italian immigrant from Davis, West Virginia, augmented the group's popularity for several years. During much of this time she was also the wife of Doc's fiddling brother Cy. In her absences Doc's wife Wanda, or "Chickie," filled in and eventually occupied the spot permanently, achieving a following that equalled and perhaps surpassed that of her husband. Both Hugh and Shug's Radio Pals and the Rhythm Rangers used Mary Ann Estes (Vasas), an Ohio girl of Hungarian ancestry, at various times as featured vocalist. Celia Mauri worked not only with Frankie More but also with Mack Jeffers and his Fiddlin' Farmers, a later WWVA act. Other groups generally had a girl vocalist—probably the precedent had been set by the Prairie Ramblers and Patsy Montana at WLS Chicago— but the Wheeling Jamboree seems to have virtually standardized the system. In too many cases, however, the girls' identity tended to be hidden in a nickname like "Brown Eyes" or "Laughin' Lindy." When World War II military service began to take its toll on male performers the girls at WWVA moved even more to the forefront.

The Jamboree also allowed generous space for rural comedy. More often than not, many of the masters of bucolic humor affiliated with the touring units of the more popular stars of any given time. Anthony Slater, who had begun his career as yodeler Smiley Sutter, endured much longer as cornball clown Crazy Elmer, appearing on WWVA off and on for some forty years until his death in the spring of 1980. Other notable comedians included Shorty "Hiram Hayseed"

Godwin, Smokey Pleacher, and Dapper Dan Martin, all associated with the Border Riders at various times. Martin and Abner Cole worked as part of the Clinch Mountain Clan. A Kentuckian, Lazy Jim Day, and a fellow known as Cy Sneezeweed also ranked among the better-known Jamboree humorists.[11]

While some of the musical groups that came to Wheeling exhibited neither the impact and longevity of a Doc Williams and a Grandpa Jones nor the professionalism of the Radio Pals or Log Cabin Gang, many did establish themselves as regional favorites. Such included Jake Taylor and his Railsplitters, led by an Arkansan transplanted to Indiana. Taylor's group included his wife Betty, a grotesque looking comedian named Ray (Quarantine) Brown, and a bass player named Herman Redmon. The Railsplitters came to Wheeling in 1936 after two years at a Terre Haute station and remained about three years before moving on to Fairmont and subsequently other locations where they could retain part of their old following while adding new fans. Joe Barker, a Clarksburg native, did virtually the same thing in reverse by coming to WWVA in 1937 after an earlier career in Fairmont and Greensburg, Pennsylvania. Barker's group, the Chuck Wagon Gang, partially a family affair since it included his wife Little Shirley, a cute redhead (four feet ten inches in height), and small daughter Nancy Lee, remained Jamboree favorites until 1950.[12]

Not all acts that came to Wheeling found commercial success. In fact, many of them moved in and out of the industry without making much impact. Unfortunately most examples come from those who did well elsewhere and under different circumstances. Johnnie Bailes and Red Sovine of Charleston, for instance, spent several weeks at WWVA in 1937 as a duet called the Singing Sailors. As Bailes later recalled, on many days they did not even eat. A few years later, however, Bailes and his brothers found wide popularity, and Sovine as a solo performer had more songs on the *Billboard* charts than any other West Virginia musical figure. Charlie Monroe and his Kentucky Pardners had a phenomenal following in the Carolinas but found things so discouraging in Wheeling that they stayed only a few months. Finally, Floyd Tillman, a Texan who had already made some impact as a western swing vocalist and later made such great hits as "Slippin' Around" and "I'll Keep On Loving You," came to WWVA in 1939 with Lew Childre's group. Although the latter did reasonably well and stayed at WWVA for three or four years (returning to Alabama in the summers), Tillman apparently drew fewer fans than Doctor Lew's trained dog "Mr. Pooch." As Doc Williams commented in 1981, some people just had bad timing.[13]

Although many Jamboree artists had played personal appearances since the time of Cap, Andy, and Flip's early days, the concept of the package tour did not arrive until April 1939. Seven bands, a pair of solo performers, and announcer Bill Thomas comprised that year's "goodwill tour" group, which must have included virtually the entire Jamboree cast. The Border Riders, Radio Pals, and Log Cabin Girls constituted the more established acts along with Big Slim and Elmer Crowe. Jake Taylor's Railsplitters and the Joe Barker unit (then called the Radio Circus) were slightly less well-known along with Shorty Fincher's Cotton Pickers and the relatively obscure Tommy Nelson Gang. Three Pennsylvania towns—Greensburg, New Castle, and Uniontown—and three Ohio cities—Marietta, Dover, and Canton— were the locations chosen. The total aggregate attendance of 19,464, or an average of 3,244 per night, illustrates the venture's success.

By the time of the First Goodwill Tour, daily shows had become nearly as important as the Jamboree, both to the station and to its audience. Sponsors such as Georgie Porgie and Pinex paid salaries to their acts to perform on the air every day. In fact, some artists worked daily without performing at all on the Jamboree. Bluegrass Roy Freeman, who sang for Hamlin's Wizard Oil, played at WWVA during 1935-36 and again in 1939, appearing only one time on the Jamboree. Frequently, those who worked for medicine firms drew salaries only from September through June, since liniment and cough and cold nostrums did not sell well during the summer. Other acts received no salaries as such but worked on the "PI" (per-inquiry) plan, which meant that they received a commission on the basis of the number of mail order products they sold via their shows. By either system, however, the participants on the First Goodwill Tour furnished three and a half to three and three-quarters hours of live music weekdays in addition to the Saturday night Jamboree. This format became roughly the standard until the early 1950s, when the daytime shows were gradually phased out and increasingly replaced by recorded music.[14]

The Jamboree management arranged for more Goodwill Tours in 1940, 1941, and 1942. Sites varied somewhat as booking agents dropped some towns from the itinerary and added new ones like Akron and Youngstown, Ohio. Greensburg, Pennsylvania, appears to have been the only city always on the schedule. Performers changed, too, as new acts came to the station and some of the older ones departed. The 1940 cast, for instance, again included the units of Doc Williams, Joe Barker, and Frankie More. Big Slim and Tommy Nelson remained, but their status reversed in that the former now led a band while the latter worked solo. Blaine Smith, Calvin "Curley" Miller,

and Mack Jeffers all boasted band units while two more solo performers, Silver Yodelin' Bill Jones, back from four years in New York,
and a popular blind vocalist from Georgia named Pete Cassell
(1917-1953), rounded out the talent lineup.

The 1941 tour group was much smaller. It was made up of Big
Slim's Happy Ranch Gang; Frankie More's Log Cabin Boys (composed
largely of personnel borrowed from the Border Riders); Lew Childre
and his Buckeyes, including Chief Redhawk, an Indian rope expert;
Bill Jones; and the Chuck Wagon Doughboys, who constituted a fu-
sion of the Curley Miller-Joe Barker bands. Solo artists Benny Kis-
singer, Brown Eyes, and Smiley Sutter, the yodeler recently arrived
from Fairmont, completed the performing unit. The 1941 Program
Tour Booklet contained the first publication of the "Song of the
WWVA Jamboree," which staff organist Vivian M. Miller had composed a few months earlier.

The 1942 group contained a mixture of the familiar in Big Slim,
Bill Jones, Doc Williams, the Barkers, Lew Childre, Curley Miller,
and Smiley Sutter, along with such newcomers as the Leary Family,
a gospel singing band from Randolph County that included Wilma
Lee and Stoney Cooper; Eileen and Maxine Newcomer, a pair of
seventeen-year-old blind twins from Pennsylvania; and Millie Wayne,
a tall attractive brunette from McKeesport, Pennsylvania, and the
sister of Curley Miller.[15]

By the spring of 1942 and the fourth annual Goodwill Tour, the
nation had been involved in World War II for several months and shift-
ing conditions soon produced a variety of changes in the industry.
Gasoline rationing in particular made it difficult for artists to get
out into the hinterlands to play showdates and equally difficult for
audiences to come to Wheeling. So, although WWVA became a
50,000-watt station on October 8, 1942, thus increasing its listening
audience, especially at night, to include New York, New England,
much of the Mid-Atlantic area, and southeastern Canada, the live audience Jamboree was discontinued from December 12, 1942, until July
13, 1946. The Jamboree and the daytime country shows flourished
as never before, but only as studio presentations. Several announcers
and performers, including Joe Barker, Monte Blake, Lloyd Carter,
Curley Miller, and for a brief period Doc Williams, entered military
service while others went into defense plants. Some who stayed in
radio found other jobs to supplement their incomes now that personal
appearances had to be curtailed. Still, country music—like major
league baseball—helped the national morale and received government
encouragement.[16]

A wave of patriotic hillbilly songs brought new attention to country music generally. As a *Billboard* columnist said, "Popularity of the fighting country tunes . . . calls attention to the fact that . . . folk music . . . far more than the pop field, has come thru with war tunes" which are "doing a fine morale job." Jamboree artists included in their songbooks such lyrics as "A Hundred Million Kisses for Hitler," "A Letter to a Soldier," "The Devil and Mr. Hitler," and "You Won't Know Tokio When We Get Through." Probably no WWVA group exemplified the wartime spirit better than the Chuck Wagon Gang. Jamboree announcer Lew Clawson wrote that Joe Barker is doing "what he can to preserve your home and your way of life." Meanwhile, Little Shirley carried on "in the traditional American pioneer manner," broadcasting "her program on the air" and "doing more than her share for victory." Referring to Joe, far away in the U.S. Navy, Shirley altered the chorus of "Remember Me" to:

Remember me, when gone I'll be yearning
For you each night far away on the deep blue sea
Don't cry for me but keep our love light burning
When I'm gone, I hope you'll remember me.[17]

The changes wrought by the war may have delayed some careers, but they accelerated others. They helped bring such new performers as Millie Wayne and Bonnie Baldwin to the forefront. Wayne had been born on October 6, 1920, and first appeared on the Jamboree in 1939. In 1943 she teamed with Ruth "Bonnie" Baldwin, a Coolville, Ohio, native four years younger, whose parents had moved to Bridgeport across the river from Wheeling. Bonnie first worked briefly with the Chuck Wagon Gang. As the Radio Rangerettes, Millie and Bonnie with their duet renderings of old hymns, sentimental ballads, and western songs quickly became one of the station's more popular acts. Another young Ohio native, Toby Stroud, who had played on some smaller stations earlier, won a popularity contest at WWVA in July 1944. Adept as a vocalist, fiddler, and rhythm guitarist, Stroud with his two young Wyoming Ranch Boys, fiddler Buck Ryan and mandolinist Bill Bailey, helped pioneer a brand of music very near to bluegrass. In fact a little later Stroud had a band which included Don Reno and Red Smiley among its members.

Another youthful act, the Davis Twins, Nial and Maxine, best known as Honey and Sonny, came from New Lexington, Ohio, and performed mandolin-guitar duets in the appealing style that had become popular in the 1930s. They had first come to WWVA with

Tommy Nelson after the Twins won a talent contest at the Ohio State Fair in 1939. Sonny, however, eventually found himself in the service.

One newer group, Gay Schwing and his Gang from the Hills, was a combo of older generation and youthful musicians led by a Marshall Countian born in 1905, guitarist Gay Wesley Schwing, who had originally played on WWVA in 1929 as a member of Fred Craddock's old Happy Five. Other band members included his brother Herman on guitar and banjo and youthful daughter Ramona on mandolin. For a time he had the services of young fiddler Flavil Miller from Guernsey County, Ohio, who also spent some time with Doc Williams while Cy was in the service. Schwing's group eventually moved on to Fairmont and Bluefield. Ramona Schwing married "Flannels" Miller, who subsequently entered the ministry.[18]

By July 13, 1946, when the "World's Original Jamboree" reopened its doors for public viewing at the Virginia Theater, the show had returned to its prewar strength with new acts as well. Unfortunately managing director George W. Smith had died two months earlier, but William Rine and Paul Miller managed to fill his shoes adequately. Although the Virginia Theater was relatively small, seating only about 1,400, the artists usually gave two shows, which sometimes filled the house twice. The immediate postwar decade was probably the brightest in Jamboree history. Thirteen acts headlined the Jamboree in 1946. The more established groups included Doc Williams and his Border Riders, with Chickie Williams now the featured vocalist and William "Hiram Hayseed" Godwin doing comedy, Shorty Fincher's Prairie Pals, Joe Barker's Chuck Wagon Gang, Blaine Smith, Pete Cassell, Big Slim, and Smiley Sutter, whose skirt-chasing, rube comedy characterization, Crazy Elmer, had nearly taken over his act. Those who had gained popularity during the war years included the Davis and Newcomer Twins, Millie Wayne and Bonnie Baldwin, and Toby Stroud's Blue Mountain Boys. Newcomers included "The Singing Mountaineer" Reed Dunn, a thirty-year-old Marshall Countian who favored older ballads, and Hawkshaw Hawkins, a honky-tonk style vocalist who soon rose through the ranks to become the show's premier performer.[19]

Born Harold Hawkins in Huntington on December 22, 1921, young Hawkshaw exemplified the new honky-tonk style that emphasized an electric lead and steel guitars in the instrumental backup. He had gained some brief radio experience at Huntington and Charleston before the war intervened, but managed to do some playing in the Far East, including a show from Manila, and returned to the States in 1945 signing with both WWVA and King Records, a new but fast-rising Cincinnati firm. Hawkshaw had an appealing voice that could sing either new songs or older ballads in a modern style, and the type of appearance that rapidly won him popularity with both male and female audiences. By the time he made the cover of the *National Hillbilly News* in July-August 1947, he had already earned something of a name as a hillbilly heartthrob in the manner that Elvis Presley would do for mass audiences nearly a decade later. At first he tended to be closely associated with Big Slim, but increasingly became a star in his own right. Except for brief absences for extensive tours and a stint with WFIL-TV in Philadelphia, Hawkins remained with WWVA as a very popular artist until 1954, when he departed for first the "Ozark Jubilee" and then the "Grand Ole Opry." He did return occasionally as a Jamboree guest prior to his untimely death in 1963, always with his popularity undiminished.

The "Hawk," or "Eleven Yards of Personality" as he became known, possessed a characteristic that would later be termed charisma. While acknowledged as a ladies' man in one sense, men—especially those interested in horses, dogs, guns, and hunting—also found him a good companion. The late Stoney Cooper and Little Jimmy Dickens recalled many pleasant hours spent on hunting trips with their fellow West Virginian. Margie Shannon knew Hawkins from his teenage days in Huntington and remembers that he always made the rough musicians around WSAZ behave like gentlemen in her presence. Wilma Lee Cooper also remembers that Hawkshaw had a puritanical streak. Once, when living in Wheeling, he stopped by the Cooper household to get Stoney to go on a short errand with him, but when Stoney insisted on wearing his Bermuda shorts—just then coming into vogue—Hawkins became embarrassed and refused to let Stoney go along until he promised to remain in the automobile. But the Hawk went through all sorts of agony when Stoney jumped out of the car and began modeling the apparel, which Hawkins considered effeminate at best and downright immoral at worst. Later, Wilma Lee nostalgically recalled, when the two old West Virginia pals lived in Nashville and Stoney suffered a heart attack, Hawkins came to their house often and helped nurse his friend back to health. On one occasion he even brought a live chicken to the Cooper home, wrung its neck, and made a pot of chicken soup which he fed Stoney with all the affection of a Jewish grandmother.

Hawkshaw Hawkins began his recording career by doing covers of Ernest Tubb hits for the Cincinnati-based King label. He soon moved on to honky-tonk songs of his own styling such as "Dog House Boogie" and "I'm Kissing Your Picture Counting Tears" as well as numbers owned by Big Slim, like "When They Found the Atomic Power," "Moonlight on My Cabin," and, most important of all, "Sunny Side of the Mountain." He popularized the latter as a theme song for at least a decade before it entered the repertoire of bluegrass artists like the Stanley Brothers and Jimmy Martin. While Hawkins continued to sing some tradition-oriented numbers such as "Little White-Washed Chimney" and "The Life of Hank Williams" along with tender-hearted ballads like Eddie Nesbitt's "Unwanted," honky-tonk material dominated his repertoire through his King recordings and also his RCA Victor sides. He switched to Columbia about the time the "saga songs" or pseudo-historical ballads became popular in the late 1950s and rejuvenated his popularity with numbers like Jimmie Driftwood's new lyrics to the traditional fiddle tune "Soldier's Joy" and the cowboy song "Patanio, the Pride of the Plains," which derived from his association with Big Slim. Meanwhile, Hawkins shifted his base of operations to the ABC-TV "Ozark Jubilee" in 1954 and to Nashville's "Grand Ole Opry" in 1955.

By 1962 Hawkshaw Hawkins had married Jean Shepherd, also an Opry star and a major female country vocalist. That September he returned to his original record label, King, waxing a dozen sides for an album including the song that turned out to be his biggest all-time hit, "Lonesome 7-7203." Unfortunately the Hawk got but a small taste of what seemed like approaching superstardom. The song began its climb up the charts on March 2, 1963, and Hawkins died in a plane crash on March 5 while returning from Kansas City, where he had participated in a benefit concert. Ironically, he feared flying and seldom traveled by air. Two other major performers who had West Virginia connections, Cowboy Copas and Patsy Cline, perished in the same accident.[20]

While Hawkshaw Hawkins best exemplified the new style coming from postwar Wheeling, other new artists and groups who came to the station continued to favor the more traditional forms of country music. One of the best and most popular, Wilma Lee and Stoney Cooper, both natives of Randolph County, had worked briefly at WWVA early in the decade as members of the Leary Family. Born at Harman and Valley Head in 1921 and 1918, respectively, the pair had married in 1941 and gone on to gain wide radio and travel experience in such locations as Grand Island, Nebraska, Indianapolis, Chicago, Fairmont, Blytheville, Arkansas, and Asheville, North Carolina. They came to WWVA in December 1947 having just cut a record session for the small but influential Rich-R-Tone company of Johnson City, Tennessee. The Cooper band, known as the Clinch

Mountain Clan, emphasized traditional acoustical sounds such as the fiddle, mandolin, and Dobro guitar played, at various times, by such masters of those instruments as Tex Logan, Blaine Stewart, James Carson, Will Carver, Buck Graves, and Stoney himself. Colorful comedians such as Abner Cole and Dapper Dan Martin also added to the Clan's appeal. Their instrumental and vocal style—slick yet old-time sounding—possessed a certain character that in one sense hearkened back to older days but was still being played by young musicians. Wilma Lee recalls that WWVA listeners had never heard anything quite like them before and they established themselves rapidly as favorites. In their duets, individual solos, and trio numbers the Coopers sang with deep sincerity, specializing in sad ballads and sacred lyrics with a few honky-tonk songs performed in their more tradition-rooted stylings.

In 1949 Wilma Lee and Stoney Cooper signed with Columbia Records. Their four-year career with that label could be considered remarkable in that while it produced no gigantic hits it resulted in a great many songs that became long lasting standards in the trade. Some of the songs had initially been popularized by fellow West Virginia radio acts, such as Lee and Juanita Moore's "Legend of the Dogwood Tree," Rex and Eleanor Parker's "Moonlight on West Virginia," and Doc Williams's "Willy Roy, the Crippled Boy." Other West Virginia songs included their own "On the Banks of the River" (about the Cranberry River region) and "West Virginia Polka," one of the best but most atypical of the Louvin Brothers' compositions. Sacred songs of lasting appeal included Odell MacLeod's touching "Thirty Pieces of Silver," about Judas Iscariot's betrayal of Christ, and the even more heart-rending lyric portrait of the crucifixion by Ruby Moody, "Walking My Lord up Calvary Hill." Finally, their cover version of "Sunny Side of the Mountain" featuring Tex Logan's fine fiddle work and one of Stoney's rare vocal solos occupies a transitory position in that song's history, being recorded after the country versions of Hank Snow, Hawkshaw Hawkins, and Big Slim, but prior to the many bluegrass renditions.

In the mid-1950s the Coopers moved to the Acuff-Rose affiliated Hickory label, where they enjoyed their two biggest hits, "Big Midnight Special" and "There's a Big Wheel." This move also led to their joining the "Grand Ole Opry" and moving to Nashville in the spring of 1957. Their career as Opry artists lasted for some two decades with short interruptions caused by Stoney's recurring heart problems. Although they continued to favor the older country sounds, record company executives sometimes tried to accommodate their style to more modernization with only limited success, as their later Hickory and Decca waxings illustrate. By the early 1970s they had moved back toward their roots and although their later recordings did not make the charts, their fans found them more satisfying. After Stoney died in March 1977, Wilma Lee Cooper carried on as a solo act with a solid bluegrass band. The older ballads, heart songs, and gospel hymns that sustained the Coopers in later years have also endeared them—along with Roy Acuff, Bill Monroe, Lester Flatt, and the McGee Brothers—to the large number of traditionalists remaining among the Opry enthusiasts.[21]

Other Jamboree acts also remained close to tradition. Red Belcher's Kentucky Ridge Runners tended to favor the brother duet stylings of the 1930s. Finley "Red" Belcher, a Kentucky native born in 1914, played a respectable old-time banjo and sang some, but displayed his best talent as a pitchman or radio salesman. Belcher employed a variety of duos to do most of the performing. The Lilly Brothers, a Beckley area team who sang in a style somewhat like the Monroe Brothers, and the Mayse Brothers, a Braxton County duet who fashioned their harmonies in the Delmore Brothers' tradition, constituted a pair of Mountain State duos who worked with Belcher. Out-of-staters included Galen and Melvin Ritchey, a Pennsylvania pair who also did Delmore material as well as such interesting originals as the "Red Arrow Train" and "Trailing Arbutus," and Mel and Stan Hankinson, the Kentucky Twins, who also worked with Hawkshaw Hawkins at times. At the end of the decade, Lee and Juanita Moore, already familiar to West Virginia audiences through their work at other stations, came to Wheeling. The Moores worked at WWVA for a decade and although their marriage broke up in 1960, Lee continued for another thirteen years as a Jamboree artist and as the all-night disc jockey until the end of the 1960s.[22]

The "World's Original Jamboree," while continuing to keep one foot in the door of tradition, kept up with the newer stylings, too. Don Kidwell, a Falls Church, Virginia, boy came to WWVA in 1949 at the tender age of twenty-one and had four professionally successful years there before moving on to the "Brush Creek Follies" in Kansas City. Jimmy Walker, born near Point Pleasant in 1915, had acquired some Hollywood film credentials on the west coast as well as record sessions. He did well with songs like "Sioux City Sue," "Detour," and the honky-tonk classic "Out of Money, Out of Place, Out of Style." Walker spent a year at the "Grand Ole Opry" as a replacement for Roy Acuff, then a couple of years at Wheeling in the later 1940s, returning in 1953 and remaining until 1964. Although they still worked with piano only instead of using full country instrumentation, the Sunshine Boys constituted in many respects the first contemporary country gospel quartet. Usually based in Atlanta, the foursome of Ace Richman, Eddie Wallace, Fred Daniel, and J.D. Sumner worked at Wheeling from 1949 to 1951 and with their four-part harmony helped to bring the Deep South quartet style to middle- and northern-Appalachian audiences.[23]

As in the prewar era, some people with stature had limited appeal or remained only briefly for other reasons. Hank Snow, the Yodeling/Singing Ranger with a fair following in his native Canada, came to WWVA. His eventual goal at the time being Hollywood, Hank made enough to invest in a tent show and returned to his large Canadian audience. But Hollywood wiped out his savings and forced him to go back to Canada. His third U.S. attempt proved more successful. Ken Curtis, a Colorado Singing Cowboy, already had solid Hollywood credentials when he came to the Jamboree about 1948-49. He too remained only briefly, returning to California to join the Sons of the Pioneers. Eventually Curtis earned his greatest fame not as a singer but as a character actor, immortalizing the role of Festus Haggen in the "Gunsmoke" television series from 1964 to 1975. Finally, George Morgan, then known as Tennessee George, worked at WWVA for a few months until the fame of his hit "Candy Kisses" brought an invitation to Nashville and the Opry. Reportedly it took some strong persuasion from Mary Jean Shurtz, a poet, songwriter, and pioneer hillbilly journalist residing in Newcomerstown, to get station officials to hire the cross-eyed country crooner from Barberton, Ohio.[24]

At the beginning of 1951 one subtle change did occur at the station's behest. They hired a staff country band that received a union contract and subsequently backed all other live artists on their daily shows. This group, called the Country Harmony Boys, did a daily show of their own and furnished backing for the other acts except for Doc and Chickie Williams, who retained their Border Riders unit. The initial staff band consisted of Gene Jenkins, lead guitar; James Carson, mandolin; Bill Chamberlain, bass fiddle; Monte Blake, accordion; and Will Carver, fiddle or dobro guitar. Roy Scott worked as their vocalist and also played guitar. Scott later took the Country Harmony Boys' name for his own band and maintained a twenty-one-year association with the WWVA Jamboree, having begun it in a brief association with Red Belcher. Members of the staff group worked showdates with whoever needed them on a first-come, first-served basis.[25]

Some idea of the popularity of Jamboree artists can be obtained from the 1952 statistics on their success on showdates. In that year WWVA acts played 761 appearances in 436 locales to a total of 526,789 persons, for an average attendance of 692. When one considers that some failures undoubtedly occurred and that many school auditoriums remained relatively small, it seems clear that the performers had considerable appeal as drawing cards. Part of the growth of the era can be attributed to the development of outdoor parks, particularly in Pennsylvania. In the period after World War II local entrepreneurs constructed parks for Sunday afternoon shows. Eddie and Millie Ruton's Hillbilly Park near Newark, Ohio, typified them. Some artists constructed their own, with Doc Williams's at Musselman's Grove and Joe Barker's at Ravine Park, both in the Keystone State, among the first. Former WWVA artists like Jake Taylor operated Radio Ranch near Grafton, and Shorty Fincher had Golden Oaks at Waynesburg, Pennsylvania. Other popular spots included Himmelreich's Grove, New River Ranch, Valley View, and Sunset Park, all in Pennsylvania, Frontier Ranch in Ohio, and Buck Lake Ranch in Indiana. The park system offered wholesome family entertainment for country fans at modest prices.[26]

Although a few Jamboree artists managed to obtain contracts with major firms making phonograph records—most notably Hawkins on King and the Coopers on Columbia—the majority of WWVA artists in keeping with station policy recorded sparingly or not at all. Those who did generally found themselves on small labels with inadequately distributed products. Big Slim's waxings from his prime years, for example, can be found on obscure labels like Dixie and Page. Gay Schwing recorded on Hug, Lee and Juanita Moore on Cross Country, Red Belcher, the Lilly Brothers, and the Ritchie Brothers on Page, and Bonnie Baldwin, Roy Scott, and Millie Wayne on Cozy. The last firm, based in Davis, West Virginia, played a key role in recording numerous locally important Mountain State radio acts although the discs have become exceedingly rare because of their limited distribution. Doc Williams, a more astute businessman than most, initiated his own company, Wheeling Records, and as a result he and Chickie did well on discs, particularly Chickie with "Beyond the Sunset," which incorporated the poem "Should You Go First" in 1947. In Canada, these same masters appeared on Quality Records, a major label there.

The 1950s brought some new acts to Wheeling and some old ones moved elsewhere. Dusty Owens constituted one of the brighter and more promising young mainstream country vocalists. He signed with Columbia Records and waxed some original songs like "Once More" and "Somewhere She's Waiting" that did quite well. But Owens became dissatisfied with his country music career and subsequently entered the ministry and later business. Skeeter Bonn, a country singer and yodeler from Illinois, came to WWVA after some initial successes on the "National Barn Dance." For two or three years Bonn recorded for RCA Victor and divided his time between the Jamboree and Cincinnati's "Midwestern Hayride." He won a considerable following in the mid-1950s before the rise of rockabilly made conditions difficult for yodeling cowboys. Gene Hooper, a straight country singer from Maine, also pleased fans in the Northeast with his appealing vocal style but, unlike Bonn and Owens, never got a contract with a major record firm.

A new face who proved more adaptable to newer styles, Sidney "Hardrock" Gunter, came to Wheeling from Alabama in 1953 and had already had a hit with "Birmingham Bounce" in 1948. Gunter continued to perform as a straight honky-tonk style singer at the Jamboree and recorded with such major firms as Decca and MGM. He also waxed what were later regarded as vintage rockabilly numbers for Sun Records. Both Gunter and Lee Moore gained something of a name for themselves as disc jockeys when record shows gradually replaced the live performances. Moore in particular became at least as famous as the Coffee Drinkin' Nite Hawk, with his 2:00-5:00 AM show (later expanded to midnight to 6:00 AM), as he had been as a singer. As an artist, Lee performed on the Jamboree from late 1949 through 1973 (the first decade with Juanita), and as a deejay from 1951 to 1969 with the exception of brief periods spent at Moncton, New Brunswick, and Mt. Jackson, Virginia. This exposure led to his ranking second only to Doc Williams as the most noted WWVA personality.[27]

Husband and wife teams within performing acts became especially popular at WWVA through the 1950s. Although some couples split up—most conspicuously Joe and Shirley Barker at the start of the decade and Lee and Juanita Moore at the end—others continued. The most notable enduring couples included Doc and Chickie Williams, whose daughters Peeper, Poochie, and Punkin occasionally joined them for shows, and Wilma Lee and Stoney Cooper, sometimes augmented by daughter Carol Lee. The Coopers moved to Nashville and the "Grand Ole Opry" in 1957. Among the new arrivals, Bud Messner and his Skyline Boys already had a wide following in Pennsylvania and adjacent states through their radio work at such locations as Hagerstown and Chambersburg. Born at Luray, Virginia, in 1917, Messner maintained a band equally at home with traditional and contemporary material. With his featured vocalist and wife, Molly

Darr, an Asheville, North Carolina, girl, they had an act which boasted considerable fan appeal. Another couple, Buddy and Marion Durham, featured soft-harmony duets along with Buddy's superb old-time fiddling and showmanship. The Durhams arrived in 1954 and remained for several years. Mabelle Seiger and her Sons of the Plains included husband, Curly Seiger, and Chuck and Jim Cook, the latter a pair of rockabilly singing brothers. Mabelle, a Pennsylvanian, played a variety of instruments including harmonica, accordion, clarinet, and fiddle. In the summer of 1953, Lone Pine and Betty Cody came to Wheeling from Maine. They had already won their way into the hearts of numerous fans with their duets and individual solos throughout upper New England and the Maritime Provinces of Canada. Although none of these couples remained at WWVA as long as the Williamses or the Coopers, they all stayed several years, long enough to give both their individual fans and those of the Jamboree a strong association with the institution.[28]

Another Wheeling act of the period constituted something of a throwback to the era of Frankie More's Log Cabin Girls. Known as Cowboy Phil's Golden West Girls, they were originally led by veteran guitar player Philip Reed, a one-time vocalist on the "Iowa Barn Dance." The girls included fiddler Abbie Neal, guitarist Tina Franzi, mandolinist Gay Franzi, and Wanda Saylor on accordion. Eventually Abbie Neal left to form her own all-girl unit, the Ranch Girls, who by 1955 consisted of June Mayse, Carol Moser, Candy Lange, and Suzy Darden. Cowboy Phil obtained a new corps of Golden West Girls in the persons of Eva Burke and the McCumbee Sisters, Carol and Phyllis, members of a multitalented family from Morgan County in the eastern panhandle. The Ranch Girls in particular enjoyed a rather prominent career extending well into the 1960s, including some regular live television shows in Pittsburgh and Wheeling and appearances in Las Vegas and Reno night clubs.[29]

Bluegrass music also made its full-fledged debut at WWVA when the Bailey Brothers and their Happy Valley Boys joined the Jamboree in April 1952. Natives of Hawkins County in East Tennessee, Charles and Dan Bailey had several years of radio experience and commercial success in Knoxville, Nashville, and other major cities behind them when they arrived in Wheeling. A mandolin-guitar duet in the old-brother tradition, Charlie and Danny's band included such outstanding sidemen as fiddler Clarence "Tater" Tate, Don McHan, adept on both banjo and lead guitar, Joe Stuart, skilled on all instruments, and bass fiddle playing comedian Slaphappy Jake Tullock. Exceedingly popular in their years at the Jamboree, the Baileys drew phenomenal crowds wherever they played. Tater Tate, recalling his early years as a professional some twenty years before, stated that he never worked with anyone who attracted fans to their shows as well as the Baileys. In the spring of 1954 ill health forced Dan Bailey's return to Tennessee, although Charlie Bailey later returned to Wheeling with bands that featured such talented musicians as the Osborne Brothers and Phyllis McCumbee.[30]

During and after the Bailey stint at WWVA, other bands playing in the bluegrass style began to appear more or less regularly on the Jamboree. Jim and Jesse McReynolds together with Hylo Brown worked at WWVA for a few months in the summer and fall of 1955. Although this brief tenure preceded their commercial successes, both had already had sessions with Capitol Records that produced some truly classic bluegrass. Of the bands that spent considerable time at the Jamboree, none have surpassed the Osborne Brothers in either quality or quantity. This Eastern Kentucky-born duo who grew to adulthood in the Dayton, Ohio, area worked as part of Charlie Bailey's group from August to December of 1955 and returned on their own as Jamboree regulars the following October. That June, Bob and Sonny Osborne, on mandolin and banjo respectively, together with Red Allen on guitar, had waxed a memorable session for MGM records which included a revival of the old Cousin Emmy song "Ruby." During the next seven years the Osbornes perfected their trio vocals and recorded what most scholars consider their most outstanding material. Unfortunately, it came at a time when country music generally and the more traditionally-oriented styles in particular faced unfavorable comparisons with the rise of rockabilly and its urban counterpart, rock and roll. Despite their beautiful music, economic necessity forced the Osbornes to supplement their incomes by part-time jobs as taxi drivers in Dayton. The Osbornes managed to survive those hard years and in 1963 moved on to the "Grand Ole Opry" and Decca, where they found the monetary rewards that had eluded them earlier.[31]

When *Billboard* magazine noted an upcoming fall tour by a young unknown named Elvis Presley in October 1954, it seems unlikely that many people in Wheeling took much notice. Yet the impact of Elvis and the style he and others of similar ilk created would wield a tremendous influence in the next two or three years. The honky-tonk styles that had dominated country music since World War II would become obsolete and the more traditional styles—hitherto commercially tolerated—suffered even more. WWVA artists found the going difficult for a few years and some dropped from the scene. By the time the Jamboree made it to network radio in the mid-1950s on a rotating basis with the "Old Dominion Barn Dance," "Tennessee Barn Dance," and "Louisiana Hayride," much of the nationwide radio audience had been lost to television. Fortunately the Jamboree itself had always operated on a relatively low budget, which also kept losses minimal. Nonetheless the "World's Original Jamboree" managed to survive as an institution and a few of its artists made some notable contributions to the rockabilly genre.[32]

Bob Gallion probably constituted the Jamboree's prime rockabilly figure. Born at Ashland, Kentucky, in 1922, Gallion first came to WWVA as a straight country singer in 1952, began doing rockabilly in the middle of the decade, and after 1960 returned to hard-country material. Gallion's material from the later 1950s, recorded on the MGM label, includes some fine rockabilly songs. One of them entitled "My Square Dancin' Mama (She Done Learned to Rock and Roll)" could in a sense symbolize the whole dilemma that country musicians faced during that era. Other Gallion rockers included such lyrics as "Baby Love Me," "Start All Over," and "I Want Her Blues." He worked as a Jamboree regular off and on for some twenty-five years, dividing his time between Wheeling and the states of Alabama and Georgia, and scoring several hits during the 1960s. By 1975 he had come to typify the "too country" artist who found it difficult to get his records played on stations that specialized in the top-forty type of pop-country. Hardrock Gunter also did a generous proportion of the new style recording under both his own name and pseudonyms like Sidney Joe Lewis and the Rhythm Rockers. In fact, his "Gonna Dance All Night" and "Fallen Angel" appeared on Sun Records a few months before Presley's now legendary Sun sessions. This and other recordings suggest that such music at least partially predated the Elvis impact. Chuck and Jim Cook, erstwhile members of the Sons of the Plains, also waxed such rockabilly numbers as "Juke Box Play for Me" and "You Gotta Go."[33]

The Wheeling Jamboree survived the rock and roll revolution in the long run not so much through the accommodation of rockabilly artists as through the dedication of older stars like Doc and Chickie Williams and Lee Moore. Such performers had built up sufficient followers through the years to sustain them in an uncertain period of changing styles. Doc was able to get steady work throughout the 1950s although he played more distantly from Wheeling—enjoying immense popularity in Canada from Ontario to Newfoundland—and did not always get to the Jamboree every Saturday. He also had some mid-week television shows in places like Altoona and Johnstown,

Pennsylvania, that broadened his exposure. Nonetheless, the Jamboree would see more fluctuation in the next decade, with more far-reaching changes in the long run, than the upheavals that resulted from the rise of rockabilly.

The changes that hit the Wheeling Jamboree—and indeed the entire country music industry—in the 1960s tended more toward the evolutionary than the revolutionary. In a sense, they came in such subtle fashion that the average listener hardly realized what was happening. The new country music got increased exposure on network television, "country" radio stations mushroomed all over the nation, and national magazines commented on the idiom's rising popularity. Only a few academics, folklorists, and cultural reactionaries (or traditionalists) commented negatively that in the process of gaining new acceptance much of the "country" in country music seemed to be rapidly fading.

That the 1960s symbolized a decade of change for the Jamboree can be symbolized partially by its repeated geographic relocation. The Virginia Theater served as the locale from 1946 until July 1962, when workmen demolished the old landmark. The Rex Theater then became the show's home, and remained so through the broadcast on January 8, 1966.[34]

In a sense the Rex Theater period represented something of a low point in Jamboree history. Even smaller than the Virginia, it seated only 800-900 persons. In the mid-1960s when the station changed ownership, the new management considered abolishing the show, but John Corrigan and Doc Williams argued instead for "revitalizing" with success. In August 1965 Lee Sutton was named Jamboree director, and in the next fifteen months he added some twenty-seven new acts to the roster. The list included several rising younger performers, including David Houston (who soon experienced a hit song in "Almost Persuaded," so popular that he quickly outgrew the show), established vocalist Mac Wiseman, hard-country singer Esco Hankins, comedian Cousin Wilbur Wesbrooks, and five bluegrass bands ranging from veterans like the Stanley Brothers (who appeared only a few times due to Carter Stanley's declining health and subsequent death) to relative unknowns like Jim Greer's Mac-O-Chee Valley Folks. Sutton retained nine acts already on the Jamboree and initiated a more prominent series of guest stars. With such an enlarged lineup, some "regulars" now appeared on the air only about one night per month. Most important of all, the site of the show shifted on January 15, 1966, to the Wheeling Island Exhibition Hall, which could easily accommodate 2,000 to 3,000 fans at a time.

Other changes took place in the station's policies. On November 8, 1965, WWVA became a full-time country station except for some news, religious, and occasional sports shows. In making the change to the "Big Country Sound," Arlen Sanders, a west coast deejay, became program director and shifted the emphasis to "the sharpest modern radio techniques with a TOP 60 country music hit parade." These alterations had numerous advantages and gave the Jamboree a decided boost, but also created a few problems that would eventually surface. Mac Wiseman came to WWVA in May 1966 and took over talent agency and booking operations, and in October initiated a post-Jamboree midnight show known as the "Mac Wiseman Record Shop," modeled after the WSM post-"Grand Ole Opry" "Ernest Tubb Record Shop." Wiseman even managed to get the legendary Texas Troubadour to appear as his guest early in the show's history. A third alteration came on November 1, 1966, when Lee Moore's "All-Night Show" went to the "more modern" format used during the daylight broadcasts. This situation, unfortunately, cramped the style of the Coffee Drinking Night Hawk, led to his feeling increasingly like a "button-pusher," and resulted in his eventual departure as a nocturnal record spinner.[35]

From January 15, 1966, until December 6, 1969, the Exhibition Hall on Wheeling Island served as Jamboree headquarters. On the first night a record crowd of 5,600 (in two shows) saw the performance with Buck Owens as special guest. Finally, on December 13, 1969, the Jamboree returned permanently to the Capitol Theater, scene of the first broadcasts and of special nights periodically thereafter. Basic Communications Incorporated had purchased the building that summer, renamed it the Capitol Music Hall, and moved the radio studios into the structure as well. By this time the show had a new name, "Jamboree U.S.A.," which seemed not only more cosmopolitan but more in keeping with the times, considering the fact that country music was now becoming accepted as something of a national institution. By this time, too, the Jamboree had reached an honored status as the only survivor (other than Nashville's "Grand Ole Opry" and "Renfro Valley Barn Dance," no longer on a major station) of the once numerous radio barn dance shows.[36]

As "Jamboree U.S.A." survived, however, the show's management accepted a degree of recognition of Nashville as the center of the industry. More and more it seemed that the biggest crowds visited Wheeling on the nights major figures from the Nashville scene did guest appearances. According to Tom Gray, then bass player for the Washington-based bluegrass band the Country Gentlemen, this trend began about the time the Gentlemen played there frequently in 1962-1963. It has continued steadily since that time, particularly since 1966. While some degree of accommodation to changing circumstances may have been necessary, the unfortunate result was the demotion of the Jamboree regulars to a status of second-rate performers on their own show. Wheeling had never become a recording center of note and various ventures into that phase of music met with only limited success. Doc Williams did moderately well with his own Wheeling label, but with few exceptions it was mostly a personal triumph for him and Chickie. Such Wheeling-oriented firms as Admiral, B-W, and Jamboree, the latter owned by "Jamboree U.S.A.," also failed to produce many hit records. Even in the 1950s, Jamboree stars who cut sessions on the major labels, such as the Coopers, Jimmy Walker, and Dusty Owens, went to Nashville to record. By the middle and later 1960s Nashville performers and styles were taking over the Jamboree. The bigger-name artists appeared as special guests while many of those struggling for recognition in Music City signed on as Jamboree artists and commuted to Wheeling partly in hopes that they could gain the attention there that had eluded them in Tennessee. For most, however, the strategy failed, partly because they found themselves overshadowed by a Tammy Wynette, Charlie Pride, Buck Owens, or Ray Price who appeared on "Jamboree U.S.A." as a special guest. A typical format for a two-hour show might feature four Jamboree regulars backed by a staff band playing quarter-hour segments. The second hour would feature the big-name guest star and his own band. A lesser known guest star might play for only a half-hour, and six Jamboree regulars would precede his appearance. In recent years, the most often heard regulars might play on the Jamboree only six to eight times annually, others even less often. By 1973 only ten Jamboree artists listed themselves as Wheeling area residents compared to eight in Nashville and twenty-one in other locales.[37]

The new system did not totally obscure the older performers. Big Slim continued to work on the Jamboree periodically until ill health and finally death overtook him in October 1966. Hardrock Gunter remained through most of the 1960s and Lee Moore stayed as a performer until 1973, although his all-night deejay show became a casualty to a more modern format in 1966. Doc and Chickie Williams have remained with the Jamboree, but their appearances have become increasingly few and far between, hitting lows of one in calendar years 1980 and 1982. Nonetheless, Doc still remains the Jamboree's single most prominent figure. His best box office years were in the mid-1960s, and tourists in town for the Jamboree have made their way in droves to his Country Store across the street from the Capitol Music Hall. Although the "Grand Ole Opry" has modernized, too, Roy Acuff, Bill Monroe, and Ernest Tubb remain as prominent symbols of the past. The newer management at WWVA has never seemed to know quite where to place their own legends, such as Doc Williams, who has been affiliated with the Jamboree longer than Acuff has with the Opry.[38]

Some of the other Jamboree artists have retained a flavor of the past. Bob Gallion held relative prominence through the early and mid-1970s, often appearing with Patti Powell. A Georgia girl, Patti sang modern solo songs and performed a type of hard-country duet with Gallion in the same tradition that found duos like George Jones and Melba Montgomery or Porter Wagoner and Dolly Parton appealing. Kenny Roberts, known earlier as a yodeler at WLW, survived on the Jamboree from 1959 until 1973 but altered his style more toward the country mainstream. Darnell Miller, a Bland, Virginia, native who earlier did extensive radio and television work in the Bluefield area, became a Jamboree regular in January 1966. Miller had earlier made a favorable impression with his Starday recording of "Mommy, Will My Doggie Understand?," a mournful original about a dying child in the vein of "Put My Little Shoes Away" and "Little Joe." Miller has remained at WWVA and sings good material, but like Vernon Oxford on the Nashville scene seems a little "too" country to become a superstar. So too does Junior Norman, a southeastern Ohioan of mixed blood who has been at Wheeling since 1970 and has become the WWVA answer to Charlie Pride. More modern in his stylings, Jimmie Stephens, a New Englander, appeared on the Jamboree for more than a decade beginning in 1963, becoming a regional favorite. Other good country performers in this vein have included Kenny Biggs, a corpulent vocalist from Sleepy Creek, West Virginia, by way of Aliquippa, Pennsylvania, who performed the hits from Nashville as well as some good original songs; Gus Thomas, a popular disc jockey by day who also did appealing vocals, sometimes with his wife, Jo Ann; Slim Lehart of Calis, West Virginia, a good crowd pleaser on the Jamboree stage who often played in his own local lounge; and Bud Cutright, a West Virginia migrant to Ohio who enjoyed a minor hit with his recording of "You Left Too Much" in 1969.[39]

Of those who used the Jamboree largely as a springboard, several enjoyed modest success although none achieved superstar status. Kathy Dee, a Moundsville girl who moved to the Cleveland area, displayed considerable promise in the 1960s. She appeared on the Jamboree off and on from 1956 and enjoyed a couple of songs on the charts,

"Unkind Words" and "Don't Leave Me Lonely Too Long" in 1963 and 1964, respectively. Then illness struck, eventually resulting in her blindness, an attempted comeback, and finally death in November 1968. The single biggest success was probably achieved by Johnny Russell, a Nashville-based Mississippian who signed as a Jamboree regular in March 1972. Russell had several minor hits and two major ones with "Red Neck, White Socks, and Blue Ribbon Beer" and "Catfish John." Although Russell had a relatively short tenure at WWVA, he strengthened his West Virginia credentials by marrying Beverly Heckel, a Randolph Countian who had been part of a popular family group the Heckels. The latter joined the Jamboree in the late 1960s and became widely known throughout the state from their role as entertainers in Jay Rockefeller's gubernatorial campaigns. In the process they did a great deal to popularize John Denver's "Take Me Home Country Roads" with its famous first line, "Almost Heaven West Virginia," throughout the Mountain State. Van Trevor affiliated with "Jamboree U.S.A." in 1967 and enjoyed the presence of eight songs on *Billboard's* charts through 1971. Mary Lou Turner, a singer based in Dayton, Ohio, worked at Wheeling from 1965 until 1973, when she went to Nashville as vocalist with the "Bill Anderson Show."[40]

Jamboree management has also kept a bluegrass band or two on their roster, although none of the later groups ever rivaled the Baileys in drawing power or the Osbornes in overall quality or impact. Jimmy Martin and the Sunny Mountain Boys headquartered at WWVA for a while and the Country Gentlemen visited often in 1962-1963. Martin, a powerful lead singer, featured a hard-driving style while the Gentlemen pioneered in the progressive style which included elements from urban-folk and non-country sources. Charlie Moore and Bill Napier appeared regularly from 1964 to 1967, and later Moore worked off and on again between 1971 and his death in 1979. Red Allen, once associated with the Osbornes, had bands on the Jamboree off and on throughout the 1960s and 1970s. Red Smiley and his Bluegrass Cutups based in Roanoke, Virginia, often played there from 1965. After Smiley dropped out in 1969 the band continued as the Shenandoah Cutups led by fiddler Tater Tate, who had played in the early 1950s as a sideman for the Baileys. Although Tate eventually joined the Opry, working for both Lester Flatt and Wilma Lee Cooper in recent years, he could boast even earlier that he had influenced Buddy Spicher, who hung around backstage at the Virginia Theater during Tater's initial sojourns at WWVA. Another bluegrass group at the Jamboree in the 1970s was Frank Necessary and the Stone Mountain Boys, a competent group who received much applause for their versions of Osborne Brothers' hits, but less acclaim because of limited originality. Finally, the Cochran Family, a pure West Virginia group from Webster County, also won fan favor partly as a result of the talented children in the band.[41]

Country gospel music also came into prominent popularity in this period. The Blue Ridge Quartet, in particular, gave gospel music a strong boost at "Jamboree U.S.A." Although based in Spartanburg, South Carolina, they played in Wheeling fairly often and won honors as the show's most popular act in 1970. Much of their success could be linked to the leadership of Fred Daniel, who had been with the Sunshine Boys two decades earlier. Eventually Daniel himself left the group to work as a solo gospel singer. Another gospel act, the Walter Bailes Singers, included Frankie Bailes and Dorothy Jo Hope (aunt of Dolly Parton and author of her hit song "Daddy Was an Old Time Preacherman") who worked at WWVA in 1973 and 1974 but eventually broke up because of Frankie Bailes's delicate health.[42]

Through the 1970's, WWVA management held a variety of special shows. On September 2, 1972, and September 1, 1973, "Truckers' Jamborees" featured specialists in that kind of song such as sometime-regular Jamboree performer Dick Curless of "Big Wheel Cannonball" and "Tombstone Every Mile" fame, Red Sovine, master of trucker recitation material, and Dave Dudley, who had made "Six Days on the Road" famous. Patti Powell added her own "Long Haul Widow." Capitol Records waxed the Curless performance for future release. Another feature, the annual homecoming reunions, brought back past stars led by Grandpa Jones and the Coopers, but also included some real old-timers such as Bill Jones and Elmer Crowe along with "evergreens" like Williams and Moore. On other occasions there were broadcasts from the Moundsville prison and a Bahamas cruise with Jamboree performers providing the entertainment to both captive audiences.[43]

Although outside of West Virginia proper, the mammoth outdoor country music festival Jamboree in the Hills constitutes an outgrowth of WWVA's activities. Initiated in July 1977, largely at the behest of Jamboree director Glenn Reeves, the open-air extravaganza held at Brush Run Park near St. Clairsville, Ohio, drew crowds estimated at from 20,000 to 39,000. Johnny Cash led the parade of stars, which has also included such Nashville luminaries as Mel Tillis, Tom T. Hall, and Barbara Mandrell. Mayf Nutter of Jane Lew, West Virginia, whose career has been divided between Wheeling and Hollywood (as an actor), recorded an official "Jamboree in the Hills" song about the event. A scattering of "Jamboree U.S.A." regulars has kept the event from being excessively Nashville dominated. To date, Jamboree in the Hills has achieved a degree of success as a country extravaganza marked by the absence of the disorder and riotous behavior that has marred many rock festivals and even a few bluegrass festivals.[44]

Wheeling and "Jamboree U.S.A.," although perhaps accepting a degree of subordination to Nashville, have endured as a regional center of country music. A 1967 survey showed that the program maintained a corps of listeners through most of New England, southeast Canada, Pennsylvania, New York, New Jersey, Maryland, and Delaware, and even points farther south. Northern West Virginia, eastern Ohio, and western Pennsylvania had the largest concentration of fans but those more remote in location also tended to be loyal. For those country music fans in the northeast—and there are many—the Opry remains far away for a weekend auto drive, but they find the Jamboree accessible. On November 27, 1976, the accumulated attendance since 1933 reached 5,000,000, which indicates that numerically the newer crowds have exceeded those in the earlier era, when the local artists had more integrity of their own. So, while Wheeling's reputation as a distinct center may have declined somewhat, and though the traditionalists say they cannot get their records played on the station with its chart-oriented format, the actual audience likely exceeds that of earlier times.[45]

Whether modern country, more traditional country, or bluegrass musicians adorn the stage of "Jamboree U.S.A.," the thousands of cheering fans in the live audience and the larger number of radio listeners bear witness to the show's continuing popularity. In 1983, as it passed its fiftieth year of existence, the Jamboree's place in history seemed assured. Even if it has become something of a "Nashville North" and more of a follower than a leader in the country music industry, WWVA and its musicians have made positive contributions. Over the years it has served as a place where northern and southern artists could meet, mingle, and even mix their styles. Sometimes they have produced a hybrid form of music that diluted the purity of the southern Appalachian strain. But in this process they have helped make the music more acceptable to those from cultures other than the rural Anglo-Saxon, Germanic, and Celtic bloodlines. Through their singing and playing, WWVA performers have brought pleasure to millions of people not only in West Virginia but elsewhere as well, particularly in areas north and east of the Mountain State.

4. Tune In: Radio to 1942

While WWVA has undoubtedly played a more significant role than any other broadcasting unit in the Mountain State, other stations have also featured a great deal of live country music in their programming. By the end of the 1920s four additional radio transmitters had gone into operation, three of which attracted many listeners in adjacent states as well as their own. Although the Great Depression hit West Virginia hard, the number of radios increased and in the middle and later 1930s more radio stations took to the airwaves.

Huntington, considerably newer than West Virginia's other cities, surpassed Wheeling as the state's premier metropolis in the 1920s, increasing its population from 50,177 to 75,572. By 1930 some 6,411 Huntingtonians owned radios and listeners also abounded in adjacent towns in Ohio and Kentucky. Unlike the northern panhandle, comparatively few owners existed in the neighboring hinterland counties, with Lincoln ranking lowest in the state, only 6.1 percent of its households owning sets. The city acquired West Virginia's second radio station in a somewhat roundabout manner. In 1923 Glenn Chase of Pomeroy, Ohio, obtained a license for WSAZ (meaning "Worst Station, A to Z"). By late 1926 Chase realized that he needed a larger city for his infant enterprise and shifted it to Huntington, where he combined his efforts with those of William McKeller, an electrical supply store operator. The show window of the McKeller Electric Company served as a studio for many of the early broadcasts.[1]

The early recording artists who came from the Huntington area along with a few associates provided WSAZ with its first country entertainers. David Miller's group, the Guyandotte Mockingbirds, generally consisting of banjo picker Cecil "Cobb" Adkins, several fiddling brothers named Baumgardner, and Belford Harvey, who played harmonica, banjo, and guitar, worked a great deal in the years prior to 1933. Miller's son recalls that Blind Davey did not have a very smooth relationship with McKeller. The Blind Soldier, forced by his affliction to support his family through music, complained about the inadequacy of his meager radio earnings which ranged from nothing to three dollars a day. McKeller argued that the publicity helped increase Miller's earning power for outside engagements. Finally after Davey complained about having to sing "Stackalee" excessively and McKeller cautioned him about his language, Miller threatened to throw the manager out the window. This ended the Blind Soldier's career as a regular radio artist, although he sometimes did guest spots on later shows and sang on Salvation Army radiothon fund raisers. By that time McKeller no longer controlled WSAZ, which had been purchased by the Huntington Publishing Company.

Following the initial appearances of David Miller and group, Frank Welling and a variety of associates were among those gaining early air exposure over WSAZ. Welling, his wife Thelma, John McGhee and daughter Alma, Miller Wikel, Tommy Cogar, and Bill Shannon all played on the station in an assortment of ensembles ranging from old-time string bands to gospel and barbershop quartets. Welling also appeared in Hawaiian groups and for a time, under the sponsorship of the Evans Baking Company, as Evans' Old Timer (a name used on some of his 1932 recordings). He sometimes did comedy and dramatic skits as well.[2]

Many of the other early country performers at WSAZ appeared only sporadically and remain relatively obscure. Local musicians from the Tri-State area provided a sort of talent reserve upon which either the station management or local sponsors could draw. Huntington newspapers in 1930, for instance, announced appearances by "guitar wizards" Howard and Roy, the Holcomb Brothers, the Kentucky Mountaineers, the West Virginia Ramblers, the Ohio River String Teasers, and the Houston Brothers of Proctorville, Ohio, who presented a "program of old-time tunes" on July 3. Jack Marlow, a Parkersburg product, sang briefly there before moving farther west where he later gained some renown as a radio singer in Sioux Falls, South Dakota. Other pickers and singers appeared as guests on the Saturday afternoon "Sandy Valley Grocery Program." Charles "Big Foot" Keaton of Ashland, Kentucky, who later became one of the area's premier old-time and western-style fiddlers, recalls making his radio debut on that show about 1932 when hardly more than a beginning pupil. Other artists appeared on the air only with listings such as "Old Time Music" or "Old Fiddlers."[3]

Three newer area performers emerged on more or less regular programs by 1935. Harmie Smith, often called the Ozark Mountaineer or with a band of that name, dated his first appearance on WSAZ to 1930. Born in Lawrence County, Kentucky, on August 19, 1908, Smith generally resided in Ashland and tended to rotate his radio base between Huntington, Charleston, and after 1935 Ashland with brief forays elsewhere. Smith built up considerable popularity in the Tri-State area and the Kanawha Valley, but according to close associates often shifted stations because "the grass looked greener" in other places. Smith also suffered from chronic asthma and had several close brushes with death. Finally in 1943 he went to KWKH Shreveport, Louisiana, and remained in that area for most of his career, dying in 1973. In Louisiana, Smith found not only a healthier climate but even wider popularity including a somewhat unexplainable appeal to black audiences. He also exercised influence on rising country artists like Webb Pierce and Hank Locklin and rockabilly pioneers like Tommy Sands and Elvis Presley.[4]

Bernard F. Henson created something of a link between an older and a younger generation of Huntington country musicians. He participated in fellow teenager Richard Cox's recording session in 1932 and had his own daily show on WSAZ the following year. David Miller sometimes guested on Henson's Rainbow Ridge show after his regular appearances stopped, and younger performers like Lonnie Lucas, Margie Shannon, and Hawkshaw Hawkins had some of their earliest radio experiences with him. Henson played both fiddle and guitar while singing such songs as "I Only Want a Buddy Not a Sweetheart" and "I Know What It Means to Be Lonesome." Never a full-time musician, "the old Cornhusker" remained in the employ of the Chesapeake and Ohio Railway and his job took him eastward as the national economy revived with the escalation of war in Europe. He also stayed in music, however, and April 1941 found him doing radio work at WHDH Boston with a group known as the Arizona Rangers. After the war Henson moved westward, reportedly dying in El Paso several years later.[5]

A third artist, Hobert Adkins, had two quarter-hour shows daily by May 1933 and a reputation as something of a loner. Like Frank Dudgeon, Adkins used "The West Virginia Hills" as a theme song. Eddie Nesbitt recalls him as a very good performer of old ballads.[6]

A band from nearby Catlettsburg, Kentucky, provided a youthful array of talent over a period of several years. Led by nonperformer Dolpha Skaggs, chief of the Catlettsburg police, the Mountain Melody Boys had a weekly half-hour show on WSAZ by 1933 and continued it after they obtained a daily show on Ashland's WCMI. Eventually sponsored in Huntington by Wonder Bread, they altered their name on WSAZ to the Wonder Melody Men. Early in 1938 the Mountain Melody Boys enhanced their reputation by playing a six-week engage-

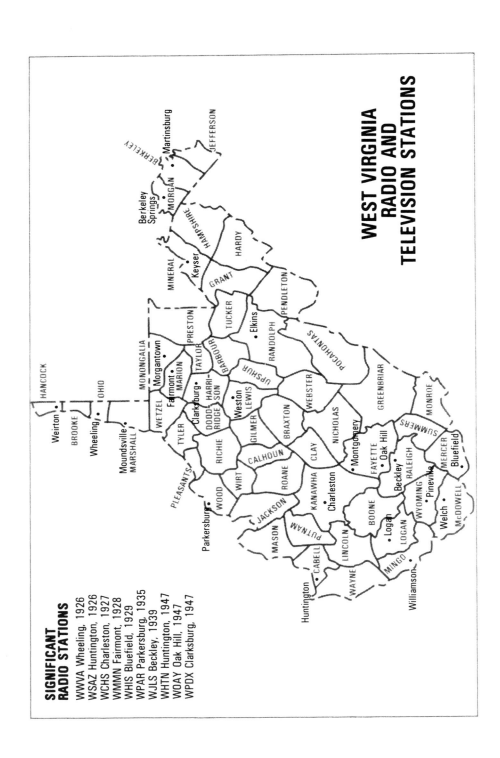

WEST VIRGINIA
RADIO AND
TELEVISION STATIONS

**SIGNIFICANT
RADIO STATIONS**

WWVA Wheeling, 1926
WSAZ Huntington, 1926
WCHS Charleston, 1927
WMMN Fairmont, 1928
WHIS Bluefield, 1929
WPAR Parkersburg, 1935
WJLS Beckley, 1939
WHTN Huntington, 1947
WOAY Oak Hill, 1947
WPDX Clarksburg, 1947

ment at the Village Barn in New York City and appeared on network radio. Early alumni of the band included Charles Wiginton, who subsequently worked for many years with Pee Wee King's Golden West Cowboys, and Slim Clere, who worked for three years with T. Texas Tyler and created the comedy character Nimrod. Later members included Big Foot Keaton, Bob Shortridge, and Curley Wellman, three young Ashlanders who after their New York experience joined forces with a bass-playing comedian named Jimmy Heaberlin from Kitts Hill, Ohio, to become the band for Curt Poulton on Knoxville's "Mid-Day Merry-Go-Round" and Nashville's "Grand Ole Opry." In 1939 they became a band for the team of Salt and Peanuts. Known as the Boys from Kentucky, the youths developed an excellent Sons of the Pioneers western-styled trio, playing radio at both Fairmont and Harrisonburg, Virginia.[7]

By 1939 a newer generation of musicians began to come of age in Huntington. These included Hawkshaw Hawkins, whose career fully matured at WWVA, and some other figures whose fame remained primarily local. Lonnie Lucas, who came from the same Guyandotte suburb as David Miller, played an excellent fiddle and organized a good band known as the Golden West Ramblers. Margie Shannon, still in her teens, became known as the Lone Star Yodeler, performing cowgirl type material somewhat similar to that done at the "National Barn Dance" by Louise Massey or Patsy Montana. Other young musicians whose careers began to blossom included the Heck Brothers—Del, Cliff, and Otis—of whom Del would eventually become a sideman at the Opry while Cliff would play in various New York country bands; Glen Ferguson, an outstanding young fiddler who alternated his career in later years between Huntington and sideman work with Hawkshaw Hawkins; and Johnnie Bias, who would later become known in locations ranging from Nashville to Hollywood as Johnnie Arizona.[8]

Not all the performers at WSAZ could be classed as local talent. As early as 1936 Riley Puckett and Bert Layne, seasoned veterans of both extensive radio work and recording sessions, came to Huntington for a few months, but left for Gary, Indiana, taking young Slim Clere and Richard Cox along in their Mountaineer Fiddler Band. The main impetus in bringing non-local hillbilly musicians to WSAZ came in 1939 with the station under the management of Meyer (Mike) Layman. According to Jenny Via, a Huntington-based country music journalist; "Mike was called in when station WSAZ was losing money and fast and after looking things over for awhile said, "What this station needs is a good group of hillbilly bands." Immediately he hired

Radio Dot and Smokey, Jake Taylor and his Railsplitters, Slim and Tex, and many others. With sponsored stage shows, PI accounts, etc., the station was soon out of the red and on a paying basis." Margie Shannon disagrees with Via's contention that WSAZ had been in financial trouble, but does point out that Huntingtonians supported outsiders with more zeal than they did home-grown artists such as Lonnie Lucas and herself. Be that as it may, the newly hired acts were ones whose prior experience had been at other stations in West Virginia. Dot and Smokey had little experience outside of Fairmont, while Taylor's had been there and in an earlier stint at WWVA. Slim Clere and Tex Tyler had broader experience but had worked together for only one season at Charleston and a few weeks each in Bristol, Virginia, and the little station at Williamson. Their sponsored stage show, the "Tri-State Roundup," took place in the Margaret Theater on Thursday nights with future sportscaster Gene Kelly announcing. It attracted considerable attention although hardly on a par with the radio jamborees held in Wheeling, Charleston, and Fairmont.[9]

The outside acts soon augmented their own talents with other performers. Jake Taylor hired "Cowboy" Copas as a featured vocalist. Copas, a tall Adams County, Ohio, farm youth, had been around several Ohio and West Virginia stations earlier, often in the employ of Larry Sunbrock, a promoter of fiddling contests, whose entourage included Natchee the Indian fiddler (Lester Vernon Storer), Indian Bill and Little Montana (Bill and Evalina Stallard), and Arizona Rusty (Arthur Gabbard). Clere and Tyler kept Orville Q. Miller, a Charleston tap dancer, in their "Gang" and also added Toot and Johnnie Sergent, a brother duo from Lincoln County who played excellent mandolin and guitar featuring the high lonesome vocal harmonies often associated with Carolina duet acts.[10]

By the time World War II opened, Huntington and WSAZ had begun to exhibit some of the characteristics of WWVA and some of the other Mountain State radio stations in promoting hillbilly music. When Mike Layman entered the navy in April 1942, Flem Evans replaced him and continued similar policies. Evans had previous experience with WPAR Parkersburg and WCHS Charleston, the latter a station whose management displayed a more consistent commitment toward country music programming, although Charlestonians also displayed similar degrees of ambivalence toward the idiom.

When the Charleston station initiated its broadcasts back on October 12, 1927, the call letters had been WOBU. Walter Fredericks, a local realtor, inaugurated it as a 50-watt operation and, like WWVA, the power slowly increased until it reached 1,000 watts in 1936. The

Huntington Publishing Company acquired ownership in 1935 and a year later John L. Kennedy of Clarksburg purchased both the Huntington and the Charleston radio outlets including them in his four-station West Virginia Network. Just before Kennedy obtained control the Huntington owners not only upgraded the power but also changed the call letters to WCHS, while moving the studios from the Ruffner Hotel to newer facilities on Capital Street. Still later, in May 1939, Kennedy bought Midelburg Auditorium, at 1121 Lee Street, to use for shows and studios, and in October boosted the power to 5,000 watts. At the beginning of the decade fewer Charlestonians than Huntington residents owned radios, but the large county of Kanawha with its numerous industrial towns and coal camps contained more sets, 10,220, than any other in the state. Dwellers in the mining counties of Fayette and Raleigh to the south owned more sets than those in the poor farm counties that surrounded Cabell County.[11]

The first country musicians on Charleston radio included the Kessinger Brothers and Bill Cox. The latter, a stationary engineer at the Ruffner, received his original impetus to record from Fredericks because of his irregular habits as a radio performer. Both he and the Kessingers did most of their work in the earlier years, although the latter apparently still had a regular show as late as 1937 under the sponsorship of the Butter Krust Bakery. In addition to Cliff Hobbs, several younger local musicians owed some musical debts to the Dixie Songbird, such as Kyle Bailes, Harry Griffith, and Cox's first cousin once removed , Woodrow "Red" Sovine, who became a major performer in Nashville for a quarter century. Cox also tended to perform risque material on occasion which allegedly terminated his radio career in the late 1930s.[12]

Other performers also graced the WOBU studio with their talent. Among the early performers, Willie Tyler, an excellent singer and yodeler, stood out in some persons, recollections while others recalled Jimmie Gravely or the duo of Jimmie Stamper and Hayes Young. The latter, a pair of railroaders, sang in a style somewhat "uptown" like that of Vernon Dalhart and Carson Robison. So too did Tommy Radcliffe, sometimes known as the Man with the Silver Throat, or the Friendly Troubadour. To more authentic down-home style performers such as Walter Bailes, the term "high class country" fit such vocalists as Stamper, Young, and Radcliffe. Bailes's preferences lay with Cox, the Kessingers, and more obscure groups such as Bob, Fred, and Fay Snider, who rendered a credible version of "When the Snowflakes Fall Again"; the duo of Smokey and Curley; or his own older kinfolks Jennings "Flash" Thomas and Kyle Bailes, who styled themselves the Mountaineer Cowboys. Thomas sometimes traveled with carnivals as a musician and Kyle, the eldest of the four Bailes Brothers, would work off and on for nearly a half-century with his brothers and other country musicians.[13]

The artist destined to have the largest single impact on the Charleston country radio scene, Buddy Starcher, made his initial entry in 1930. Born near Ripley on March 16, 1906, but reared primarily in the isolated sections of Nicholas County, Buddy learned the fundamentals of Appalachian music from his old-time fiddler father. Later he picked up some elements of commercialism from phonograph records and first sang over the airwaves at WFBR Baltimore in the fall of 1928. Something of a wanderer in his earlier years, Starcher remained at WOBU for only a few months, receiving no salary. In 1932 he spent part of the summer hanging around Washington, D.C., as a sympathizer of the Bonus Army during their weeks of protest, and singing a couple of compositions, "Hoover Blues" and "Bonus Blues." Recalling the latter song, which exposed him to a national audience—albeit anonymously—Buddy wrote: "This song was printed in Washington, D.C. by a veteran who had a printing shop, and we was told that he printed 5,000,000 copies. These were than given out to the veterans that made up the bonus army and they would sell them on the streets of Washington. Many sent them home to be sold by friends all over the USA . . . I sat on the steps of one of the make shift cabins and sung a few verses of the song for the Pathe News, which was shown in theaters all over the world."

The Bonus Blues

Hoover said go home boys, and dry up your tears
For you won't get your bonus for thirteen more years
Bid your wife goodbye boys and fall into line
For thirteen years boys, is a mighty long time.

When we were in France boys, you remember very well
And fought for our country, we sure had hell
Then we were heroes, and blessed by our land
But when we want money, no one offers a hand.

Go talk to old Hoover, with tears in your eyes
Just ask him for money and he'll look surprised
He'll say "Go home boys, that's where you belong"
And that is the reason, I'm writing this song.

When we were in France boys, fighting for our lives
And think of our mothers, our sweethearts, and wives
Hoover was at home boys, and he made himself rich
Now we fight for our bonus, and sleep in a ditch

I've counted the bed-bugs, I've counted the lice
I've counted the insects, I've counted the mice,
I've counted the soldiers, that left with goodbyes,
But I never have counted, Old Hoover's big lies.

So join in the chorus, let's sing this little tune
We may get our bonus by sometime next June
So come on and sing boys, help sing this little rhyme
For thirteen years boys, is a mighty long time.

With the failure of the bonus marchers, Buddy abandoned his fledgling career as a protest singer and social activist and drifted southward where he lingered for several months at radio station WSOC in Gastonia, North Carolina. There a musical trio known as the Three Tobacco Tags learned his song and likely recorded an unissued version of it for Champion on August 9, 1932. In the fall of 1933 he returned to Charleston and finally managed to land not only a sponsored show but also a regular position as announcer. Like the early artists at Wheeling, Buddy seems not to have realized the potential of personal showdates. When the former vaudeville duo of Salt and Peanuts came to WOBU and began booking theaters, they responded to inquiries about Buddy by bringing him along. Starcher soon got the idea and began booking himself. He and an announcer named Gene Ferguson also auditioned amateur talent on Wednesday evening and aired those approved on Friday night. In time this program, augmented by regular performers and a live audience, evolved into the "Old Farm Hour."

After two years in Charleston, Buddy grew restless again and moved to Washington where he had a daily show broadcast over the Dixie Network. He then went to WMMN Fairmont for the first time, staying six months, and then spent the winter of 1936-37 at WPAY Portsmouth where he survived the Great Ohio River Flood. In the summer of 1937 he returned to WCHS for the third time and organized Starcher's Mountaineers. A good unit, the group consisted of Jack Carter, a guitar picker; Robert (Georgia Slim) Rutland, an up and coming fiddler who had been at WCMI Ashland, Kentucky; Lee Moore, who had been a cowboy-style singer at both WPAY and WCMI; Smiley Sutter, a versatile musician who specialized in yodeling songs; and

Budge and Fudge Mayse, a duet from Braxton County who had been coming down on Friday nights to play on the "Old Farm Hour." Together with an occasional girl vocalist, Starcher's Mountaineers found themselves in great demand for personal appearances for the next fifteen months.

Although Buddy Starcher would not return to Charleston for twenty-two years after his 1938 departure, he managed to keep his popularity high in West Virginia by headquartering two more times in Fairmont, twice in Harrisonburg, Virginia, which had many West Virginia listeners, and once in Clarksburg. He also had radio stints in such distant locations as Shenandoah, Iowa, Philadelphia, and Miami. Whenever Buddy went he built up and retained a large number of fans and often kept his following by having transcriptions played in his former locations. By the mid-1940s he had built up a fan club of several thousand members and finally in 1946 began a recording career with the independent Four Star label. He waxed some four-teen sides including his most famous composition, "I'll Still Write Your Name in the Sand," which eventually became an often-recorded bluegrass standard, and his then-popular theme song, "Bless Your Little Heart." In 1949 he moved on to Columbia records and did ten numbers for that firm. Although many of his recorded songs featured an almost pop-style instrumental accompaniment, those that seemed most effective had only his own guitar backing. After a session with DeLuxe in 1954 that resulted in only one released single, he moved on to the Starday label at the end of the decade and did some more of the low-keyed but highly appealing vocals for which he became known. In 1960 he returned to Charleston with an early morning television show that had higher ratings locally than NBC's "Today" show. In 1966 he had his only really big hit with a recitation entitled "History Repeats Itself," a piece of nostalgia that detailed coincidence and similarity in the lives of Abraham Lincoln and John Kennedy. A nationwide infatuation with the Kennedy mystique helped catapult the song to not only a high position on the country charts but even the pop top-forty as well. After a brief fling in the national limelight, Buddy returned to radio as a station manager and eventually retired to a quiet life in his beloved Nicholas County hills.

One other aspect of Buddy Starcher's career deserves mention and that is his writing talent. Somehow only "Sweet Thing" and "I'll Still Write Your Name in the Sand" became standards among his song compositions, but another one apparently became something of a model for Hank Williams's "Cold Cold Heart." His recitations re-vealed a talent for prose as well. In 1944 he began serializing his autobiography in his fan club's journal and also authored a regular column in the magazine *Mountain Broadcast and Prairie Recorder.* In a sense this presaged the activities of artists like Jimmie Osborne, Bobby Gregory, and Bill Anderson, who became writers for other country music journals in later years.[14]

At about the same time that Buddy returned to WCHS, Frank Welling also came over from Huntington and joined the WCHS staff as an announcer and musician. As the Pow-a-Tan Old Timer, he performed on a daily quarter-hour show for Pow-a-Tan Tonic. The WCHS engineers also piped the show to the Parkersburg and Clarksburg stations via the West Virginia Network. Welling also gave numerous recitations and, having already introduced this variation of country song on record, further spread its appeal on radio. As Buddy Starcher had done earlier, Welling auditioned amateurs for possible guest spots of the "Old Farm Hour," which he emceed in the personage of his comic characterization Uncle Si.

Frank Welling pretty much directed the hillbilly music aspects of Charleston radio during his early years with the station. A 1940 promotional booklet for the West Virginia Network identified him as "in charge of our old-time talent and the Old Farm Hour in addition to his staff announcing duties," which generally ran from 6:00 to 8:00 each morning. The WCHS management reserved those hours almost exclusively for country music and made a positive albeit apologetic endorsement of the style with "We West Virginians like hillbilly music . . . but not all day long. Since the early days of WCHS these old melodies have had a place on our schedule." Certainly WCHS alloted more space to it in the booklet than any other on the network since Huntington and Parkersburg each gave it one-third page while Clarksburg gave it none. Welling's knowledge of the music and the dignity with which he approached it—in spite of the fact that his own style tended to be diluted, by pure hillbilly standards—no doubt contributed to this relatively enlightened outlook.[15]

During Frank Welling's initial year at WCHS, one of the more memorable events in Charleston's country music history took place. Promoter Larry Sunbrock staged a large number of fiddling contests from coast to coast in the mid-1930s and held one of these picturesque extravaganzas in the WCHS Auditorium on October 17, 1937, which he advertised as the "West Virginia String Band, Fiddlers, and Yodelers Championship Contests." A writer for *True* magazine later dubbed Sunbrock "the Greatest Cowboy Con-Man." He made use of radio to build up suspense for a promised showdown between the already legendary Clark Kessinger and Natchee the Indian, whom Sunbrock kept on his payroll most of the time. Other contestants also participated, including Ralph "Stuttering Zeke" Hamrick, a Roane Countain then working with the Dixie Ramblers; Big Foot Keaton, then only sixteen and called "the Wonder Fiddler" by Sunbrock; Fiddlin' Bob Rutland, better known as Georgia Slim; and a somewhat obscure character labeled Fiddlin' Johnnie. The stringband entries included the aggregations of which the fiddlers were part, such as Natchee's Tribe, Kessinger's Butter Krust Bakers, Al Hendershot's Dixie Ramblers, and the Mountain Melody Boys, but also lesser known groups bearing colorful names like the Cabin Creek Wildcats, Trail Blazers, Texas Cow Hands, and finally the unnamed band of future "National Barn Dance" star Bob Atcher (then performing for a brief stint at WCHS). Lee Moore, Smiley (Lonesome Singer) Sutter, Bob Atcher's wife, Bonnie Blue Eyes, and Gertrude Miller (who became the wife of former Georgia Wildcat Jack Dunigan) comprised the yodeling contestants. Sunbrock's ballyhoo pre-contest publicity paid off because a large enthusiastic crowd attended, but hardly anyone can recall who won the contests.[16]

The following year saw many changes in the talent lineup at WCHS. Having played out the territory, some bands broke up or went elsewhere while others remained. Starcher's Mountaineers split in late summer with Buddy and Smiley moving to Fairmont and the Mayse Brothers to Bluefield. Lee Moore, however, lingered in Charleston for another year, earning enough money, as he later recalled, to buy his first new D-45 Martin guitar. A girl whom he had met in Ashland, Juanita (Pickelsimer), the Gal from the Hills, and her "Sister Ann" came to Charleston, and when Lee and Juanita married after a few months they formed one of country music's more memorable radio duets. Grandpa Jones came to Charleston for a few months in 1938 and then moved on to WTIC in Hartford, Connecticut, but on May 13, 1939, settled in for a long stay at WMMN Fairmont. Cap, Andy, and Flip left Fairmont after September 16, 1939, evidently settling permanently at WCHS. The noted trio had their only recording sessions shortly afterward, waxing about a dozen sides which they subsequently released on their own Fireside Melodies label. By that time Lee and Juanita had relocated in Bluefield. In the meantime, Harmie Smith, formerly of Huntington and Ashland radio, had come to Charleston and persuaded former Mountain Melody Boy Slim Clere to move up from WSB Atlanta to play fiddle for him. Having accomplished that feat, Smith then got homesick for Ashland, leaving Clere to look for new associates and to develop his comic character Nimrod.[17]

Amongst all this shuffling of musicians, still more hillbilly groups came to Charleston, including two that already ranked among the best known in the nation. The Delmore Brothers, an Alabama duet, had five years of "Grand Ole Opry" experience and enough Bluebird Records on the market to make their vocal and instrumental stylings together with their original songs among the most copied anywhere when they arrived in Charleston in mid-March 1939. On Sunday, March 19, they appeared in two shows at the WCHS Auditorium with Natchee the Indian, Clark Kessinger, and Nimrod. The Delmores had two quarter-hour shows daily at 7:45 and 10:00 AM, but found the local economy hurting when a coal strike began on April 3 and continued for several weeks. Cliff Carlisle and his brother Bill, both veterans of radio in Louisville and the Carolinas and with about as many record sessions as the Delmores, found themselves in the same financial squeeze. Alton and Rabon Delmore held on for a few months, made one tour of showdates through southern West Virginia, and finally secured a spot at WAPI Birmingham, although they returned to West Virginia on Labor Day to fulfill a commitment at Huntington's Camden Park. The Carlisles held out until late July when they went to New York for two days of Decca recording sessions and then relocated at WNOX Knoxville.[18]

One group of young relatively unknown performers—Deacon Wayne and his Melody Boys—contained so many people that they were unable to make much from personal appearances because they had to split their meager profits among so many. As a result the group slowly faded in number and finally became the Red River Rangers, consisting solely of Ace Richman, Tennessee Smith, Smitty Smith, and a comedian known as Snoozy. After several weeks of tough times in Charleston, they managed to land a spot at Atlanta, where they gained more success as the gospel singing Sunshine Boys. The Smith Brothers also had considerable prosperity in Atlanta, but as Alton Delmore later wrote, "we all starved together" in Charleston in the spring of 1939. The one survivor of the Wayne group, T. Texas Tyler (David L. Myrick), an Arkansan, teamed up with Slim Clere to form the Slim and Tex duet. Once the economy recovered sufficiently, they enjoyed a year of modest prosperity, remaining in Charleston until July 1940.[19]

Slim and Tex came back to West Virginia in the fall of 1940 and worked at WSAZ until the spring of 1942 after which time Tex went on his own and eventually achieved national fame. He spent a few months in Fairmont and then went to Indianapolis, where he teamed with Jimmy Dickens, a southern West Virginia boy he had met earlier. They each had a solo program and then did a gospel program of duets. Tyler entered the service in 1944 and after the war ended up in California where numerous entertainers found prosperity playing to the Oklahoma, Texas, and Arkansas migrants whose economic status had improved via wartime and defense plant prosperity. Like Buddy Starcher, Tyler signed with Four Star records and soon became one of their top recording artists. Songs like "Remember Me" and "Oklahoma Hills" did quite well for Tyler, whose records generally featured western swing style accompaniment and a line or two of his good-natured growl in virtually every song except for his gospel and recitation numbers. Like Cowboy Copas, he helped to popularize Billy Cox's "Filipino Baby."

T. Texas Tyler's biggest hit, however, came in 1948 when he did an inspirational recitation entitled "Deck of Cards" which became one of the year's most popular country hits. According to Slim Clere, Tex had recomposed the number from an old poem about Wild Bill Hickok's gambling habits (possibly by Captain Jack Crawford, "the Poet Scout"), but the roots of "Deck of Cards" apparently go back into medieval Europe. Whatever its original source, his "tale about a soldier boy and a deck of cards" in the little chapel in North Africa did indeed bring some reality to his already widely used subtitle of "the man with a million friends." He remained one of the most popular country stars on the West Coast with a national following on records through the early 1950s. His last major hit in 1954, "Courtin' in the Rain," also came from the old-time repertoire, but Tyler managed to sing, growl, and recite his way through it to what was for him a somewhat atypical bluegrass accompaniment.

The middle 1950s have generally been considered a difficult period for Tyler and he apparently had some problems with alcohol and near brushes with the law, but eventually came out of it a changed man by 1957. In that year he wrote his old West Virginia pal Slim Clere about his changed attitude and hope for the afterlife (apparently in response to a letter from Slim telling him about the recent deaths of Warren Caplinger and Frank Welling). He joined the "Grand Ole Opry" for a time, but eventually turned extensively to evangelical work and became a Church of God minister and gospel singer with his headquarters in Springfield, Missouri. When he died from terminal cancer in January 1972 at the age of fifty-six, it was said that none of his once numerous Nashville and Hollywood friends attended his funeral. However, with the return of his remains to Huntington, where he was buried beside his first wife, a few of his old pals from the "Old Farm Hour" and the "Tri-State Roundup," including Clere, Margie Shannon, Molly O'Day, and Lynn Davis, paid their last respects to a man whom all agreed could never be surpassed at conveying his dynamic personality to a live audience.

The coming of a new decade saw six musical groups entrenched at WCHS along with announcer Welling, who had his own Pow-a-Tan Old Timer Show at 6:15 AM. The Trail Drifters, a group of younger performers led by Curley (later Rex) Parker and Tommy Cantrell, opened the daily broadcasting schedule at 6:00 AM. After Welling's program, Harmie Smith and his Ozark Mountaineers (then consisting of Ray Ross on bass and Big Foot Keaton on fiddle) came in at 6:30 AM. The next group, Bob Biddle and his Buckaroos, played semi-western swing. Later they had the misfortune to lose two members in World War II. Red and Raymond (Anderson), a father-son duo, followed and although new to Charleston had several years of experience behind them including WSB Atlanta. By this time, however, their days were numbered as little Yodeling Raymond, hitherto billed as "radio's littlest cowboy," was about to outgrow his cuteness and become (as one critic said) "just another fat adolescent." Slim and Tex held the 7:15 AM slot with a variety of western solos, duets, comedy, and fiddling accompanied by the tap dancing of Orville "Q" (for Quickstep) Miller. After a short newsbreak Cap, Andy, and Flip came on at 7:40 AM for twenty minutes. More often than not the popular trio also had a second show later in the day. By now the group did virtually all hymns and continued this format after Flip left later that year to be replaced by Andy's sixteen-year-old son Milton Patterson. Fortunately the three originals managed to preserve a few of their numbers on some custom recordings made in 1939 by Starr for their own Fireside Melodies label. Their own hymns included some real gems such as "I'm Taking My Audition to Sing Up in the Sky," "Star-Lit Heaven," and a lovely parody of "Will the Circle Be Unbroken" entitled "Television in the Sky," which contains a hopeful message that if people on earth could only behold the beauties of heaven via television they would surely seek salvation.[20]

The "Old Farm Hour" on Friday evening drew about 2,000 spectators weekly to the WCHS Auditorium. All the regular daily acts participated, with Welling as Uncle Si doing the emcee work. Here T. Texas Tyler introduced his famous "growl" technique by singing a special version of "El Rancho Grande" to a cheering audience. Youthful guest performers like the Lilly Brothers (as the Lonesome Holler Boys), who would someday introduce Boston brahmins to mountain duet singing, and the Bailes Brothers, who brought a "pentecostal" fervency to harmony duets at the "Grand Ole Opry," made their radio debuts. An existing program of a June 15, 1940, "Old Farm Hour" roadshow played at East Bank High School probably typifies the program as heard on the air. Following an opening chorus by the group and the introduction of Uncle Si, each act came out and did a couple of numbers: Bob Biddle's Buckaroos, Harmie Smith, Cowboy Copas (now known as the Gold Star Ranger and on his own from Sunbrock and Natchee), Red and Raymond, and Slim and Tex. Orville Q. Miller then did his "boy with the musical feet" routine, twelve-year-old Jackie Lee Miller sang, and the duo of Check and Curley did likewise. Comedy skits followed, one entitled "The Old Farm Hour Revue" and the other a "Specialty by Uncle Si." The "entire company" then did their "Grand Finale" and "round and square dancing" commenced after the floor was "cleared of seats."[21]

With the coming of World War II and gas rationing, the "Old Farm Hour," like the WWVA Jamboree, curtailed its live audience broadcasts, although not so drastically. Once a month the public performance broadcast continued from the WCHS Auditorium. To a greater degree than elsewhere, however, the war seemed to take something out of country music in Charleston. Cap, Andy, and Milt remained, evidently as popular as ever, and Frank Welling went on with his Uncle Si role. A few acts continued, but otherwise the Kanawha Valley entered a slow decline into a lackluster period of its musical history that would not undergo a real revival until about 1960.

Even before Charleston had hit its peak in the 1939-1941 period, a smaller northern West Virginia city evolved into an important center for hillbilly radio activity. Fairmont occupied the central geographic location in a string of three Monongahela Valley municipalities whose combined population and radio-set count in 1930 rivaled those of Charleston. Like Wheeling, the Fairmont station also had a reserve of listeners in southern Pennsylvania.

Radio had its origins in Fairmont when a local firm, the Holt-Rowe Novelty Company, purchased some used equipment from a Chicago station and set up a studio in the Fairmont Hotel. Taking its call letters from local resident and U.S. Senator Matthew M. Neeley, WMMN began broadcasting on December 22, 1928, with 500 watts of power. In December 1935, some months after control was bought by Fort Industry Incorporated of Toledo (later known as Storer Broadcasting and also owner of WWVA and WSPD Toledo), the power was increased to 1,000 watts and again to 5,000 in December 1938. By this time station publicity suggested that WMMN also signified "Where Miles Mean Nothing."[22]

   As in the other localities, country music on WMMN grew slowly from rather modest beginnings. Two of the earliest entertainers,
Mr. and Mrs. Lorain Gainer, had a Sunday evening program of old-
time hymns. Known as Gainer and Gainer, the couple featured
Lorain's tenor voice while his wife sang contralto and accompanied
their singing on piano. A regular station employee from 1929, Gainer
worked in the commercial department in addition to his singing
chores. Other early performers were announcer Herb Morrison and
fiddler Chuck Satterfield, who later played in the bands of other acts
at the station. String bands included the Puddle Jumpers from St. Leo
and the Critchfield Brothers from West Union. The Yerkey Twins—
Edward and Edwin—were an early duet who played at WMMN. But
one early artist overshadowed all the others because of his later prominence. Scott Wiseman (1909-1981) combined his radio performing
with academics at Fairmont State College. Born at Ingalls, North
Carolina, young Skyland Scotty played banjo and sang mountain songs
on a regular basis from early 1929 until 1933. After completing his
B.A. degree in 1932, Scotty also worked for a year as WMMN program director before moving on to WLS Chicago in 1933. By that time
he had also waxed a session for Bluebird Records. Making good use
of his West Virginia radio experience, Scotty combined forces with
Myrtle (Lulu Belle) Cooper and they soon married.
   The team of Lulu Belle and Scotty soon became the most popular
husband-wife duet in radio and perhaps in the entire entertainment
field. Lulu Belle pulled something of a surprise in 1936 by winning
a nationwide poll as the most popular girl in radio over several well-
known New York and Hollywood stars. Later they appeared in films
with people like Roy Rogers and Roy Acuff. They had nationwide
hit recordings including "Have I Told You Lately that I Love You"
and "Remember Me." By the time they retired from show business
and returned to their North Carolina homeland, Scotty had obtained
a Master of Arts Degree from Northwestern University. In their post-
retirement careers Scotty served as a bank director, and local voters
sent Lulu Belle to Raleigh for two terms in the state legislature. Few
if any other country music duos have ever matched the popular
esteem that Lulu Belle and Scotty achieved in both entertainment
and public service.[23]
   In 1934 Al Hendershot organized his initial hillbilly band, then
known as the Health and Happiness Gang. Hendershot, a native of
Grantsville, born March 20, 1899, moved to Akron about 1911 and
after several years of labor in a rubber factory entered radio work. The
original group consisted of Vic Marcin, fiddle; Al Poling, guitar; Ruby

Purkey, vocals; and Hendershot on guitar, comedy, and emcee. The following year the Gang moved on to Charleston and took the name Dixie Ramblers, a name Hendershot maintained for more than a dozen years on stations in many states including several in West Virginia (twice more in Fairmont). During that time numerous musicians spent brief stints with the Dixie Ramblers including two of Hendershot's own children.[24]

Through the earlier years, however, WMMN seems to have programmed relatively minimal amounts of country music. Buddy Starcher worked there for the first time on a sponsored show for six months beginning in the fall of 1935. He recalls a few other entertainers around the station, including Tommy Radcliffe, Joe Barker, Gertrude Miller, Audrey Tennant, and Hillbilly Bill Kirby. Nonetheless, at the end of 1935 only the duo of Tommy and Joe (probably Radcliffe and Barker, respectively), could be strictly identified as a hillbilly act, although the name of the sponsor can sometimes conceal the type of program in a listing. In succeeding months this situation underwent a gradual change. By early June the trio of Cap, Andy, and Flip had arrived on the scene and broadcast twice daily for a quarter-hour, at 7:45 AM and 1:45 PM. Three other country acts graced the station with regular programs: a string band, the Young Old Timers; Curley the Ranch Hand (Calvin "Curley" Miller); and Hillbilly Bill Kirby, now sponsored by Certified Crystals. The CBS Network carried a quarter-hour program three days weekly by Wilf "Montana Slim" Carter at 10:15 AM and a half-hour of the Indiana-based "Hoosier Hop" on Monday afternoons. One might conclude that the new management, having observed the potential in hillbilly music emerging at WWVA, endeavored to emulate their own performance by escalating the same process at their Fairmont property now that the latter station's power had been increased.[25]

Evidently the plan succeeded because in the next five years more and more radio time went to live performances of down-home style music from the WMMN studios. On August 10, 1936, the West Virginia Mountain Boys moved into the 7:30 AM time slot. Led by Frank Dudgeon, already a recording artist and veteran of radio work at WWVA and a couple of midwestern states, the band also included Fairmont fiddler Chuck Satterfield, banjoist Leroy (Pep) Saurborn, and guitarist Pink Saurborn. Other new acts who arrived at WMMN in the latter part of 1936 and earlier were the Mountaineer Girls, the Kentucky Hillbillies, and the much-traveled Tweedy Brothers, pioneer recording artists. Curly Miller acquired a band, the Ranch Hands, which included one Cowboy Jack. Some of these groups remained for relatively brief periods.[26]

The team at Blaine and Cal Smith constituted the major new act at Fairmont in terms of up-and-coming popularity. Blaine Smith, a native of Dickens, Iowa, had been born on September 2, 1915. Reared in Ohio, Smith performed both by himself and with Cal, his older brother by three years, and at times also led a group called the Boys from Iowa. At the time of his arrival at WMMN, Smith had already appeared regularly on stations in Cleveland, at KDKA Pittsburgh, and at WWVA. He likely achieved more fame and success at Fairmont than in the larger cities, however. Strikingly handsome, Smith won an especially large following among female listeners. His vocal style, amazingly soft and smooth for a country singer (almost in the popular vein), along with his looks won followers among younger feminine clientele some of whom probably cared little for other country singers. At the same time his favoring of old songs, reverence for motherhood (he apparently sold huge numbers of pictures of his own West Virginia-born mother over the air), and his championing of the old values made him equally popular with more mature women. In February 1939 he and Cal had a session with the American Record Corporation in Chicago and they subsequently spent a year at WLS and the "National Barn Dance." Returning to Fairmont in November 1940, Smith took up where he had left off earlier with a new band that included Bill Hatfield on mandola, Ted McCoy on steel guitar, and the Davis Twins as a featured duet.[27]

Some of the other artists who came to WMMN had pretty well established their reputations by the time of their arrival. Cowboy Loye Pack spent nearly four successful years at WWVA in addition to radio experience elsewhere. The size of his Blue Bonnett Troupe gradually expanded from the time of his arrival in September 1937 until it sometimes included more than a dozen members. French Mitchell, who had worked with Loye at WWVA, returned from his Putnam County home, fiddle in hand. Loye carried a second fiddler, one James "Sheepherder" Moore, who also played harmonica and was one of the oldest performers of his time, having been born back in 1869. Moore came from Nebraska and must certainly have been one of Loye's associates from his ranch-hand days. Custer Allen, Just Plain John Oldham, and Smiley Lowe constituted three other members of Loye's band. A trio-singing sister group from the hamlet of Hundred in Wetzel County probably made up the most popular members of the group other than the Cowboy himself. Known as the Blue Bonnett Girls, Sylvia, Lillian, and Florence Curry delighted audiences with harmony renditions of old ballads and hymns and even managed to continue by themselves for several years after their mentor's untimely passing. Loye had suffered from ulcers for several weeks when he went to the Cleveland Clinic for an operation on March 12, 1941. He survived the surgery but died early on the morning of March 15, reportedly from bleeding when he ripped his stitches after regaining partial consciousness. At a memorial program held at WMMN on March 19, announcer Uncle Bill Taber told among other things of the irony he had experienced in introducing the popular artist at his first radio appearance in York, Nebraska, in 1929, and at his last show at WMMN on March 3. Unfortunately Cowboy Loye, who ranked as one of the most popular country singers of his era, never made a single phonograph recording.[28]

A frequent associate of Loye's, Ray Myers, won wide acclaim as "the world famous armless musician." Born near Lancaster, Pennsylvania, on January 2, 1911, young Myers adjusted amazingly well to his handicap from birth, contending that he could do virtually anything his brothers and other neighborhood children did. After receiving widespread publicity at the Chicago Exposition of 1933 via Robert Ripley's "Believe It Or Not" exhibit and writings, Myers went into radio. He soon gained a name for his ability to boost attendance at stage shows. Myers had a creditable singing voice, played harmonica, and chorded a Hawaiian guitar with his toes well enough to accompany his vocals and please audiences. He also demonstrated his abilities to handle such tasks as opening cans, grooming hair, and doing carpentry. Since his act generally had what one might call high intensity but short-term appeal, Ray tended to relocate every few months. He had worked on Pennsylvania stations and with Loye at WWVA prior to coming to Fairmont in the fall of 1937. Romance entered Ray's life at this point and his December 22, 1937, marriage to Eleanor Jane Sturm on stage in the Fairmont High School Auditorium attracted thousands of fans and well-wishers. A few months later the Myerses moved on to Reading, Pennsylvania, but he later returned to WMMN and other Mountain State stations as well.[29]

A female band leader who strongly came into her own at WMMN after working briefly in Cowboy Loye's unit at WWVA gained fame as Radio Dot. Born Dorothy Maxine Henderson on August 27, 1916, at Hundred, West Virginia, she organized her Jubilee Boys in October 1937. Initially the band included Big John Stockdale on fiddle, Fred Wells on tenor banjo, and Little John Graham on guitar. Dot sang, emceed, and provided leadership while the boys joined in various vocal combinations. Graham recalls that in the early days of the group's struggle for livelihood, they shared equally in the profits, but when their popularity and showdate receipts soared upward, Dot put the band members on a weekly salary of twenty dollars. By mid-March 1938, Radio Dot's standing at WMMN reached a rough equality with Cowboy Loye's in terms of mail and far ahead of Blaine Smith's and Curley Miller's, the other high-ranking hillbilly acts at that time. In terms of her artistry and style Radio Dot could almost be considered a female counterpart of Blaine Smith. Her youth, soft voice, and attractive features appealed to younger men while her old songs, hymns, and brief homespun homilies found favor with the older generation of both sexes. Unlike Smith, however, who tended to veer away from a brother duet toward a solo performer image, Radio Dot found a husband in the person of Louis W. "Smokey" Swan and became half of a team. Various members entered and left the Jubilee Boys over the next several years, the most notable being Dot's younger brothers Jack and Ted Henderson, and Webster Countian Ray Anderson. Each of the Hendersons gained some renown on his own, largely at Nashville's other major station, WLAC, where Ted also worked with his wife Wanda. Dot and Smokey also eventually wound up in Nashville by way of Huntington, Charleston, and Shreveport, Louisiana.[30]

One Wheeling personality who came to Fairmont found his career cut short by tragedy. Murrell Poor came to WMMN in 1937 working primarily as an announcer but also giving recitations and singing an occasional song. He gathered a band known as the Tradin' Post Gang that consisted of Little John Graham, Jimmie Smith (called the Virginia Vagabond) and tenor banjo player Howard "Big Eared Zip" Binnix. Binnix was one of the few musicians to actually come from the Fairmont area, working in the bands of numerous WMMN artists up into the 1950s. Returning from a personal appearance at Mill Creek in Randolph County, the band's auto crashed and Poor died in a Philippi hospital although the others survived with minor injuries. The Old Pardner's death on June 1, 1939, and his subsequent funeral drew a crowd estimated at 10,000, while another 17,000 had viewed the body earlier. Mel Cox, Hal Harris, and Red Kidwell from WWVA sang at the funeral and the entire incident produced a wave of mass sorrow like that later associated with the death of Hank Williams. Joe Wright, a WMMN janitor, composed a memorial poem later recited (and possibly sung) in tribute to his well-liked friend which demonstrates something of the esteem held by the common man toward his radio pals:

> The Old Pardner
> The old pardner was a real entertainer,
> With hillbilly down deep in his soul

He traveled the hills and valleys,
Pleasing friends was his one great goal.

He gave a show worth seeing,
Sang real folk songs every day;
He went smiling on personal appearances,
And always returned that way.

Until one night deaths grim reaper
Came and took him by the hand;
He was killed in a wreck on the highway,
And everyone lost a true friend.

Thousands attended his funeral,
Thousands still miss him today;
He was really a friend to many,
So good bye "Old Pardner" we say.

And if hillbillies go to Heaven,
The old pardner is there today;
Looking forward to a great reunion
Somewhere along the Heavenly way.[31]

Some of the musicians who came to Fairmont had prior experience in locations other than WWVA. Buddy Starcher came back in September 1938 after his success at WCHS. In Fairmont he teamed up with the Connecticut-born yodeler Smiley Sutter, who had been part of his Mountaineer group in Charleston. Starcher frequently did a quarter-hour daily program solo and a half-hour one with Sutter as "Buddy and Smiley." Ted Grant, once trained as a violinist and a former member of Hugh and Shug's Radio Pals, also joined them. During this sojourn at WMMN, Buddy first met Mary Ann (Vasas) Estes, who worked as a vocalist with the Hickory Nuts. Some time later she joined the group and also became Mary Ann Starcher. The groups associated with Buddy Starcher could always provide a wide variety of entertainment.[32]

By the end of 1938 the WMMN program schedule featured at least two and a half hours of live hillbilly music between 6:00 AM and 6:00 PM. Cap, Andy, and Flip moved to Charleston permanently in September 1939 and Curley Miller went to Wheeling, but other acts remained while more continued to arrive. The notion of an evening live audience show like that at WWVA, WCHS, and other stations across the country loomed in the near future. Known as the "Sagebrush Roundup" and first presented at the Fairmont Armory on Saturday, December 10, 1938, the program became an almost instant success. Murrell Poor and Uncle Nat Royster, a vaudeville veteran newly arrived at WMMN with his Smoky Mountaineers, put the first shows together. Unlike the WWVA Jamboree which generally required all of its regulars present each Saturday night, only half of the "Sagebrush Roundup" cast appeared on a given show. This permitted outside showdates roughly half the time. Station officials charged admission, with the artists sharing in the gate receipts. In 1941 the CBS Network auditioned the show for possible nationwide broadcast and although they did not place it on the network, the mere fact of consideration demonstrates that the program carried substantial prestige. Except for the "Renfro Valley Barn Dance," the other hillbilly radio jamborees of major reputation all originated in cities much larger than Fairmont—Chicago, Nashville, Des Moines, Atlanta, Cincinnati, Wheeling, Charlotte, Charleston—and generally over radio stations more powerful than WMMN.[33]

Several new musical groups came to Fairmont in 1939. Grandpa Jones and his Grandsons, consisting of Lennie Aleshire, Loren Bledsoe, and Harold Rensler, proved to be highly popular. Jones already had a following in the state from his prior stints at WWVA and WCHS, and increased it by remaining at WMMN for nearly two years and then returning to Wheeling. Jake Taylor's Railsplitters proved as popular in Fairmont as they had been at WWVA and would later be at WSAZ. With featured band members like the Harmony Brothers (Bernard Lohri and Bob Steele), comedian Jewel "Shorty" Sharpe, and bassist Herman "Tex" Redmon, long a familiar sideman with Wheeling and Fairmont acts, the Railsplitters had considerable appeal to WMMN listeners. Jimmy James (real name Vincent Gamelli), born in Springfield, Massachusetts, on August 10, 1912, had a dance band background but had also worked with H.M. Barnes's Blue Ridge Ramblers before coming to WMMN, where he organized his Hickory Nuts group. Yodeling cowgirl Mary Ann Estes and Enoch "Eli" Haney, a smooth vocalist from Smithfield, Pennsylvania, handled most of the singing with the Hickory Nuts while James did comedy augmented by zany sounds he extracted from trombones, hot water bottles, and a variety of other instruments. Their material varied from humorous and novelty numbers to sad laments of dying children such as "Will There Be a Santa Claus in Heaven?"

Perhaps the most significant of all the traveling acts that served time at WMMN—Salt and Peanuts—had much respected radio and vaudeville experience. Frank Salt (Franklin Kurtz) bore a long-standing reputation as a real professional in terms of quality entertainment.

With Salt and Peanuts (Margaret McConnell) doing their comic novelty tunes assisted by son Buddy Frank and a youthful but talented trio, the Boys from Kentucky (comprised of ex-Mountain Melody Boys Curley Wellman, Bob Shortridge, and Big Foot Keaton), the act gave a road show of real quality—so good, in fact, that Clayton McMichen tried without success to hire the Boys away from Salt.[34]

By February 16, 1940, live hillbilly programming at Fairmont increased to the point that the station was broadcasting five hours and forty-two minutes of music daily, plus at least another hour via transcription. Cowboy Loye, Buddy and Smiley, Jake Taylor, and Grandpa Jones had forty-five minutes each, usually in two shows. Radio Dot and Smokey and Uncle Nat had half-hour programs while the Hickory Nuts had twenty-seven minutes. Frank Dudgeon, the Rhythm Roundup, Slim Mays, Arizona Rusty Gabbard, and Clem's Ranch Hands each had a quarter-hour. The station also carried forty-five minutes daily of transcriptions by the Carter Family, and the Ralston Purina Company's Checkerboard Time thrice weekly. Some of the other shows may have included live country music. This means that more than half of WMMN's daily programs consisted of country music in addition to an hour of the "Sagebrush Roundup" on Saturday evening.[35]

One of the newer acts at Fairmont in early 1941 was Jack Dunigan's Trail Blazers. Dunigan, born near Alton, Missouri, in 1909, had once been a member of Clayton McMichen's Georgia Wildcats and worked on some major stations solo as well, including a year at WWVA. At the time of his brief Fairmont experience, he had recently recovered from a lung operation and his wife, Gertrude Miller, did much of the vocalizing. Although somewhat "high-class country" in her style, Gertrude could yodel and did a lot of older songs such as "Sweet Kitty Wells" that proved popular with fans. Red Herron, who became one of the more prominent fiddlers of the 1940s and early 1950s, also worked with the band. They figured prominently in the WMMN schedule at the time the "Sagebrush Roundup" received its network audition. Perhaps their departure in late April 1941 for WKBN Youngstown, Ohio, was one reason CBS decided not to use the program. Mack Jeffers and his Fiddlin' Farmers also had something of a name, although a less prestigious one than the Dunigan group. Jeffers came from east Tennessee and the band included his two sons Slick and Sleepy, the latter of whom married Maxine (Honey) Davis of Davis Twins fame and became a noted performer and comedian (as Little Willie) in his own right. Bill "Shorty" Godwin (1889-1959), already a veteran of tent and vaudeville shows in the Deep South and a 1929 Columbia recording session, remained in West Virginia after the Farmers disbanded and spent the twilight years of a more than half-century career as a comedian for Doc Williams under the name Hiram Hayseed, a character he had already portrayed for several years. Another hillbilly comedian, Uncle Rufe Armstrong of New Bern, North Carolina, also had a vaudeville background, while his wife Norma (or "Petunia") had worked at WSM and with Grand Ole Opry road shows. Their unit, the Coonhunters, consisted of local West Virginians like the veteran "Hillbilly Bill" Kirby, May "Boots" Minner, and Moundsville native Earl (Little) Sampson, a sideman with many WWVA and WMMN acts. A new act to show business, the Campbell Sisters Trio—Jane, Evelyn, and Lorene—came to Fairmont from Ohio with little professional experience. Overall, the WMMN hillbilly talent lineup displayed a rather rare and varied combination of geographic diversity, a broad range of experience, and age differences in their performers that added depth to the roots of country music, then as always in a state of evolution and change.[36]

Other new acts at WMMN grew out of personnel changes as some people moved on and others remained. Little John Graham, only twenty in 1940, had worked with Radio Dot, Murrell Poor, and Buddy Starcher before obtaining his own show. In that year the Monongalia County native met an eighteen-year-old girl singer from Youngstown, Ohio, with the unlikely country name of Hattie Dickenhoff. Using the stage name Cherokee Sue, however, she proved quite popular, especially with children. John and Sue married in Buckhannon on June 22, 1941, before a crowd estimated at 14,000. From then on John and Sue generally had a duet program as well as their own separate shows, and often they combined with Budge and Fudge Mayse on their showdates. The Mayse Brothers had come to WMMN late in 1939 and worked with Buddy Starcher for a few months before getting their own show in November 1940. In the spring of 1942 John and Sue went to WSAZ Huntington for a brief period before John entered military service, and T. Texas Tyler took their spots at WMMN when Slim and Tex split up about this time. Little Jimmy Dickens had also come to Fairmont. Another group with past West Virginia experience called themselves Hill-Billy Varieties. Arthur (Rusty) Gabbard worked with that group, as well as solo, with his dad as the Singing Gabbards, and briefly with Buddy Starcher as a Smiley Sutter replacement. The remainder of Hill-Billy Varieties was composed of Indian Bill Stallard, Little Montana, and for a short time Natchee the Indian. None of this last group remained quite as long as Arizona Rusty (who had never set foot in Arizona at the time, much less punched cows or ridden broncs in the Desert State).[37]

The fall of 1941 and the following winter brought some changes to WMMN. Buddy Starcher spent the summer in Indianapolis and did not feel quite the same when he returned. His close friend Cowboy Loye had died in the spring and many of his old "All-Star Roundup" touring unit had gone their separate ways. Loye's death in particular had unnerved him and he sought new territory, accepting a job at WSVA Harrisonburg, Virginia. This station went on the air in 1935 and had a large audience in the Shenandoah Valley and along the eastern fringes of West Virginia. Over the next several years numerous acts from WMMN and WSVA exchanged places. In addition to T. Texas Tyler and Little Jimmy Dickens, Lee and Juanita Moore comprised the new acts at Fairmont while the Franklin Brothers, who had worked earlier in Buddy's group, got their own show. Lee Moore recalls an interesting baseball game that spring between teams representing the radio station and the Fairmont newspapers. Members of the victorious WMMN team included himself, Tyler, and Dickens, the latter as shortstop. As the impact of World War II began to be felt in the Monongahela Valley, Fairmont continued its position as Wheeling's chief rival as a live country talent station and as a location where ethnic influences entered Appalachian music. (Pennsylvania stations had a role here, too.) As early as June 1941, the WMMN program director reduced the time given to hillbilly broadcasts from five hours and forty-two minutes to four hours and fifteen minutes, but this was still higher than at most stations.[38]

A station on West Virginia's southern border that fulfilled a function similar to that of WMMN in the north was WHIS Bluefield. This city increased in population from 15,000 to 19,000 during the 1920s and maintained its position as the urban center for the Pocahontas coalfields. Radio set ownership in that section tended to lag behind the less isolated northern counties, although a higher percentage of Bluefield residents owned receivers in 1930 than was true in Huntington. In the later 1920s Hugh Ike Shott, publisher of the *Bluefield Telegraph* and Republican party leader, aspired to add radio to his communication network. Shott secured a license and WHIS (from his initials) began broadcasts on June 24, 1929. The station operated with only 100 watts and for three and a half hours daily in its first two years of operation. Gradually as the station increased its power and programming, the local management learned of the appeal of downhome music to potential listeners.

In the mid-1930s WHIS began to boom as a hillbilly station. The early performers tended to be local. Two area youths in their late teens, Jimmy Barker and Gordon Jennings, worked as the duo of Gordon and Jimmy. Barker also frequently did comedy using the name

"Elmer, the Hillbilly Kid." Frequently subordinating himself in other groups, he eventually left WHIS with the Lynn Davis band, first for Beckley and then for Birmingham, Alabama.

Ordon Lafayette "Gordon" Jennings was born in Freeman, West Virginia, on October 21, 1916. Although he never attained national stature, Jennings remained a pivotal figure on the Bluefield scene for several decades. After Barker joined Lynn Davis, Jennings did some solo work and also worked as part of Ezra Cline's group, the Lonesome Pine Fiddlers. Jennings did much of their lead singing in the early years and also learned some booking skills which he made use of not only for the Fiddlers but for other Bluefield acts. When gasoline shortages curtailed personal appearances during the war, he sought work at a larger station and joined the Carson Cowboys, who had a network program based in St. Louis. He spent five years with this group and enjoyed a brief flair of national publicity at the end of the war by singing a parody of "Wabash Cannonball," about the Japanese surrender, on all the major radio networks.

In 1951 Gordon Jennings returned to Bluefield as a deejay and singer at WKOY. During the ensuing decade he made a few recordings, all for small firms with limited distribution. His most popular effort was a slightly modernized version of Arville Reed's old Victor solo "The Telephone Girl" on the Kingsport label. He also recorded a fine original song entitled "Monday Morning Blues" in a Hank Williams styling. When WHIS expanded into television, Jennings emceed their Saturday jamboree show and sang occasionally in addition to weekday deejay chores. He maintained a highly respected reputation as a regional country music figure until he passed away in the spring of 1982.

Another important early figure at Bluefield and WHIS, Joe Woods, ran a place called the Hillbilly Barn where he hosted dances and live stage shows. Although Woods himself was classified more as a promoter than as a musician, the Joe Woods Harmony Band included a number of outstanding musicians who worked on and off at WHIS in a variety of bands and solo groups for many years. These included Joe's son Otis Woods, Lyle Keeney, Tex McGuire, and Garland Hess. Hess saw a better future in radio management, however, and soon moved into sales work, subsequently becoming owner and manager of his own station in Tazewell, Virginia.[39]

Fiddler Leslie Keith was the outstanding musician to work for Woods, at least in the early days. A native of Pulaski County, Virginia, born March 30, 1906, Keith lived in Tennessee for several years and developed a fine fiddle technique, winning several contests in that state. In 1936, while visiting his cousin, Woods asked Keith to join his group at WHIS. Billed as the Champion Tennessee Trick Fiddler, Keith proved to be an outstanding attraction with his superb skill and showmanship and his original tune "Black Mountain Blues" (later called "Black Mountain Rag"). In the spring of 1938 Keith and Woods sponsored a fiddler's contest at Glenwood Park near Bluefield which drew 9,400 people and twenty-seven entries. The crowd saw Keith and famed WSM fiddler Arthur Smith finish in a tie which four runoffs failed to break.

After World War II military service, Leslie Keith continued his fiddle work, mostly at radio station WCYB in Bristol. He played with the Stanley Brothers when that now legendary bluegrass duo organized their first band, and helped them learn the business. He recorded on their early Rich-R-Tone sessions. Later he also worked with the harmony duet of Bill and Earl Bolick—the Blue Sky Boys—and with Curley King's Tennessee Hilltoppers. Eventually he retired to Arizona but returned east to play at the Carter Stanley Memorial Festival a couple of times. By the time of his death in 1977 he had finally managed to get an album of his fiddle work released and began to gain some recognition from folklorists as a historic figure in the commercialization of old-time fiddle music.[40]

Some of the musicians who came to WHIS to work for Joe Woods arrived from more distant locations. Kentuckians James and Martha Roberts, newlyweds in late 1939, came to West Virginia and worked for six months with Woods's group, now known as the Pioneer Boys. Martha also worked in a trio with her sisters Opal and Bertha as the Sunshine Sisters. A couple of years later the Robertses gained considerable attention at WSB Atlanta as James and Martha Carson—the Barn Dance Sweethearts—while Opal became a successful vocalist and writer under the names Mattie O'Neal and then Jean Chapel.[41]

Another stimulus to country music at WHIS occurred when the Jeffries Drug Company started an early "Morning Jamboree" from 5:00 to 7:00 AM to advertise their line of Bi-Tone Products, which included cough syrup, tonic, and liver pills. Also about this time WHIS became a 1,000-watt station. Lynn Davis, a veteran of weekly shows at WSAZ and WCHS along with a lengthy tour with Shorty Fincher's Prairie Pals in the fall of 1936, returned to Bluefield at the end of the year and organized his Forty-Niners. Davis sang and played an excellent lead guitar while a pair of Pennsylvania yodeling cowgirls, Sue and Ann Mason, and fiddler Georgia Brown rounded out the group. Gordon Jennings and Jimmy Barker also joined the cast of the "Morning Jamboree," as did Claymon Foster, a local vocalist and folksong authority, Sleepy Perkins, a tenor banjo-playing comedian, and Sky

Buck, a fiddler with considerable past radio experience. Two brothers from Mingo County, Esmond and Esland Stepp, sang songs in the Delmore style, and one Cowboy Jack Morris boasted a wide reper- tory that included about every song. The show proved popular, but Bi-Tone Products had their problems. As Gordon Jennings humorously told his biographer, once customers saw the word strychnine on some of the labels, you could not even give them away.

Some shuffling also occurred in band personnel. Jimmy Barker joined the Forty-Niners, and Gordon Jennings combined forces with the Cline Boys, who came down from Gilbert. Ezra Cline, a thirty- one-year-old bass player, came to WHIS in 1938 with his teen-aged kinsmen Ireland "Lazy Ned" Cline on banjo and "Curly Ray" Cline on fiddle. With Jennings on guitar and doing the lead vocals, the band became known as the Lonesome Pine Fiddlers. They remained at WHIS with varying personnel off and on until 1952 and in existence until 1968, becoming one of the most influential pioneers of bluegrass from 1950 onward.[42]

Some new groups also came to Bluefield in 1939. Lee and Juanita Moore, another pair of recent newlyweds, proved very popular, receiv- ing mail literally in bushel baskets for the friendship ball-point pens they sold on a PI basis. The Buskirk Family, veterans of Parkersburg and Fairmont radio programs, also did quite well with their ballads, old-time hymns, and young Paul Buskirk, already a wizard on the mandolin. Judie and Julie Jones, a sister duo from Mullins, worked at both WHIS and WJLS Beckley. With a singing style closely resem- bling Millie and Dolly Good of "National Barn Dance" fame, the Jones Sisters landed a recording contract with Bluebird and spent stints at both WLS and WLW.[43]

Many of these artists and possibly others also worked on Bluefield radio under names associated with various sponsors. The Lilly Moun- taineers, for instance, always worked for the Lilly Land Company, the J.F.G. Coffee Boys for that firm, the Rock Cliff Musical Moments for the Rock Mineral Springs Company, and the Purity Maid Bakers for the bread of the same name. Lee Moore recalls that transcriptions also were occasionally played for some of these shows, and particular- ly remembers Sons of the Pioneers' material being used on the J.F.G. Coffee time slot.[44]

Woody Williams also led a popular group in Bluefield for several years. The band included among others Woody's brothers Jack and Buddy. Curly Ray Cline recalls that they played an older style of music featuring a lot of guitar and old-time fiddle with a vocal style not great- ly different from that of Cap, Andy, and Flip.[45]

The Holden Brothers constituted a well-liked act at Bluefield that originated some distance from the Mountain State. Fairley Holden and Milton Jackson, although unrelated, used the names Fairley and Jack, the Holden Brothers. Of Georgia origin, they had been born there in 1916 and 1915, respectively. The Holdens circulated extensively through several states after meeting in a CCC camp, and played in Charleston as part of Al Hendershot's Dixie Ramblers. At Bluefield, Jack met his wife and sometime singing partner, Frances Kay. The Holdens also usually had a fiddler in their group, the spot at various times being occupied by Curley Parker, Skeets Williamson, and Ralph "Zeke" Hamrick, who also did comedy. The Holdens played twice at Bluefield, leaving the second time in April 1941, although Jack and Frances returned for a time following World War II with a band known as the Georgia Boys.[46]

One promising Bluefield artist's career ended in tragedy. Cecil Dale Roseberry, usually known as Smilin' Dale, was born near Ripley on April 9, 1913. A brother Bob, sometimes associated with Dale, came along two years later. The Roseberrys guested at WCHS and in 1935 teamed up with Roane County's Ralph and Bert Hamrick at WPAR. Dale worked as an announcer for the Buskirk Family in Fairmont and on a variety of other stations. Bob went to work with Lee Moore, and Dale later worked with him also. Dale organized a band, the Campfire Boys, and his success proved indirectly fatal. Rushing to his third showdate of the day at Grundy, Virginia, on Sunday, September 14, 1941, Roseberry's car overturned en route and he died instantly, crushed under his own vehicle. The Campfire Boys carried on the show for a time and Bob Roseberry also continued as a radio artist. Smilin' Dale Roseberry's memory lingered on in the Bluefield area for many years as an outstanding interpreter of sad country songs and sentimental poetry such as "The Drunken Driver."[47]

Lynn Davis and the Forty-Niners returned to Bluefield in the fall of 1940, but without Sue and Ann Mason, who had left the group. A new girl singer, Dixie Lee Williamson of McVeigh, Kentucky, soon took their place more than adequately and in April 1941 became Mrs. Davis as well. Dixie Lee had gained some radio experience as Mountain Fern at WCHS and had appeared briefly on the new stations at Williamson and Beckley. Not quite eighteen at the time of her marriage, Dixie Lee would soon become the star of the show and, as Molly O'Day, a name she adopted in 1942, make a larger impact upon the country music world than any previous female.

By the advent of World War II, country music had become firmly established in the programming at WHIS Bluefield. Generally the station carried some three to four hours of country music daily. The 5:00

to 7:00 AM space tended to be all live shows. Another hour and a half to two hours scattered throughout the day also featured hillbilly acts although two or three fifteen-minute segments might come from transcriptions. With appreciative audiences through southern West Virginia and adjacent sections of the Old Dominion, WHIS became a significant conveyer in the commercializing of traditional music.[48]

After 1929 no new West Virginia radio stations took to the air until 1935. The economic hard times no doubt accounted for this situation. By 1935 a modest recovery encouraged the formation of WPAR Parkersburg. The following year the station affiliated with the West Virginia Network and somewhat later with CBS. WPAR never became a significant country music station although some artists began careers there and achieved a degree of noteworthiness. Among the first of these, the Hamrick Brothers from Roane County—Ralph (born 1909) and Bert (born 1915)—worked for a time with the Roseberrys and also had an association with the much-traveled Al Hendershot's Dixie Ramblers. Ralph also performed comedy as Uncle Zeke. The Hamricks' chief contribution came through their songs "Why Not Confess" and "Sweetheart Mountain Rose," which became standards for duets, particularly the former, eventually being recorded by the Blue Sky Boys.

The Buskirk Family, made up of Parkersburg area natives, probably ranked as the most important group to get their start locally. J. Everett Buskirk married Lottie Memel in 1916. As the Buskirk sons Wilbert, Buster, and Paul reached adolescence, their musical talents mushroomed. Lottie and the boys featured a wide variety of down-home flavored ballads, hymns, and some good originals such as "Station G-L-O-R-Y" and "Strand From a Yellow Curl." From WPAR the Buskirks moved to WMMN and WHIS. By this time Paul's reputation as a mandolinist reached proportions far ahead of the others, who were quite good by all accounts. In mid-April 1941 Lottie went to Beckley as a solo performer and Willie, Buster, and Paul, together with Skeets Williamson and the Holdens, headed for KRLD Dallas, Texas, where Paul played his first recording session with the Callahans on April 23. Willie later returned to Huntington and Paul to Harrisonburg, Virginia, where he worked with Buddy Starcher. Only Paul continued in music after the war, working as a sideman with vocalists ranging in diversity from Johnnie and Jack to Lefty Frizzell.

Paul Buskirk eventually settled in Texas and became known for his instrumental virtuosity. From mandolin he broadened his instrumental expertise to include mastery of the fiddle, tenor banjo, and dobro guitar. Although not famous in the sense of a Bob Wills or a Waylon Jennings, Buskirk still managed to have a major influence on Texas styles of country music. Willie Buskirk remembers spending several weeks in Houston with Paul in 1960 and pleasantly recalls how he, Paul, and a then unknown Willie Nelson put together the tune and lyrics to the song "Night Life," which subsequently became a Ray Price hit. (Nelson and Paul had already written the country gospel standard "Family Bible.") Paul recorded a tenor banjo album for RCA Victor in 1970 which showed his capability to transcend the bonds of traditional country music, and through the ensuing decade recorded some tenor banjo and Dobro albums for the Texas-based Stoneway label. At the end of the 1970s he renewed his association with Willie Nelson, both as a sideman and as a record producer.[49]

Another Parkersburg native, Bobby Cook, never gained wide fame outside of West Virginia but did perform significantly in the Mountain State. Born on August 31, 1922, Robert Lee Cook first joined a group known as Bob Wright's Juvenile Jug Blowers. He later reorganized it as the Texas Saddle Pals, which included local fiddler Jackie Miller and steel guitarist Herman "Jiggs" Lemly. Getting their start about 1940, Cook and his band remained prominent in West Virginia through most of the decade.[50]

In the WPAR listening area the Burroughs Trio undoubtedly constituted the main local group. Headed by young Billie Jean Burroughs (1922-1976), they obtained a 6:00 AM show in the station's early months and held it for several years. Usually the "trio" had a half-dozen or so musicians in their entourage, led by Billie, Betty, and Charlie Burroughs, and furnished valuable experience for several local performers. By 1940 station public relations literature expressed some pride in the program, calling it "a favored morning feature . . . nearing its 800th broadcast."[51]

Management of two other northern West Virginia stations showed relatively minimal interest in live country music. In Clarksburg, WBLK went on the air on April 12, 1937, becoming the fourth outlet in the West Virginia Network. The station's power increased from 100 to 250 watts in August 1939 and also affiliated with NBC at that time. Beyond an occasional live country group and Frank Welling's show from Charleston, such network programs as "The Ranch Boys" and "The Prince Albert Grand Ole Opry" from the network remained their hillbilly offerings. A similar situation prevailed at WAJR Morgantown, which started in 1940. The latter station had an occasional show by a local performer such as fiddler Ellis Hall and carried "The Shady Valley Folks" via MBS for many years. Probably their management and that of WKWK Wheeling (1941) saw little point in trying to compete with established 5,000-watt entities like WWVA and WMMN.[52]

Newer broadcasting outlets in southern West Virginia programmed more hillbilly music. In Beckley, WJLS in particular did a great deal. On the day the station opened, April 5, 1939, several aspiring musicians participated, including Uncle Howard and his Dixie Ramblers and Everett and Mitchell Lilly. The former group soon retreated into oblivion, although some of their musicians stayed around, such as young Charles "Rex" Parker, who also worked in a duet with Tommy Cantrell at WCHS and similarly with Tex McGuire at WHIS before settling down in Bluefield for a long career with his wife Eleanor. The Lillys, then eighteen and fifteen, also gained valuable experience at WJLS with their high-harmony duet that would eventually take them all over West Virginia and even to Japan.

Many of the young musicians who came to WJLS had been guests on the "Old Farm Hour" in Charleston or found themselves too overshadowed by more established performers to make good at WCHS. These included people like Johnnie Bailes and Skeets Williamson, who faced near starvation as members of Ervin Staggs and his Radio Ramblers, but did well enough in Beckley to eat three meals—always hot dogs with different trimmings—daily. In the spring and summer of 1940, Dixie Lee Williamson came up and worked with them before joining Lynn Davis in Bluefield. Walter Bailes came down and also organized a group which included young local musicians Ed "Rattlesnake" Hogan and George "Speedy" Krise, the latter recently graduated from high school in Hinton and possessor of a unique two-finger Dobro style. Krise later became an important sideman and songwriter.[53]

Although largely unheralded at the time, Jimmy Dickens from the coal camp of Bolt probably emerged as the major solo performer from among the numerous aspiring artists in the early days of Beckley radio. James Cecil Dickens, born on December 19, 1920, reached only four feet eleven inches in height when full grown (he grew five inches of that after he was old enough to vote), and walked several miles daily to bring the station on the air each morning with his rooster-crow imitation. Dickens gained most of his early experience at WJLS by working with Mel Steele (born 1909), a Pennsylvania native who worked there with a band that also featured his wife, Blue Eyed Jeanie. When Steele move on, Dickens joined up with Johnnie Bailes and his Happy Valley Boys and often received billing as "the Singing Midget" and "Jimmy the Kid." In 1941 Little Jimmy moved northward to Fairmont.

Although he briefly attended nearby West Virginia University when he relocated in Fairmont, Dickens already had his heart set on an entertainment career. Soon his activities at WMMN surpassed academics and he began working full-time with Mel Steele, who had also come north. Interested in sports and something of a novelty on the basketball court and baseball field, he played shortstop on the station's baseball team, which included Lee Moore and T. Texas Tyler among its stars. When Tyler moved on to Indianapolis in the fall of 1942 he soon talked Dickens into joining him. Jimmy recalls that he and Tyler each had a thirty-minute solo program and also did thirty minutes together as a gospel duet. During this time Dickens learned a song from a banjo picker named Sonny Grubb, who worked at the station, called "Take an Old Cold Tater and Wait." Although it had actually been written back in the 1920s by an Arkansas gospel composer and recorded by a man named Clarence Ganus, it had achieved relatively little attention, and it soon became one of Dickens's most requested songs. The lyrics describe a runt kid being pushed away from a full dinner table with company coming. For an artist of his physical stature it seemed almost autobiographical.

Eventually T. Texas Tyler entered military service and Little Jimmy continued as a solo for another year at Indianapolis before moving on to the 50,000-watt WLW Cincinnati for a year. Here he worked on the major Saturday night show, the "Boone County Jamboree," which changed its name to the "Midwestern Hayride" during his tenure. In 1946 he shifted to another large station, this one in Topeka, Kansas. Here he found the radio fans receptive and he continued to make money via his long-time PI sponsors such as Sunway Vitamins and Coco-Wheats. But the more scattered population made personal appearances less frequent, although the entire cast of the station's jamboree show, the "Kansas Roundup," did work some county fairs. After a year he moved again to Saginaw, Michigan, where he met the Nashville superstar Roy Acuff, who helped Dickens secure a Columbia contract in November 1948. He did his initial session for Art Satherly the following January and joined the "Grand Ole Opry" two months later.

Prior to his first Columbia recordings, Little Jimmy Dickens had sung few comic novelty numbers other than "Old Cold Tater." But the success of that number and a newly composed Boudleaux Bryant song "Country Boy," of similar ilk, influenced Satherly to have Dickens specialize in this type of song. The Columbia people generally paired them on releases with more serious heart songs like "Pennies for Papa" and "My Heart's Bouquet," but it was largely the humorous pieces that made Little Jimmy a major star. Follow-up hits of this nature included "Cold Feet," "Bessie the Heifer," "Then I Had to Turn Around and Get Married," "It May Be Silly but Ain't It Fun," "Walk Chicken Walk," "I'm Little but I'm Loud," and "Out behind the Barn," all from the pen of Boudleaux Bryant. "Sleepin' at the Foot of the Bed" (another old timer), "Hillbilly Fever," and "The Galvanized Washin' Tub" came from other sources, but they fit in with the image of the brash but pint-sized hillbilly that has sustained "Ma Dickens' little tater eatin' boy" for some thirty-five years. No doubt the lasting popularity of the songs also stemmed from the fact that the vignettes of rural life contained within the lyrics of many of the songs struck a responsive chord with thousands of rural-reared southern and midwestern Americans.

While turning out a string of popular hits, Little Jimmy Dickens also established himself as an appealing personality with fellow artists, fans, and promoters. His experiences working around persons like Hawkshaw Hawkins and T. Texas Tyler who, as he said, "never tried to make themselves better people than their audience," made a deep impression on him. As a result he never maintained an attitude of aloofness from those who attended his shows. He never charged excessive fees, trying to make money for his promoters as well as for himself. Dickens also helped young struggling artists such as Marty Robbins, whom he met on a far west tour in the spring of 1951. Dickens helped the young Arizonian get his initial contract with Columbia Records. So grateful was Robbins that one of his last public statements was an expression of regret that he had been chosen for the Country Hall of Fame before his mentor, Little Jimmy Dickens.

In the mid-1950s, Dickens left the Opry but always managed to stay active. He worked in the Philip Morris Caravan for a time and had some moderate success with rockabilly songs such as "Rockin' with Red," "Black Eyed Joe's," "Salty Boogie," and "I've Got a Hole in My Pocket." But his only real hit in that period was an uncharacteristic one for him, the Mel Tillis composition "A Violet and a Rose." Then in 1965 a newly-written novelty song with the unlikely title "May the Bird of Paradise Fly Up Your Nose" catapulted him to the top again and even ranked high on the pop charts. He followed with another string of humorous songs that included "When the Ship Hit the Sand," "Truck Load of Starvin' Kangaroos," and "Country Music Lover." He rejoined the Opry in the 1970s and had some minor hits with a silent-majority tribute song, "The Every Day Family Man," and a final novelty number entitled "Try It, You'll Like It." In recent years he has remained active both on the Opry and doing road tours, often working package shows with Merle Haggard. Dickens has also moved gracefully into the ranks of the elder statesmen of his art.[54] Finally, in October 1983, the Country Music Association selected him for the Hall of Fame.

Another southern West Virginia station that opened in 1939, WBTH Williamson, in theory had a good location for attracting hard-core country fans. Located on the Tug Fork adjacent to Pike County, Kentucky, as well as the Mingo County coalfields, its mountain audience unquestionably loved their music. However, the low power—100 and later 250 watts—in early years created difficulties for musicians because only in a small area could the station be heard. Dixie Lee, Duke, and Skeets Williamson worked there briefly, as did the Mayse Brothers and also Slim and Tex, but all found the concentrated audience a handicap in obtaining showdates.

The same situation probably prevailed also at WLOG Logan and WBRW Welch. These stations managed to attract a few musicians when they took to the air in late 1939 and August 1940, respectively. Artists like the Blankenship Brothers worked at the latter station as part of Al Hendershot's Dixie Ramblers. Frank "Hylo" Brown and Doug Saddler came over from near Paintsville, Kentucky, to play a weekly show at Logan, and Kyle Bailes and Stoney Mason, the former a veteran of the "Old Farm Hour," came to Welch. But with the low power and the coming of World War II with its gasoline shortages, only limited opportunities for showdates developed.[55]

There seems to be little doubt that from the mid-1930s, country music and radio in West Virginia became heavily intertwined. Doc Williams recalls that it was at about this time that the technical quality of broadcasting equipment became such that listeners could hear the sound of individual instruments better than before. Numerous aspiring musicians showed a willingness to work cheaply and station management found the PI system profitable in an economically depressed area and era. Jane Chambers, a WMMN secretary, remembers that the station's management, while not necessarily fans of the music, "generally looked upon" their format "as good business." As a result, hillbilly music flourished on West Virginia radio stations with varying degrees of economic success. Management prospered without really getting rich in times when numerous businesses lost money or failed. A few musicians perhaps did as well, although most seem to have maintained themselves at the poverty level. But most were also young and optimistic enough to hope that with a little luck, what had befallen a Jimmie Rodgers or a Gene Autry could also happen to them. In the meantime they could survive on songbook and picture sales, personal appearances, PI accounts, and the support of fans who loyally listened.[56]

While the response from fans, musicians, management, and advertisers attested to the popularity of hillbilly music on the airwaves, critics also made themselves heard. Generally those elite self-appointed guardians of culture expressed their concern for the Mountain State image. Ned Smith, editor of the *Fairmont Times*, became the chief spokesman for this group and his writings were reprinted in the *Parkersburg Sentinel* and also the *West Virginia Review*. Calling "hill billy music one of the worst nuisances a free people ever were subjected to" Smith in 1939 wrote:

This is the imposition upon our people of the stigma of being the Hill Billy state, and if the name of West Virginia is mentioned, it is immediately associated with hill billy music and a suggestion of a social inferiority which constitutes nothing short of libel upon the name of the state. We seriously doubt if West Virginia ever produced a genuine hill billy of the current variety. Certainly he is not native here. From the time the state was settled just prior to the Revolutionary War, it is hard to find an historical connection between the music and dances of the early settlers and what passes off as the West Virginia "mountain music" of today.[57]

One wonders if Editor Smith and the officials of WMMN, such as Raymond Warden and Howard Hopkins Wolfe, ever encountered one another in polite Fairmont society or at the Rotary Club, and if so what they discussed. No doubt the dignified editor could have learned that people out there in radio-land must like what they were hearing. He could also have learned that while some musicians, such as Cowboy Loye, Jake Taylor, or Grandpa Jones, may have been imported from neighboring states, it would be well nigh impossible to find anyone with stronger West Virginia mountaineer credentials than those exhibited by Buddy Starcher, Radio Dot, Al Hendershot, or Warren Caplinger right there on their hometown station, not to mention Big Slim at WWVA, the youthful Lilly and Bailes boys just starting at WJLS, or the Clines—Ezra, Ned, and Curly Ray—down at WHIS. There, the *Bluefield Telegraph* writers would and could treat a program by Mingo County's Stepp Brothers with as much dignity as a review of the Metropolitan Opera. In Bluefield, of course, both WHIS and the *Telegraph* were owned by the same family, but whether because of broad taste or good business sense, the radio station managers learned what the "folk" liked and gave it to them.[58]

5. Stay Tuned: Radio after 1942

World War II caused many alterations in the pattern of hillbilly radio entertainment that had evolved prior to the December 7, 1941, attack on Pearl Harbor. Gasoline shortages curtailed or ended personal appearances by musicians and the large crowds that had flocked to jamboree shows like the "Old Farm Hour" or "Sagebrush Roundup." Manpower shortages led many musicians into defense plants or military service. The music itself increased in popularity, however, and, as has been shown by developments at WWVA, served as a morale booster. Those musicians able to remain active found more popularity and prosperity than before and the immediate postwar years witnessed even greater prosperity for hillbilly radio acts, both returning artists and those active in the war years. Then in the 1950s increasing competition from television and changing patterns in the entertainment industry forced new adjustments.

At Huntington, country music programming, somewhat reversing the general trend, probably hit its zenith during the war. Flem Evans, who followed Mike Layman as station manager at WSAZ, continued his predecessor's policy of maintaining good hillbilly acts. In terms of artistry, the Bailes Brothers suddenly found themselves exceedingly popular after a half-dozen years of bare subsistence. Natives of Kanawha County, Johnnie and Walter Bailes, born in 1918 and 1920, respectively, had worked around WCHS, WJLS, and other stations with minimal success. But when they came to WSAZ and put themselves under Evans's guidance, their careers began literally to boom. Beyond the WSAZ listening area, Evans managed to get their transcriptions placed at both Logan and Williamson. The brothers could now afford band members like bass player Evelyn Thomas, who with her sister had come to Huntington as half of the Dot and Evy duo in Uncle Nat Royster's Smokey Mountaineers. Most significant of all, they acquired the services of Fiddlin' Arthur Smith, an already legendary bow wielder whose erratic habits had made him something of an itinerant wanderer after the "Grand Ole Opry" management dismissed him in 1938. Following Smith's departure, local fiddler Del Heck joined the Bailes group. Since numerous opportunities for showdates fairly close to Huntington existed in the Tri-State region, the Bailes group managed to play extensively.

More important, they attracted the attention of such outsiders as John Lomax, the folk music authority, who got the boys on a BBC presentation. Then Roy Acuff worked a show in Huntington, saw the Baileses' potential, and in October 1944 induced them to come to Nashville and the Opry. Johnnie and Walter by now had many original songs in the repertoire along with their numerous old-time duet numbers and hymns. Acuff and Fred Rose, then in the process of launching their publishing firm, signed the Baileses as writers for Acuff-Rose and persuaded Art Satherley to contract them with Columbia records. Soon Bailes Brothers' songs like "Dust on the Bible," "I Want to Be Loved But Only by You," and "I've Got My One Way Ticket to the Sky" were on their way to becoming standards that figures like Acuff himself and RCA Victor's Blue Sky Boys would cover. Johnnie and Walter Bailes, a pair of poor boys from north Charleston, found themselves the first West Virginians to star on the "Grand Ole Opry" and obtain a major-label record contract in the post-Depression era. Their arrival in Nashville was a well-timed one for it occurred in a period when the "Grand Ole Opry" was about to emerge as the principal country show, displacing the "National Barn Dance."

Although the Bailes Brothers blazed the trail to Nashville for West Virginia musicians, somewhat ironically they did not remain there permanently. Late in 1946 the group relocated at KWKH Shreveport, where they reached the pinnacle of their success and helped found one of the last major radio jamboree shows, "The Louisiana Hayride." At times the Bailes Brothers had as many as four programs daily on the station, all of which paid union-scale salaries rather than mere exposure time. Their band, styled the West Virginia Home Folks, included some influential musicians, such as Clyde Baum and Ernest Ferguson, both of whom played mandolin, and Harold "Shot" Jackson, who played either Dobro or electric steel. Jackson later became a partner in the influential Sho-Bud Company. For a time Sleepy Jeffers and the Davis Twins came down from Charleston and worked with the Bailes' touring unit. In 1947 Walter Bailes dropped out to enter the ministry and fiddler Homer Bailes became Johnnie's duet partner. But when "The Louisiana Hayride" premiered on April 3, 1948, Walter returned long enough to put all four brothers on the stage at once. If anything, the duo of Johnnie and Homer equalled and perhaps surpassed the earlier Bailes combinations in popularity. The Bailes Brothers continued as a top act at KWKH until late 1949, when the group fragmented.

Since that time various combinations of the Bailes Brothers have remained active in either the country or the gospel music scene. Johnnie and Walter worked together in 1953 and 1954 and recorded some fine duets for King. Kyle and Homer worked on radio in Arkansas and later in Ohio prior to Homer's entering the ministry. Johnnie Bailes managed a radio station in Swainsboro, Georgia, for many years and did some solo recording for Decca in 1957 and 1959. Walter would occasionally work with the other brothers through the later 1950s and 1960s and as a duet with his wife Frankie. His most significant contribution through this period was authorship of the song "Give Mother My Crown," which became a bluegrass gospel favorite through the recording by Lester Flatt and Earl Scruggs. The song presented an accurate portrayal of the Bailes Brothers' poverty-stricken childhood in the slums of Charleston, and how their widowed mother had taught them "the right way to go." In 1976 Johnnie, Homer, Shot Jackson, and Clyde Baum got together again at the Red River Bluegrass Festival for a reunion concert and in 1977 all four brothers (and also sister Minnie), together with Ernest Ferguson, recorded a gospel album. Kyle and Walter also did an album together and they and Ferguson have worked at several bluegrass festivals in recent years, including Beanblossom, and did a tour of Holland in 1982. Walter and Kyle organized a Bailes' Reunion Festival at Summersville, West Virginia, in June 1983. Homer Bailes, a pastor in Louisiana, recorded a pair of albums in the early 1980s. Although the Baileses' later activities have never been as influential in country and gospel circles as they were in the late 1940s, they have managed to remain visible, and Walter's evangelistic work has led to his being dubbed the "Chaplain of Music Row."[1]

Although the Bailes Brothers dominated country music in World War II Huntington, other groups shared a portion of the limelight with them. Fiddlin' Arthur Smith, on the skids somewhat from the previous decade when he had ranked as one of the two or three major fiddlers of the era, still held considerable prestige and carried some reputation as a vocalist too with such songs to his credit as "Beautiful Brown Eyes" and "More Pretty Girls Than One." By the time the war ended Smith had departed for Hollywood, where he engineered a comeback of sorts via Jimmy Wakely films. In a sense the Huntington phase of Arthur Smith's career represented a beginning of the climb back up the ladder.[2]

Three other groups rounded out the WSAZ performers of the war years. Deacon Wayne, whose oversized band at WCHS had fragmented in the winter of 1938-39, flourished for a time. Members included Judy Wayne and musicians whose real identities remained hidden behind such nicknames as Denver Dan, Sagebrush Bob, and Drifty. Indian Bill Stallard along with his wife, Evalina (Little Montana), and Natchee the Indian divided their wartime activity between WLW Cincinnati and Huntington. Young Parkersburg performer Bobby Cook brought his Texas Saddle Pals band to Huntington, absorbing into its ranks some local musicians, such as Bud Nelson, fiddler Glen Ferguson, and Yodeling Red Watkins. Cook also developed a park at nearby Ona for Sunday afternoon shows. Camden Park, the local amusement center, also featured country programs on weekends. Finally, the duet of Ralph and Ruth Blankenship gained considerable appeal as WSAZ artists. Flem Evans revitalized the old "Tri-State Roundup," moved it to Wednesday nights at the State Theater, and renamed it the "WSAZ Jamboree," which generally played to capacity crowds for both evening shows.[3]

The departure of key acts like the Bailes Brothers and the exit of Flem Evans from the WSAZ management led to declining enthusiasm for live country music in Huntington radio circles. As Jenny Via of the Huntington-based *National Hillbilly News* lamented, "Our present station doesn't seem to believe in nor support a hillbilly act." But hope for the future loomed bright, with both Flem Evans and Mike Layman contending for a license to start a rival radio station. Evans won the first round and in 1946 WPLH took to the air, but musically something went amiss. In July 1947 Layman too got his license and set out to make WHTN the hillbilly station in Huntington. The only limitation to his goals resulted from the fact that the days of live radio were numbered—at least in all but a few locations.[4]

For a few years, however, things went well for both musicians and listeners at WHTN. Bobby Cook and his Texas Saddle Pals, popular in the war years, returned for a time, although Cook traveled a bit, once going as far west as Kansas City and St. Joseph, Missouri. Slim Clere even came out of retirement briefly with a new band, the Melody Rangers. Margie Shannon organized her Starlite Ranch Gang and played one or two daily shows for quite some time. They also played several nights weekly at the Starlite Ranch, a large nonalcoholic dance hall across the river in Chesapeake, Ohio, and did other personal appearances as well. As the band name suggests, western and honky-tonk sounds with electric guitar and steel had pretty well replaced the older styles that had dominated the prewar era. The fiddle remained as the strongest link with the past. Margie at one point appeared on all three radio stations and television until she left for WBT Charlotte in 1954.[5]

Chuck Bridges, a farm lad and war veteran from nearby Pedro, Ohio, achieved considerable popularity by winning a talent show and began daily broadcasting in January 1949 with a six-piece band, the Radio Playboys. By summer, Bridges managed to get booked on area county fair circuits, and by all accounts his rise in popularity looked promising. That fall he signed with King Records, and officials on 50,000-watt stations such as WLS Chicago and WSB Atlanta attempted to hire him, the latter apparently successfully. Although Bridges seems not to have made much of a success in Atlanta or elsewhere, his rise to local prominence via WHTN and the attention he attracted demonstrated that a radio act on a 1,000-watt Tri-State station could and did command notice.[6]

One artist who performed at WHTN achieved a degree of national prominence as a writer and vocalist. Jimmie Skinner (1909-1980) of Berea, Kentucky, moved to southwestern Ohio as a youth and worked as a part-time performer until after World War II. Generally accompanied by an electric mandolinist named Ray Lunsford and possessed of a rather distinctive voice, Skinner created a unique blend of older and newer country highlighted by original songs like "Doin' My Time," "Let's Say Goodbye Like We Said Hello," "You Don't Know My Mind," and "Don't Give Your Heart to a Rambler." Except for his Huntington live radio work and a similar experience in Knoxville, Skinner spent most of his professional career in the Cincinnati area and had some excellent recordings on Capitol, Mercury, and Decca as well as the smaller labels.[7]

Another WHTN performer and West Virginia native experienced a long career but never achieved as much prominence as Skinner. Ray Anderson, a Webster Countian born in 1924, went to Nashville after his release from World War II service but had to settle for sideman status with Radio Dot and Smokey. Coming to Huntington he performed at WHTN both solo and with his wife Maxine. He even served as program director for a time. By the mid-1950s he had become a popular disc jockey at WCHO Washington Court House, Ohio, and continued as a part-time performer, often at WWVA with the Osborne Brothers. A decade later he entered the ministry and thereafter did gospel music. Anderson, a prolific songwriter, recorded extensively on smaller labels and, although he never had any hits, has deservedly attracted scholarly attention for his topical songs such

Participants in a fiddlers' contest at the Pocahontas County Fair in August 1926. Courtesy of Guthrie Meade.

Unless otherwise indicated, photos are from the author's collection.

Opposite. Top, the Kessinger Brothers, Luches (guitar) and Clark (fiddle), at WOBU Charleston, ca. 1930. Courtesy of County Records.

Bottom, the Tweedy Brothers at WWVA Wheeling, ca. 1930.

Left, Billy Cox at age sixteen, ca. 1913. Courtesy of Ken Davidson.

Below, John McGhee (left) and Frank Welling, ca. 1928. Courtesy of Anna Lee McGhee Schrule.

Right, Cap, Andy, and Flip at WWVA Wheeling, ca. 1933.

Below, the Bluebonnet Troupe at WWVA, 1937. Standing, l-r, James "Sheep Herder" Moore, French "Curley" Mitchell, Dorothy "Radio Dot" Henderson, Betty Taylor, Jake Taylor, Custer Allen. Seated, l-r, Ray Myers, "Just Plain John" Oldham, "Cowboy Loye" Pack.

Right, "Big Slim" McAuliffe, the "Lone Cowboy," ca. 1937.

Below, the Buskirk Family Band at WMMN Fairmont, 1938: l-r, Dale Roseberry, Paul, Wilbert, Buster, and Lottie Buskirk. Front, "Hank" Williams.

Left, Natchee the
Indian, Little Montana,
and Indian Bill Stallard
at WSAZ, ca. 1943.
Courtesy of Clifford
Heck.

Below, Blaine Smith
and his gang at WMMN
Fairmont, ca. 1940:
l-r, Marty McCoy,
the Ol' Sheriff, Blaine
Smith, Billy Steed, and
Brother Cal Smith.

Right, Wilma Lee and
Stoney Cooper, late
1950s. Courtesy of
Wilma Lee Cooper.

Below, Doc and
Chickie Williams,
Brother Cy Williams,
and blind accordionist
Marion Martin, ca.
1947. Courtesy of
Doc Williams.

Above, Millie Wayne and Bonnie Baldwin, the Radio Rangerettes, at WWVA Wheeling, 1945. Courtesy of Ruth (Bonnie) Baldwin. *Below*, the Chuckwagon Plowboys: l-r standing, Joe Barker, Willie, Smilie Sutter, Curly Miller; seated, Jimmy, Little Shirley Barker, Sonny.

Above, the Trading Post Gang, ca. 1939: l-r, Murrell Poor, John Graham, "Big Eared Zip" Binnix, Jimmy Smith (seated). *Below*, the Davis Twins, Sonny and Honey, ca. 1946. Courtesy of Honey Davis Jeffers.

Left, Lee Moore at WCHS Charleston, 1938. Courtesy of Slim Clere.

Below, the original Lonesome Pine Fiddlers at WHIS Bluefield, ca. 1938: l-r, Gordon Jennings, Ned Cline, radio announcer Stewart Odell, Curly Ray Cline, Cousin Ezra Cline. Courtesy of Ezra Cline.

Above, Buddy Starcher (left) and Grandpa Jones (right) at WMMN Fairmont, ca. 1940.

Right, Slim Clere and T. Texas Tyler at WCHS Charleston, 1940. Courtesy of Slim Clere.

Above, Fiddlin' "Fudge" and Bashful "Budge" Mayse at WMMN Fairmont, ca. 1940. *Below left,* Cherokee Sue at WMMN Fairmont, 1940.

Below, the Franklin Brothers at WCHS Charleston, ca. 1939. Courtesy of Slim Clere.

Above, Mack Jeffers and his Fiddlin' Farmers, ca. 1939: l-r, Mack, Slick, and Sleepy Jeffers; seated, Shorty "Hiram Hayseed" Godwin. *Below,* the Bailes Brothers at KWKH, 1947: l-r, Homer, Walter, Johnnie, Kyle. Courtesy of Kyle Bailes.

Woodrow Wilson (Red) Sovine, ca. 1960. Courtesy of Walter Darrell Haden.

Rex and Eleanor Parker at WHIS Bluefield in 1946. Courtesy of Lynn Davis.

Musically yours,
Rex and Eleanor

Above, the cast of the 1947 "WWVA World's Original Jamboree": l-r, front row, Smokey Pleacher, Hiram Hayseed, Hawkshaw Hawkins, Sunflower, Jimmy Hutchinson, Wilma Lee, Big Slim, Little Shirley, Stoney Cooper, Cy Sneezeweed, Chick Stripling. Middle row, Paul Myers, Melvin Ritchie, Red Belcher, Chuck Henderson, Monty Blake, Budge Mayse, Galen Ritchie, Fudge Mayse, Curley Reynolds, Bill Carver, Jiggs Lemley, Uncle Tom. Back row, Doc Williams, Bonnie Baldwin, Marion Martin, Millie Wayne, Cy Williams, Joe Barker.

Above, John and Lucy Bava, ca. 1950. Courtesy of John Bava. *Below*, The Smiling Mountain Boys: l-r, Paul Taylor, B. Lilly, Everett Lilly, Burk Barbour, at WNOX Knoxville, 1947. Courtesy of Everett Lilly.

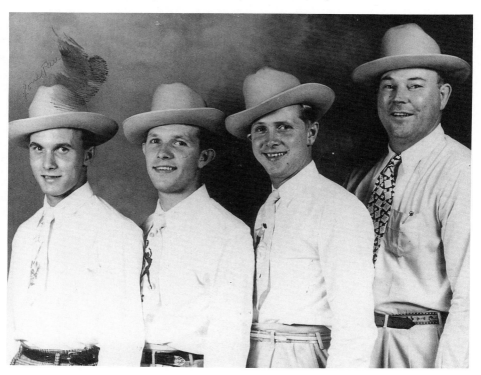

Little Jimmy Dickens and Hawkshaw Hawkins on the set of TV's "Classic Country," 1956. Courtesy of Jimmy Dickens.

Above, Jimmy Walker at the Grand Ole Opry in 1945. Courtesy of Ernest (Jimmy) Walker. *Below,* The Goins Brothers band, ca. 1973: l-r, Joe Meadows, Melvin and Ray Goins, Harley Gabbard, and George Portz. Courtesy of Melvin Goins.

Above, Billy Edd Wheeler, ca. 1980. Courtesy of Billy Edd Wheeler.

Left, Cecil Surratt, WHIS-TV Bluefield, ca. 1960. Courtesy of Cecil Surratt.

Above, Trapezoid, 1981: rear, Ralph Gordon and Loraine Duisit; front, Paul Reisler and Freyda Epstein. Courtesy of Trapezoid. *Below,* Frank George, 1982. Photo by Rick Lee, courtesy of *Goldenseal.*

Jenes Cottrell, ca. 1979.
Photo by Rick Lee,
courtesy of *Goldenseal*.

Bill Jones at the Vandalia
Festival, 1979. Photo by Rick
Lee, courtesy of *Goldenseal*.

Above left, Penny DeHaven, ca. 1982. Courtesy of Jackie Monaghan and Morning Star Public Relations. *Above right,* Lori Lee Bowles of WCHS-TV Charleston, ca. 1971. Courtesy of Mr. and Mrs. Harold Bowles.

Above, Terry Gregory, ca. 1981. Courtesy of the Country Music Foundation.

Above, the Perry Sisters, ca. 1990. Publicity still. *Below*, Mayf Nutter, ca. 1972. Courtesy of the Country Music Foundation.

Above, left, Little Jimmy Dickens, ca. 1982. Courtesy of Jimmy Dickens. *Right*, United States Senator Robert C. Byrd, ca. 1980. Courtesy of Senator Byrd.

Left, Kathy Mattea, ca. 1990. Publicity still.

as "Draft Board Blues," "Stalin Kicked the Bucket," "Sputniks and Muttniks," and "The Silver Bridge Disaster."[8]

Several other artists worked at WHTN with varying degrees of commercial success. Al Hendershot's Dixie Ramblers, back in West Virginia again, augmented their act with the much-traveled armless Ray Myers. Two new groups also worked at the station. The Ohio Valley Boys featured the singing of Claude Eldridge while Fred and Ollie Cook led a band known as the Skyline Patrol. Charlie and Honey Miller, a husband-wife duet featuring electric steel, divided their time between WHTN and WCHS. In addition, Glen Ferguson, Bud Nelson, and Red Watkins often worked as the West Virginia Nite Hawks when not associated with Bobby Cook or at WWVA as a band for Hawkshaw Hawkins. Finally, a nonmusician sometimes featured on personals, "Little Mose, the Human Lodestone" (real name Lewis Moses), a ninety-six-pound midget who possessed the amazing ability to make himself virtually impossible to lift, appeared with many WHTN acts on showdates.

Something of WHTN's quick-rising popularity can be demonstrated by the benefit show held for Ashland guitarist Blind Bob Hall on December 7, 1947. Hawkshaw Hawkins, back in Huntington for the weekend, made an unannounced appearance and most of the active groups, such as the Texas Saddle Pals, Skyline Patrol, and Dixie Ramblers, plus prewar favorites like Tommy Cantrell of Charleston and local favorite Lonnie Lucas, participated. After expenses Hall had more than $936, over three times the announced goal of $275 required to purchase and train a seeing-eye dog. As long as live country music remained practical, WHTN's Mike Layman and his program director Ted Arnold gave it their best.[9]

Meanwhile the management at WSAZ made a modest effort to counter the WHTN threat. In the fall of 1947 they induced Al Rogers, a Pennsylvania artist who had eight years of radio experience, to come to their station. Known as America's Balladeer, Al had a strong baritone voice, a petite attractive vocalist named Betty Pearl, and a versatile band, the Rocky Mountain Boys. Rogers's credits included two Pittsburgh stations, Denver, and Amarillo by the time he arrived in Huntington. He gave the local artists from WHTN the impression of being a big-time operator in contrast to their provincial appeal, but apparently got along with them, as he participated in the Bob Hall benefit concert. Rogers remained in Huntington about a year and then moved on to WAVE Louisville. Later live acts on the station were Texas Slim and his Prairie Buckaroos and Lee Bailey's Mountain Melody Boys. Otherwise WSAZ countered the rise of WHTN by offering transcribed shows such as those of current country superstar Eddy Arnold and western star Jimmy Wakely. The second Huntington station, WPLH, offered listeners an occasional live show, such as Margie Shannon or the Echo Valley Boys, or a transcription, such as "Tennessee Jamboree." Actually the management of WSAZ had their goals oriented toward the future and had begun to explore the possibilities of television, as later events demonstrated.[10]

Meanwhile at Charleston, WCHS continued to dominate the live country music radio scene. The trio of Cap, Andy, and Flip saw one personnel change when young Milt Patterson, a son of Andy, replaced Flip about 1941. According to a persistent rumor, Flip Strickland had some nervous problems and dropped out of show business to start a chicken farm. Something caused his chickens to die, however, and he later returned to music, working with Texas Ruby and Curley Fox among others before falling into obscurity. Meanwhile Cap, Andy, and Milt became almost totally a gospel group. Occasionally joined by Cap's son Omer Caplinger, a skilled mandolin player, or by featured acts like Charlie and Honey Miller, the veteran performers continued as Charleston's dominant country group until 1949. Andy's declining health and subsequent death in 1950 brought the legendary trio to a tragic end although their memory as one of West Virginia's finest musical groups lingers to the present. Fortunately they did record a few of their numbers at custom sessions in 1939 and again in 1945. Milt Patterson returned to Harriman, Tennessee. Warren Caplinger briefly had a band called the Melody Boys and then turned to deejay work, first as host of "Cap's Trading Post" on WKNA and finally in 1955-1956 on WGNV with "Saturday in the Valley." When Cap died in July 1957 an alert cemetery caretaker pointed out that the plot adjacent to Patterson's remained vacant, and the musical pals of twenty-two years now rest side by side for eternity in the Cunningham Memorial Gardens (where Clark Kessinger is also buried) at St. Albans.[11]

Frank Welling also continued at WCHS into the 1950s. By now his announcing duties and "Uncle Si" homespun philosophy-comedy skits had virtually supplanted his musical talents. For a time he had two sisters in his act, known as Uncle Si's Youngins. The "Old Farm Hour" revived for a time in the later 1940s and Frank continued to emcee. He also made a recording about 1949 for the local Red Robin label on which he included a bit of his Uncle Si talk and electric instrumentation along with his singing. Welling left WCHS about 1954, working afterwards as a radio announcer in Chattanooga and Biloxi. The Welling family planned to move to California in May 1957, but

Frank became ill and died on January 23, 1957, following some gross malpractice by the physician and hospital, in the opinion of his wife and children. Except for an already married older daughter, the Wellings relocated in California, where daughter Margie enjoyed several small roles in some major films, such as Elvis Presley's *Blue Hawaii*.[12]

Lee Moore returned to WCHS in 1947, after an eight-year absence, with wife Juanita and son Roger Lee. Leslie Keith, the one-time fiddler at WHIS, joined him as well as two musicians whom Lee had met during his 1946-1947 stay at KFNF Shenandoah, Iowa—Daniel "Zag" Pennel, billed as the Ozark Mountain Boy, and Jolly Joe Parrish. Both remained at WCHS for several months. Moore recalls, though, that the situation at Charleston had been better back in 1937-1939, and when an opportunity came for a spot in Harrisonburg, Virginia, the entire group took it. Both Harmie Smith and the Radio Dot and Smokey team spent part of the war years at WCHS, but finally went to Shreveport. Johnnie Wright and his Tennessee Hillbillies, consisting of Jack Anglin, guitar, Ernest Ferguson, mandolin, Emory Martin, banjo, and Paul Warren, fiddle, stayed part of 1941 and 1942 in the state capital with a brief stint at Bluefield in between. The group, all of whom made their mark in country music, moved on to Knoxville in June, where wartime conditions broke up the band and they did not regain their upward movement until after 1945, winning much acclaim as the duo of Johnnie and Jack. Johnnie's wife Kitty Wells, also associated with the band, sang relatively little during their West Virginia period because of the birth of son Bobby. Another group at Charleston that encountered difficulty, Jim and Jesse McReynolds, failed to obtain enough showdates to sustain them. Although young and relatively inexperienced, the brothers were a high quality guitar-mandolin duet and had a fiddler of proven excellence in Marion Sumner.[13]

Three newer Charleston stations featured some country groups in the postwar period but, except for Harmie Smith, who made one last sojourn in Charleston in the later 1940s, only one ever had more than a local reputation. WKNA (1947) featured the Magic Valley Boys, the Poling Trio, and the Kanawha Ramblers. Buddy Wilson, Ed Yerke, and Buffalo Bob Entley's Ranch Hands all appeared on WGNV at one time or another. Finally, WTIP (1946) had Bill Browning and his Kanawha Valley Boys from late 1947 to 1950. After military service, Wayne Countian Browning relocated in Cleveland in 1955, where at the age of twenty-four he formed the Echo Valley Boys and recorded both vintage rockabilly and country material for the regional Island label and also for Starday in Nashville. His best-known songs came to be the bluegrass standard "Dark Hollow" and the rockabilly rarity "Washing Machine Boogie." Sleepy Jeffers, earlier a member of his father's Fiddlin' Farmer band and later a television celebrity, also worked at WTIP for thirteen years, primarily as a country deejay, although he too did a Starday session in this period. Charleston-based country music, it seemed, had entered a lull that took the combination of Buddy Starcher's return and television to revive it in 1960.[14]

Conditions for radio remained much more favorable at Fairmont into the early 1950s. Although during the war military service claimed many of the musicians who had been there in 1941, including Budge and Fudge Mayse, Blaine Smith, Cal Smith, Jake Taylor, and Little John Graham, many remained at WMMN. Lee and Juanita Moore went to Harrisonburg for a year but returned early in 1944. The Moore Family, who now included little Roger Lee in their act, generally played three times daily, a half-hour at 5:30 AM and a pair of shorter presentations at 9:30 AM and 3:00 PM. The first group at 5:00 AM, the Happy Hoedowners, consisted of two veterans, Grandpa Wilson and W.H. "Hiram Hayseed" Godwin, along with two newcomers, Yodeling Joe Lambert from Pendleton County and Rosa Lee. The group had a total of four shows daily, all before noon.

After Lee and Juanita, a pair of oldsters, Grandad and Grandma Hite, took the air for the first of three daily shows. This couple had one of the most unusual backgrounds in country music history. Grover C. Hite, born in Nelson County, Virginia, on November 21, 1884, labored in the coal mines and lumber camps of his native state and West Virginia for twenty-two years. In 1924 he took up the ministry, having taken extensive correspondence courses and received his ordination from the Greenbriar Presbytery. During the Depression his earnings from preaching declined and he and two sons, Ed and Grover, Jr., took up country music to supplement their incomes. He continued as a church pastor but also played on radio shows, first at WHIS and then at WJLS. When Ed entered the service in 1943 and Grover, Jr. died from an auto accident, Myra "Grandma" Hite became his singing duet partner. They then came to Fairmont where they remained for more than three years. Ed Hite, when released from military life, joined them and married Florence Curry of Blue Bonnett Girl fame. Buddy Starcher, who knew the Hites well, said of their hymn singing programs, "A radio visit from them is as refreshing as a drink of cool, sparkling mountain spring water."[15]

The Franklin Brothers came to full musical maturity during the war. Clyde, Bill, and Delmas, natives of Fayette County, first entered radio at WCHS billed as "Cap, Andy and Flip, Junior," and worked summers with acts as early as 1940. As children the Franklins gained an offstage reputation as a hillbilly version of the Katzenjammer Kids. An older musician recalls that in their early days at WMMN they silently sneaked onto the porch of an old gentleman and set his newspaper afire while he read it. Nonetheless, the boys perfected an exceedingly beautiful slow-harmony trio with guitar and mandolin accompaniment that connoisseurs of the roots of bluegrass find especially appealing. The Franklins eventually left Fairmont and worked on stations in Virginia and North Carolina before breaking up about 1950. Unfortunately they recorded but sparingly and their discs are exceedingly rare. Bill Franklin continued in gospel music for a time, subsequently writing and waxing a song entitled "That Moon's No Stopping Place for Me," which contained some of the earliest hymn lyrics dealing with space travel. Like the Hites, the Franklin Brothers played for an hour daily, on a half-hour show and on two of fifteen-minutes each.[16]

Little Art Haggerty completed the talent lineup at WMMN in 1944, having three quarter-hour programs. Buddy Starcher commented that "his individual style of singing the well-loved ballads of the hill country and the plains, has brought him a rapid rise in the affections of the folks in the Monongahela Valley. We look forward to a bright future for little Art."[17]

In addition to the live acts working at WMMN, the playing of phonograph records over the air provided another type of country music programming. Lee Moore announced the records but recalls that a station engineer in the control room actually played the discs. Little did Lee realize that in the next ten or twelve years this kind of format would become the standard form of country radio and replace most live performers. The popular music industry had already expressed some concern for musicians' losing jobs because of the playing of phonograph records by radio stations, but as yet it made little impact on hillbilly musicians. Oddly enough, when Lee and Juanita Moore left Fairmont for Harrisonburg at the end of 1944, their replacements at WMMN, Wilma Lee and Stoney Cooper, had just lost their position at WJJD Chicago when station management decided to go wholly with phonograph records rather than yield to a union demand that the station double its staff of musicians and play no discs.

The Coopers stayed at WMMN for about a year. They picked up Abner Cole of Mannington, formerly of the Cole Brothers, as a bass player and comedian and also temporarily absorbed Yodeling Joe into their act. Two other associates included Bob Autry and Sonny

Gillian. With four-year-old Carol Lee Cooper in their Blues Chaser group, the Coopers, well-known in the area already from previous work with the Leary Family and Rusty Hiser, found themselves in demand for shows almost nightly.[18]

Grandpa Wilson also remained at WMMN heading a group called the Green Valley Boys. Yodeling Joe returned along with the familiar Big Eared Zip Binnix and a twenty-year-old singer/comedian freshly arrived from the Harrisonburg, Virginia, area named William "Dusty" Shaver (1925-1982). Shaver developed a comic character named Oscar August Quiddlemurp who laughed uncontrollably while singing funny songs like "Ticklish Reuben" and cried mock tears on sad love lyrics like "Nobody's Darling But Mine" and "Thinking Tonight of My Blue Eyes." Working later with various groups, Shaver spent several years around WMMN and other stations including even WWVA briefly, specializing in comedy before turning to deejay work.

Radio Dot and Smokey also returned to Fairmont, having worked the latter years of the war at KWKH Shreveport. They picked up French Mitchell, who had labored in a Nitro chemical plant during much of the war, and also Ray Myers, who had come back to WMMN. The Blue Bonnett Girls, now only a twosome—Florence and Sylvia—also had a couple of quarter-hour shows.[19]

Buddy Starcher returned to WMMN in September 1945 after an absence of four years. In addition to Harrisonburg, he had worked for a year at KMA Shenandoah, Iowa, and for about six weeks at WSAZ Huntington while cutting transcriptions. Back at Fairmont he quickly absorbed the Franklin Brothers into his "All-Star Roundup," which already included Red Belcher, Curly Watts, a comedian known as Stroupy, and Buddy's future wife Mary Ann Estes. Early in 1946, Watts and Stroupy left the show and were replaced by French Mitchell and Dusty Shaver, Herman Redmon, Jackie Osborn, and Marjorie Lee. Buddy also did some announcing and had become a virtual master at PI work by this time, having a 10:45 AM show of his own sponsored by Peruna and Kolor-Bak and then the "All-Star Roundup" sponsored by Sunway Vitamins, all products made famous nationally via the PI system. Dusty Shaver, who later worked with Starcher, remarked that Buddy through his years of experience knew that he had to look like a prosperous professional. He always drove a Cadillac and wore a business suit. There might be times when he had very little ready cash, but he knew if he always looked and acted like a successful professional, he would be treated accordingly. Buddy Starcher, therefore, commanded a great deal of respect.

A pair of acts from the distant Midwest came to WMMN in 1946.

Bob and Jim Raines constituted a father-son duo who had done radio for years, with the elder Raines picking a fine old-time banjo. Folks around Fairmont liked their music, but some believed Bob was excessively mercenary even for the PI system and told some blatant falsehoods to encourage sales. Furthermore, like the late Stringbean, he did not believe in banks, kept a great deal of cash concealed on his person, and bragged about it, which some feared might encourage robbery or burglary. The other new group, Zeke Williams and his Ramblin' Cowboys, included Joan Williams, who sang duets with her husband, Jolly Joe Parish, and David Stanford, generally known as Hank the Cowhand. The entire Williams band did not remain long at WMMN, but Stanford became a durable figure and in a sense Fairmont's last country radio star.[20]

David Everett Stanford, born on October 9, 1912, in Mexia, Texas, did ranch work in west Texas and first appeared on radio in Lubbock. He worked with the Zeke Williams outfit prior to his World War II service and got out of the army just in time to make an extensive tour that included a "Grand Ole Opry" appearance. After Zeke left Fairmont, Hank lingered and formed a band called the Foggy Mountain Boys (this pre-dated the Flatt and Scruggs band by roughly a year). Hank took Grandpa Wilson into his group and for a time even had the services of Colleen and Donna Wilson, a Pennsylvania duo who would soon become "National Barn Dance" stars as the Beaver Valley Sweethearts. As other radio performers drifted away from WMMN and the Saturday night shows ended after October 2, 1948, Hank took the name Sagebrush Roundup for his band and maintained live radio artistry into 1955. In that year he moved to WKYR Keyser as a deejay and worked there, in Oklahoma, or at WMSG Oakland, Maryland, until his death on October 2, 1966. He continued to play personal appearances for the rest of his life and even incorporated rockabilly into his straight country style. In fact, some of his best remembered songs, such as "Popcorn Boogie" and an up-tempo version of the old Jimmie Davis song "She's a Hum-Dum Dinger," fell into that genre along with such more standard western numbers as "My Brown Eyed Texas Rose." Hank's death occurred in Petersburg, West Virginia, following his last personal appearance.[21]

Throughout the remainder of the 1940s live country programming remained strong at WMMN. As late as July 1949 the station broadcast it for three hours and twenty minutes per day, but it faded quickly in the early 1950s. Old Brother Charlie and Daisy Mae, although not a new duet, gained considerable attention for a few years. Charles E. Arnett, born at Chester at the tip of the northern panhandle on

September 30, 1913, acquired a college education before entering radio. He traveled extensively, meeting his future wife Ethel Irene in Ft. Worth, Texas. A native of St. Louis and a veteran of the "Shady Valley Folks" program, Mrs. Arnett took the stage name Daisy Mae, probably from the character in Al Capp's popular comic strip "Li'l Abner." The couple worked with John Lair's "Renfro Valley Barn Dance" and also toured with a company known as the All American Barn Dance. In 1946 Charlie put together a band called the Haymakers at WMMN which for a brief time included the reunited team of Cherokee Sue and Little John Graham. Although the Arnetts did a few excellent duets on numbers like "Sparkling Brown Eyes," Charlie tended to specialize in snappy piano playing and recitations, both sentimental and humorous, while Daisy handled most of the singing in a manner not greatly different from that of such contemporaries as Molly O'Day and Wilma Lee Cooper. In 1947 the Arnetts moved on to WHIS and eventually achieved their greatest success at WDAE Tampa, Florida, while recording for Mercury and Columbia.[22]

Jake Taylor and his Railsplitters returned to Fairmont in 1947 after a six-year absence. Actually the group had been disbanded during most of that period. Taylor himself experienced two narrow escapes in the war and spent ten months in a military hospital following his November 1944 release. The Railsplitters included Blaine Stewart on mandolin, bass-playing comedian James "Froggie" Cortez, fiddler John Stockdale, and two other people. The group later changed its name to Radio Ranch Hands after Jake opened his park of that name near Grafton.[23]

A pair of newcomers to Fairmont radio in 1948 and 1950, respectively, were two of the younger artists to have daily morning shows. Eddie Snider, known as the Plainsman, first had his own program over WWVA in the last year of the war. Snider came from Steubenville, Ohio, and developed a vocal style very similar to that of western film star Tex Ritter. This gained him a great deal of initial attention, but he proved unable to sustain a lengthy career. Unlike Ernest Tubb and Gene Autry, who began as Jimmie Rodgers stylists, or Hawkshaw Hawkins whose early sound resembled that of Tubb, Snider never broke away from the image of being a second Ritter. Changing his name to Dan Snider and moving to Memphis did not help although he did snare a contract with Majestic records during that interlude. Back in West Virginia, the Plainsman at WMMN reverted to the name he had been known by in Wheeling, which did little to promote his recordings. The second youngster to enter the picture, Dorsie Lewis, a Morgantown youth, became known as "The Scared Coal Miner" from an original song that he popularized in northern West Virginia and southern Pennsylvania. An effective protest song performed in a talking blues style, it expresses quite well the misgivings of a youth entering the mines. Lewis also did straight country material and later turned toward rockabilly and bluegrass, but could never repeat the success of "The Scared Coal Miner." In a sense, Snider and Lewis became victims of two peculiar forms of minor success. Snider could never quite escape from the image of being a second Tex Ritter while Lewis always remained "The Scared Coal Miner."[24]

Ellis Hall represented another type of limited commercial success. An older man, born in 1893, and a skilled glass-blower at the Quality Glass Company in his Morgantown home, Hall played one of the finest old-time fiddles anywhere and composed original tunes, most notably "My Little Home in West Virginia." Since he had a good job, Hall never aspired to become a full-time professional, but did fiddle a great deal locally and off and on at WMMN from the station's early days. In May 1952, when nearing sixty, Hall and guitarist Bill Addis obtained an RCA Victor contract and recorded four fine numbers, but more than twenty years after this type of music had major commercial appeal. Despite brisk sales of 18,000 on "My Little Home in West Virginia," Hall never recorded again and lived quietly in Morgantown until his death in 1977.[25]

A few other musical acts worked at WMMN in the declining years of live country radio. Gay Schwing and his Boys from the Hills came over from WWVA. The Green Valley Boys—probably another Grandpa Wilson band—worked for quite a while, as did an obscure group, the Buckeye Ramblers, which may or may not have been the same as Slim and his Ramblers. The Rhythm Rascals featuring Mannington's Fluharty Brothers worked from time to time. John Bava also had a country gospel act.

Among individuals, Rosa Lee, who had worked with the Happy Hoedowners during the war, had a show in 1949, as did the old team of Salt and Peanuts, who continued making their rounds. A lesser known duo, Snap and Ginger, did likewise. Blind Bob Hall of Ashland, Kentucky, had a show for a time and so did Dusty Shaver. In 1952 Jack Henderson, the brother of Radio Dot, came back to WMMN for a few months. Buddy Starcher had left Fairmont at the end of 1946 and although he never made it his base again, he did have transcriptions played at WMMN during much of 1951. Sunshine Sue, a perennial favorite at WRVA Richmond, Virginia, also had some transcribed shows. From the latter part of 1952 onward, only Hank the Cowhand and a few associates continued. Blaine Stewart, a mandolin player from New Martinsville who had once worked with Jake Taylor and then with Wilma Lee and Stoney Cooper, did some duets with Hank. Blaine, Hank, Big Eared Zip with his tenor banjo, and fiddler Bill Huffman were all that remained at a station that had boasted a staff of forty-six entertainers in 1945. By 1954 Hank's live performing had been reduced to one half-hour show daily, then to a quarter-hour in 1955. That fall he moved to Keyser, and the most distinguishing feature of WMMN's history as a station ended.[26]

Since few of the musicians had actually been from the area, little evidence of this phase of Fairmont's history remained visible. Paul Crane, who had worked with various groups from the late 1930s, lived in the city, as did Charles Satterfield, fiddler for the West Virginia Mountain Boys among others. Big Eared Zip labored as a custodian at the school in nearby Farmington until his death in 1967. At Mannington, old-timers like Russell Fluharty, Abner Cole, and their brothers still entertain listeners with tales of the good old days of radio. In downtown Fairmont a new generation of country music fans walk daily past the glaze-fronted building with the inlaid WMMN lettering, unaware of the sound that once emanated from it. They also amble by the huge courthouse across the street without realizing that the building houses a marriage record of Hall of Fame member Grandpa Jones, whom they see regularly on "Hee Haw," or the complex estate documents of the Old Pardner and Cowboy Loye, people who within a hundred miles of Fairmont were as much stars as anyone could have been.[27]

Meanwhile, 204 miles to the south, country music had continued to flourish at WHIS Bluefield during and after World War II, but the Shott family expanded into television at about the time live radio programming declined. This caused Bluefield to remain a regional center for a longer period.

Numerous musical aggregations played at WHIS from 1942, but two dominated the scene. The Lonesome Pine Fiddlers continued for a year or so after Pearl Harbor, but wartime conditions eventually forced temporary disbanding. Gordon Jennings left the Bluefield area for St. Louis, and Ezra Cline assumed the leadership. Ned Cline died in the June 1944 Normandy invasion, but young Charlie Cline replaced him and soon displayed a knack for playing practically any instrument. He and brother Curly Ray sang as a Delmore-style duet. By March 1948 the group had four quarter-hour shows daily, with the last one ending at 9:00 AM. Band personnel apparently fluctuated because late in 1949 during the absence of Charles and Ray Cline, Ezra hired Bob Osborne and Larry Richardson, a pair of young Appalachian migrants from southwestern Ohio seeking work in a hillbilly band. Osborne sang with a high lead voice and Richardson picked a three-finger style banjo in the fashion of Earl Scruggs, and sang lead on the duets, Osborne switching to tenor. With Ray Morgan on fiddle and himself on bass, Ezra Cline brought a complete bluegrass band to the Mountain State. Although they had been popular before, the Lonesome Pine Fiddlers now reached new heights of acclaim. In March 1950 they recorded four sides on the small Cozy label, two of them—"Pain in My Heart" and "Lonesome, Sad, and Blue"— subsequently leased to Coral.

Despite the popularity of the Lonesome Pine Fiddlers, some of their efforts at commercialism seem somewhat primitive. Like other artists, they played showdates in schools sponsored by local organizations, but their specialty came to be termed the "candy show." Usually held on a vacant lot or town square, the Fiddlers would publicize their show time and location with a loudspeaker, a process known as ballyhooing. No admission would be charged, but during the intermissions the musicians sold small boxes of candy for 25 cents each. Prizes in the boxes served as a further inducement to purchase, particularly an occasional wrist watch. The audience learned that only about one watch went out per night and band members exercised care so as not to sell that box until late in the evening. One former Fiddler tells that Curly Ray accidentally sold the prize box early one time and Ezra, realizing the crowd would drift away, said in dismay, "Boys, we're ruined!"

In the spring of 1951, Bob and Larry left the Fiddlers, but Ezra secured other competent musicians to maintain the bluegrass sound. In addition to Curly Ray Cline, he hired a pair of talented teenagers, Paul Williams singing lead and playing guitar, and Ray Goins picking banjo. He secured an RCA Victor recording contract and after a time Charlie Cline returned to the group after working with Bill Monroe and his Blue Grass Boys. In the fall of 1952 the Fiddlers moved to a newer station, WOAY in Oak Hill, West Virginia. At this time Ray Goins dropped out of the group, but both he and brother Melvin Goins rejoined it a year later. During much of 1953 the band headquartered at WJR Detroit, but in the fall came to WLSI Pikeville, Kentucky. The latter location served as home base for the Lonesome Pine Fiddlers for the remainder of their existence as a group, although they continued to play often in southern West Virginia and also did some television there. Through their excellent music and recordings the Lonesome Pine Fiddlers gained recognition as one of the great early bluegrass bands although they never achieved the fame of a Bill

Monroe or Flatt and Scruggs, let alone the latter's commercial success.[28]

The other dominant Bluefield act probably acquired greater local but less national fame than the Lonesome Pine Fiddlers. Charles "Rex" Parker, a native of Maplewood, West Virginia, born in 1921, had varied earlier experience with groups at Beckley, Bluefield, and Charleston, including duets with Tommy Cantrell and Tex McGuire. On July 31, 1941, he married Eleanora Niera, born at Beard's Fork of Spanish parents in 1922. The young couple came to Bluefield and subsequently took over the spot vacated by Lee and Juanita Moore and sponsored by Tomchin's Furniture. The Parkers, in a sense, succeeded the Moores as Bluefield's premier duet act. Like Charlie Cline, Rex displayed a remarkable instrumental vituosity. Less smooth than the Moores in their singing, Rex and Eleanor projected an authenticity and sincerity in their mountain-styled harmonies with which WHIS listeners could identify.

Rex and Eleanor apparently curtailed their performing during the war years. The period immediately following 1945 proved an especially active one, however, as radio and personal appearances kept them busy. For a time they had live daily programs on stations at Bluefield, Princeton, Welch, and Pineville simultaneously. Although the Parkers generally maintained a band, the Merrymakers, which at times included musicians such as Ralph "Joe" Meadows, Bob Osborne, and Larry Richardson, they never put together a bluegrass unit but relied on Rex's instrumental talents and a wide variety of arrangements using fiddle, mandolin, electric lead guitar, and three-finger banjo. They recorded for both Cozy and Coral, waxing four songs on each label, but neither had adequate distribution to make them well-known outside the WHIS listening area. Nonetheless, the Parkers managed to endure as regional favorites, simultaneously and successfully switching from a duet to a family group, from secular to gospel music, and from a radio to a television act.[29]

Several other musical groups headquartered at Bluefield from time to time, but none remained as long as the Cline and Parker acts. Salt and Peanuts worked there for several months as part of their constantly on-the-move operation, as did Daisy Mae and Charlie Arnett. Burt Edwards led a group known as the Virginia Playboys that included his son Billy, later a bluegrass sideman of considerable significance. Budge and Fudge Mayse played there again after recovering from war injuries. Woody Williams continued at WHIS too, although not steadily. During his service absence, brother Buddy worked with Curley Sizemore. A group from Ronceverte that played more modern material than most Bluefield-based bands, the Whispering Strings, managed to get on Cozy records and later moved to WLOH Princeton. Slim Carter, once popular at WWVA, and wife Brown Eyes worked out of Bluefield for a time in 1945. Ralph and Ruth Blankenship proved popular at WHIS; they also worked in Huntington for a time and even operated a tent show. Ralph (earlier known as Gona) had once worked as part of Al Hendershot's Dixie Ramblers with brother Jess and Ruth Cline, whom Ralph married in 1933, constituting an excellent and pure country duet. They had some good original songs like "A Thought Crossed My Mind" and "Why Do You Weep Dear Willow" as well as the standard range of popular duets. Salt and Peanuts, returning again, did some of their last live radio work at WHIS in the early 1950s. Peanuts operated a dance studio in downtown Bluefield for a time before the venerable show business couple retired to Florida. Both died within four months of each other in 1976.[30]

A number of lesser known musicians or those with local popularity—sometimes in western Virginia—broadcast from the WHIS studios. Individuals included Curley Sizemore, Charlie Meadows, and Joe Emmerson, the latter being primarily a gospel singer. Bands that played there included Mason Ayres's West Virginians, the Arizona Drifters, Jim Scott's Virginia Sky Liners, Elmer's Gang (which also played at Princeton), the Rhythm Pals, and the Virginia Mountain Rangers.

Transcribed shows also continued to be used heavily at WHIS. The Korn Kobblers, a hillbilly novelty group based in New York, ranked among the most popular. Southland Echoes featured Judie and Julie Jones, who had formerly been there in person. Black Draught, a laxative, and other products of the Chattanooga Medicine Company became widely used nostrums through their "Tennessee Hoedown" shows. Louise Massey and the Westerners also received wide exposure over WHIS.

As late as 1953 new groups tried to get started using WHIS as a vehicle for advancement. In August, Melvin Goins, a twenty-year-old Bramwell youth, organized the first Goins Brothers band consisting of himself, younger brother Ray, who had played banjo with the Lonesome Pine Fiddlers after Larry Richardson departed, and Ralph (Joe) Meadows, a nineteen-year-old fiddler from Camp Creek who had once been with both the Parkers and the Whispering Strings. Financial success eluded the boys but they managed to subsist partly by cooking their meager food on an electric hot plate in the Drake Hotel room where they lived. Hotel rules forbade cooking in the room and in one instance Melvin had a hard time explaining to the maid that the smoke she smelled came from out on the street when fumes were pouring from the dresser drawer in which Joe and Ray had hidden the hot plate. By November the gang gave up trying to make it on their own. Melvin and Ray joined the Lonesome Pine Fiddlers at WLSI Pikeville, where each could count on the five-dollar daily wage that Ezra paid on days they played shows. Joe soon accepted an offer to fiddle for the Stanley Brothers at WCYB Bristol.[31]

Competition came to WHIS in December 1947 and May 1948 as WLOH Princeton and WKOY Bluefield, respectively, went on the air. The former station offered shows by Rex and Eleanor (who also remained with the older station), the Rhythm Pals, and the Whispering Strings for a time. As WAEY in recent years, the station carries one of the surviving remnants of earlier days as the Parkers have continued a Sunday morning gospel show there. Bluefield's second station arrived on the scene almost too late for much live programming but did for a time have the services of Fiddlin' Bud Kurtz, the son of Salt and Peanuts, as well as WHIS pioneer Gordon Jennings. Back at WKOY from 1951, Jennings did primarily deejay work with occasional performing and eventually television.[32]

To the north, WJLS at Beckley continued its pattern set in 1939 as a station with numerous hillbilly musicians. Neither Walter and Johnnie Bailes nor Jimmy Dickens ever returned to Beckley after their early experiences, but Speedy Krise, Paul Taylor, and Rattlesnale Hogan remained for at least part of the war years with the Blue Ribbon Boys. This band also included the Lilly Brothers when they were available and the Barbour Brothers, Roy and Carl, at other times. Lottie Buskirk, billing herself as "The Gal from the Mountains," worked there for a year or so. Early in 1944 Lynn Davis and Molly O'Day worked there for a year. They revived their old West Virginia band name, the Forty-Niners, which they had dropped in 1942 for the Sunshine Hillbillies. Their band included Burk Barbour, a top-flight fiddler from Lynchburg, Virginia, and some local musicians like Pap Jones, the Lillys, and for a brief time harmonica player Lonnie Glosson. Via a hookup with WHIS, their programs were also heard on the Bluefield station.

Of the various Beckley musicians who worked with the Forty-Niners, the Lilly Brothers unquestionably made the largest long-range impact other than Lynn and Molly themselves. Everett and Mitchell B. (usually just known by his middle initial, B., or sometimes Bea) had been born in remote Clear Creek in 1924 and 1921 respectively. They had played around WJLS from the early days and made brief forays to other West Virginia stations at various times. They later joined Lynn Davis and Molly O'Day, whose band had been renamed the Cumberland Mountain Folks, at WNOX Knoxville, where they also worked in a group called the Smiling Mountain Boys. Returning to West Virginia, the Lillys subsequently went to Wheeling where they worked as a duet within Red Belcher's Cumberland Ridge Runners and made their first recordings. In 1951 Everett worked as tenor vocalist and mandolinist for Lester Flatt and Earl Scruggs. In this role he made some classic recordings with this band including the original cuts of "I've Lost You," "Over the Hills to the Poorhouse," and "Don't Get Above Your Raising" (recently revived by Ricky Skaggs). Everett also observed the rapidly growing popularity of the Scruggs-style banjo, and when the Lilly Brothers reorganized the following year he added a young banjo picker, Don Stover, from the nearby company town of Ameagle. Going to Boston the Lillys found a radio job at WCOP's "Hayloft Jamboree" which had recently been inaugurated by eastern promoter Aubrey Mayhew, and added a fancy Texas fiddler to their band in the person of young Tex Logan, with whom they had worked and recorded at WWVA.

The Lillys, Stover, and Logan first called their group the Confederate Mountaineers and almost from the beginning they made themselves heard in Boston with their pure brand of bluegrass. The band soon found nightly employment at a small nightclub called the Hillbilly Ranch, where they attracted sailors on shore leave and those of southern working-class origins. They also began to gain a following among collegians, at least when the folk revival and hootenanny craze swept the nation's campuses in the later 1950s. No doubt many of the more educated folks thought that, compared to the Kingston Trio and the Greenwood County Singers, this was indeed the pure stuff. To be sure, nobody had a more down-home sound than the Lillys. Everett himself reported that when he and his brother first went to New England many folks invited them to play at private parties just to hear their pure mountain accents, and Tex Logan relates a tale with respect and affection for the Lillys about their initial look at the huge Bonwit-Teller Department Store. After some discussion they decided it was a place where people "got their clothes tellered." The band probably made their best recordings in 1956 and 1957 for the small Event label (since reissued on County), but then went on to do an album for Folkways and two for Prestige-International. These efforts sold primarily to urban and intellectual audiences who came to regard the Lillys as among the purest and finest bluegrass bands.

Aside from Everett's early stint with Flatt and Scruggs and a second shorter one in 1958-1959, the Lilly Brothers remained a little-known group, but to northerners who became bluegrass fans the Lillys became almost legendary. Oddly enough they also played a major role in the spread of bluegrass music to Japan through a tape recording made by one Robert Tainaka, who had it released on a Japanese label, entitled "Live at Hillbilly Ranch." In 1973 Tainaka promoted the first of two tours of Japan by the Lilly Brothers and Don Stover, and their reception in the Far East could be described as nothing less than phenomenal. Three album releases on the Japanese Towa label resulted from their concerts there. Somewhat ironically the Lillys were playing but little in the United States by that time. Following the death of a beloved son in a January 1970 accident, Everett decided after some hard soul searching to go back to rural West Virginia, and did. Meanwhile B. remained in Boston and Don Stover went on to form his own band. Still, they periodically got together for an occasional concert or festival. In 1979 they became the subjects of an educational film, *True Facts in a Country Song*, which premiered in the West Virginia State Culture Center in Charleston with numerous notables among the guests. The Lillys followed with one of their rousing concerts that included not only the standard bluegrass fare but lost gems from earlier generations such as "The Forgotten Soldier Boy" from the bonus marcher era and "That Star Belongs to Me" from World War II.

The departure of Lynn and Molly from Beckley a second time in the early spring of 1945 hit WJLS a blow from which their country programming never quite recovered. The Lilly Brothers remained a few months longer while Lynn and Molly experimented with their mountain style at KRLD Dallas, but when Lynn and Molly came to WNOX Knoxville the Lillys rejoined them and so too did Speedy Krise when he received his military service discharge. Everett and Bea put in a few brief stints at WJLS in later years, sandwiched in between their services on larger stations, but their major radio work at Beckley ended. Although in quantitative terms numerous musicians continued to work at Beckley they never achieved more than a brief and local popularity. A mid-1949 roster of WJLS acts, for instance, listed Jack Hunt and the Ranch Hands, the Lilly Brothers, the Oklahoma Trail Blazers, the Ridge Runners, Sleepy Holt, Stan Smith, Rattlesnake Hogan, and Jim Fain. Except for the Lillys (who had already gone to WWVA by that time) and the locally durable Hogan, none of the others made a particularly lasting impression.[33]

A similar situation prevailed at WNNR, Beckley's second station, which began broadcasting on July 14, 1946. Their mid-1949 listing showed two bands, the Mountaineers and the Ramblers, and two duets, George and Mary and the Stacy Twins. Of these, only the latter gained any sustained reputation. Born in Grundy, Virginia, on March 10, 1923, Fred and Ted Stacy did some entertaining in Hawaii during their military careers. They came to WJLS after the war and switched to WNNR in 1948. The Stacys attended the local junior institution, Beckley College, and later entered the insurance and real estate business. Ted Stacy also served in the West Virginia legislature. In fact, the later local economic and political prominence of the Stacy Twins may have helped—after the fact—to fan memory of their musical careers. By the same token their local renown as radio performers gave them a degree of name recognition which worked to their benefit when entering the sales and political fields.[34]

At Logan, WLOG had a spurt of live country programming during the war years. Local geography probably contributed to this situation. Logan is a small but congested city surrounded by coal camps and relatively isolated from more distant towns and cities. With coal mine work picking up during the war, people suddenly had a little extra cash but few places to spend it. The Red Rock Cola Company sponsored a "Logan County Barn Dance." Listeners to WLOG could also hear the Bailes Brothers via transcription and the J.F.G. Coffee Boys, although it is unclear whether the latter were a local live group or a transcribed one. Logan did not get its second station (WVOW) until 1954.[35]

Three newly established stations made some notable contributions to live country music programming in the postwar years. The first, WMON Montgomery, took to the air on July 14, 1946, and soon boasted such musicians as the Happy Mountain Gang, Buddy Childers, and the Robson Boys. By 1950 the latter converted to gospel music and as the Robson Quartet rendered some quality four-part harmony singing with only guitar and mandolin accompaniment. They did a session for Cozy and also worked at WOAY.[36]

The second notable new station, Oak Hill's WOAY, began broadcasting in 1947. One of the earliest groups to play there, the Western Ramblers, featured Bill Carpenter (who later became a significant Dobro player) on the electric steel guitar. The Lonesome Pine Fiddlers came to Oak Hill from Bluefield in 1952 and worked at WOAY until going to Detroit early in 1953 to be on Casey Clark's "Big Barn Frolic." Elmer Hickman, the Blue Mountain Yodeler, did some performing but more deejay work. Billie Jean and Radio Red Lydick enjoyed the longest run of all the Oak Hill acts. With their band, the Dixie Drifters, the Lydicks remained for several years and eventually did television as well. Speedy Krise returned from Knoxville and worked with the Dixie Drifters for a couple of years. A pair of country gospel singing preachers, Freddie Steele and Mont Carr, also had programs in Oak Hill for long periods of time.[37]

The last new station in southern West Virginia to program live country music extensively, WWYO Pineville, did not go on the air until 1949. Nonetheless, it managed to accomplish quite a lot in the next five years. The duo of Scotty and Tar Heel Ruby headed a long list of artists who worked there both on daily shows and on the Saturday night "Wyoming Hayride." Born Perry Edward Scott at Jesse, West Virginia, on April 2, 1912, Scotty married Ruby Fay Ellidge, a native of Walnut Grove, North Carolina, whose family had moved northward to work in the mines. The couple had some early radio experience primarily as part of other groups from 1939 to 1941 in Huntington, Beckley, and Welch. Their work at Pineville began in the station's early days and continued until 1955. They employed a band, the Dixie Border Boys, which included Huntington veteran Junior Ruggles on bass, Cecil (Ray) Morgan on fiddle, and J.B. Rose on guitar, and did two sessions for Jim Stanton's Rich-R-Tone records. After the live radio era ended, the Scotts settled in Oceana before eventually retiring to North Carolina, where Scotty died on April 9, 1983.

Numerous other musicians worked at WWYO and appeared on the "Wyoming Hayride." Cecil Surratt, a native of Coalwood born in 1926, gained three years of valuable experience at Pineville before moving on to Bluefield, where he worked some radio and even more television. Surratt displayed sufficient versatility to make an impact in the areas of bluegrass, country, and the commercial brand of folk music that flourished in the late 1950s and early 1960s. Rex and Eleanor Parker included Pineville among stations on their circuit for a time. Other artists working locally included Theodore Effler, Sunshine Danny, Eddie Robinson, and Gene Bailey, while bands bore such names as the Sunshine Sweethearts and the Rhythm Nite Hawks.[38]

In northern West Virginia, Parkersburg's WPAR continued to maintain its modest level of country music activity through the 1940s. In a late 1941 letter to the *Mountain Broadcast and Prairie Recorder* Bobby Cook described four acts on the station in addition to his own Texas Saddle Pals. These groups consisted of the ever present Burroughs Trio, Ray Thomas and the Rodeo Rangers, the Rushing Family, newly arrived from Knoxville, and that youthful but experienced duo from Raleigh County, the Lilly Brothers. Cook's group included local fiddler Jack Miller, Don and Blaine Stewart, and a singer known as Little Betty Lou. In addition to their daily shows the whole array held a Friday night "Jamboree" at the Parkersburg Coliseum that sometimes featured guests from neighboring cities such as Cap, Andy, and Flip. For Parkersburg this situation probably ranked as the high point of the city's musical development, but it quickly became a casualty of wartime conditions.

Through the ensuing years some local acts played daily shows at WPAR. The Blue Valley Pioneers included Richard Boring, a Meigs County, Ohio, fiddler and vocalist, among their number. A 1949 listing showed the Dixie Drifters, Joe Williams, and the Burroughs Girls, Betty and Billie, headquartered there. Later the Burroughs Girls' brother Charlie worked solo under the name Charlie Carroll. Also, just as the Lillys repeatedly returned to WJLS between more lucrative engagements elsewhere, Bobby Cook seems to have periodically come back to WPAR.[39]

One new station in northern West Virginia featured extensive live hillbilly programming in its early years, and a few others had some such shows. Radio station WPDX at Clarksburg went on the air August 18, 1947, with a goal of emulating and rivaling the format that WMMN Fairmont found so successful. Buddy Starcher, who had been absent from radio for several months, and Cherokee Sue and Little John Graham, who had been relatively inactive since 1942, joined the entertainment staff at the beginning. Within a few months Budge and Fudge Mayse, also former Fairmonters, came into the fold, as did Cindy Coy (Evelyn Carpenter), a vocalist born in 1919 who had some WMMN experience. Later other Fairmont veterans—the Davis Twins, Jake Taylor, Sleepy Jeffers, and William "Dusty" Shaver, the popular comedian—also came to the staff and Ray Myers headquartered there for a time. Starcher won a nationwide contest as the best local station PI salesman for Sunway Vitamins and moved on to WCAU Philadelphia in 1949. John and Sue went to the WWVA Jamboree in October 1950, but their timing for the move coincided with the hard winter of 1950-1951 and the duo returned to Clarksburg where they were already established. John Peters, an announcer, did some singing on WPDX, and two other announcers, De Wyatt and Russ Gardner, also had a close liaison with the hillbilly entertainers.

In a sense WPDX became one of the last bastions of live daytime country entertainment. Known collectively as the West Virginia Hillfolks, John and Sue, Budge and Fudge, and to a lesser extent Cindy Coy—like Hank the Cowhand at WMMN—held on as the other live acts vanished from local stations. Dusty Shaver recalls that Cherokee Sue, working for Coco-Wheats under the PI system, on an unusually good day got 5,000 letters, each containing a box-top and a quarter in response to a children's belt-buckle offer.

As early as December 1951, however, the trend away from live programming had become apparent. A *Country Song Roundup* article on Cherokee Sue reported that "her greatest following comes from the disc jockey show," the "Record Bench." About 1957 the live shows ended but the deejay work continued. Fortunately for the WPDX artists, they had prepared themselves for the changes ahead. Even while his daily shows continued, Little John Graham served as a plumber's apprentice, subsequently becoming owner of Graham's Plumbing and Heating, while Budge and Fudge attended classes at Clarksburg Business College which paved the way for post-radio careers in auto and insurance sales, respectively. Cherokee Sue continued as a deejay at WPDX and then at WBOY until fatally stricken with cancer in 1967. Cindy Coy spent years as music librarian at the radio station where she had once performed as a singer.[40]

Located in the heart of a county that had produced such musical notables as the Learys and Stoney Cooper, WDNE Elkins began broadcasting in February 1948. Although this station equalled neither WMMN nor WPDX in quantity and quality of live performers, it did produce some notable figures in its programs. Bill Carpenter, a Webster Springs native and veteran sideman at WJLS and WOAY, led a group called the Elk Mountain Rangers before moving to Michigan, where he played Dobro in some significant bluegrass combinations. Fiddler Woodford Simmons, a local Randolph Countian born in 1911, played regularly for quite a time with an early bluegrass band that included his son William singing high lead and playing guitar, Arnold Selman on banjo, and Rusty Helmick on bass and doing comedy. Simmons had earlier worked with radio bands at Harrisonburg and Fairmont and humorously tells about being unable to compete commercially with the Lonesome Pine Fiddlers and the Parkers during a brief stint at WHLS in 1949. Nonetheless, Woody Simmons played an excellent old-time fiddle, as he aptly demonstrated at numerous contests and folk festival appearances in the 1970s.[41]

John Bava was undoubtedly the most significant performer at WDNE, although his importance to West Virginia music ranges far beyond his own artistry. Born at Thomas in Tucker County of Italian parentage in 1913, Bava worked as a coal miner and minister, played guitar and accordion, and led a hillbilly gospel group, the Country Cousins, which featured the singing of his wife Lucy. In addition to their work at Elkins, the band also headquartered at WMMN Fairmont for a time and had taped broadcasts on several other stations. Bava's major contribution to music, however, came from his initiating his own hillbilly magazine, publishing firm, and record company. Orville and Jenny Via of Huntington with their *National Hillbilly News* preceded Bava's *Musical Echoes,* and Dixie Music of New York had already published the songs of numerous West Virginia performers, but Bava's Cozy records waxed some Mountain State artists unrecorded elsewhere. In addition to Bava's own group, Cozy managed to get people like Hank the Cowhand, Bobby Cook, Cherokee Sue and John Graham, Cindy Coy, Dorsie Lewis, and Ralph and Ruth on disc. At least one popular local performer, Harrison Booher (1914-1976) of Tyler County, not widely known via radio but a fine interpreter of Jimmie Rodgers's songs, did a Cozy session. Later important local rockabilly performers such as Keith Anderson, Dale Brooks, and Bruce Lambert preserved their material on Cozy, as did sacred singers including Fred Steele, the Robson Quartet, and Dave Kidwell. Finally, a few West Virginia artists recorded by Bava found their way to the major labels, including Rex and Eleanor Parker, Daisy and Charlie Arnett, Jake Taylor, and the Lonesome Pine Fiddlers. Although poorly distributed, Cozy records did get local sales for significant radio artists who found it increasingly difficult to get contracts with the larger firms.[42]

A few other postwar stations in northern West Virginia featured live country music. In Martinsburg, WEPM had Bill Peer and the Melody Boys. Moundsville's WMOD at times boasted the services of performers as well known as Jake Taylor, Bonnie Baldwin, Joe Barker, and rockabilly Keith Anderson although they tended to do more deejay work than live shows, especially during a period in the later 1950s when Taylor and Doc Williams owned the station.[43]

Outside the borders of West Virginia proper, Mountain State artists of note broadcast back to their own. Harrisonburg's WSVA, which served an audience along the eastern fringe, continued playing a key role although the best-known artists there, including Buddy Starcher, Blaine Smith, and Red Belcher, also worked almost as extensively at West Virginia stations. In Hagerstown, Maryland, station WJEJ had been on the air since 1932 and had a large audience in the eastern panhandle. One particularly important artist, Elwood "Woody" Liggett, born in 1925, organized the West Virginia Revelers in 1944, working primarily out of WJEJ but occasionally also WFMD Frederick, Maryland, and WINC Winchester, Virginia. Liggett's group played personal appearances throughout the region until the group disbanded in 1949. The band provided early experience for musicians like the McCumbees of Morgan, who later worked at WWVA. Liggett subsequently went into booking and promoting for Southern Attractions. Another eastern panhandle musician, Sammy Moss, provided some early experience for future Hall of Famer Patsy Cline.[44]

But whether an old station or a new one, by the mid-1950s changing times and particularly competition from television led to a change in radio formats. Country music continued to be heard but via phonograph record rather than live performance. Back in the early 1940s members of the American Federation of Musicians had feared this development. Congress in 1946 enacted the Lea Act prohibiting strikes against radio stations by musicians. Older union officials such as Ned Guthrie of the Charleston local contend that this law sounded the death knell for live radio entertainment. Yet many, perhaps most, stations continued their live programming until television competition made it impractical. Since many AFM locals ignored or opposed hillbilly artists anyway, this restrictive labor law does not seem relevant in most instances. As the PI system declined and television expanded, salaried musicians became a luxury no radio station could afford.[45]

In response to the changing realities many older musicians successfully converted to disc jockey work. For musicians such as Lee Moore, Buddy Starcher, and Cherokee Sue, who had already performed in such a role, this came easy. For others like Dusty Shaver, Bobby Cook, Gordon Jennings, Bonnie Baldwin, Hank Stanford, Zag Pennel, and Joe Barker, the transformation may have been more difficult. One friend of Shaver's pointed out, however, that the deejays could continue to play personals and plug them on the air just as they had on the live shows earlier. Far beyond the borders of West Virginia, people who had made their original names as singers in the Mountain State, such as Johnnie Bailes, Rusty Gabbard, and Harmie Smith, also drifted into deejay work. Here and there a young deejay like Keith Anderson or Dale Brooks gained some renown as a performer, too. Brooks in particular, an Upshur County native born in 1933, even did live and taped shows under the sponsorship of Martha White Flour in the 1960s. This in a sense made him the last significant live radio artist in West Virginia with the exception of those persons associated with the still thriving Wheeling Jamboree.[46]

At first recorded country music on radio tended to be associated with certain periods of the day—such as early morning hours—in a fashion similar to the earlier pattern of live programming. In the 1960s the trend toward the full-time country music station developed and that pattern persists to the present. Some stations continue to be identified as partial country stations, or as noncountry but with several hours of country programming weekly. By 1981 nineteen West Virginia stations, including the two 50,000-watt operations (WWVA

Wheeling and WCAW Charleston) were classified as country. These extended from the northern panhandle to Princeton and from Berkeley Springs in the eastern panhandle to Matewan on the western border. Two more stations, both country, took to the air in 1982. Five additional stations now list themselves as part country and six more include six to eighteen hours of country music weekly in their schedules. Although the product often has little of the old pure hillbilly sound associated with some of the earlier live artists, no West Virginian—or indeed American—today lacks access to country music via the radio.[47]

6. Country Comes to Television

Television came slowly to West Virginia. The decade of the 1950s proved to be a transitional period from one form of home entertainment to another although developments generally lagged somewhat in the Mountain State. This was so in part because, to a much greater degree than with radio, television receivers depended upon local stations. A radio owner in West Virginia did not have to listen to local stations, but unless a television station existed within a hundred miles, and usually less (because of the rough topography) little reason existed to own a set. Thus, neither the geography nor the continuing decline of the coal industry in post-World War II America offered much encouragement for television in West Virginia. Once television arrived, however, the format for country music programming developed much more rapidly than had been the case in radio.

On November 15, 1949, WSAZ-TV Huntington began broadcasting as Channel 5 (later as 3). Since fewer hours of network broadcasting and fewer syndicated programs existed then than in the 1980s, a greater amount of time was available for local shows. Country music, having proved itself on radio as a popular type of home-produced program, offered definite possibilities. Although it would be years before television had more viewers than radio had listeners, believers in the old saying that "the early bird catches the worm" meant that many aspired to succeed in the new medium. Several performers and programs came and went, but two country shows at WSAZ-TV eventually met with phenomenal success.[1]

Three bands pioneered country music on WSAZ-TV. The first, Texas Slim and his Prairie Buckaroos, came to television by way of radio. Slim (James Dees) had been one of the final performers on WCHS radio when that station terminated live hillbilly acts. Slim had two quarter-hour programs a week when WSAZ-TV began, but soon expanded to five shows a week. The Prairie Buckaroos consisted of George Trumbell on electric steel, Junior Ruggles on guitar or fiddle, Ale Smith on electric lead guitar, and John Webb on bass and spoons. In addition to their television work, the group also did a half-hour of radio daily and Slim did another quarter-hour solo and a half-hour of deejay work each morning beginning at 6:30.[2]

Richard Cox and the Harvesters were led by one of the early radio performers. Cox, who had left Huntington at age twenty-one in 1936 with old-timers Riley Puckett and Bert Layne, returned in 1949 and formed a modern band. Its members at various times included seasoned fiddlers Charlie "Big Foot" Keaton and Junior Ruggles and guitarist Curley Wellman, all radio veterans, along with relative newcomers Ray Daniels and Jerry Gildea. By 1953 the Harvesters had two weekly quarter-hour shows on WSAZ at 6:15 PM and also appeared on a Saturday afternoon jamboree-type program. Later, however, when station officials planned to upgrade the jamboree and move it into the more favored 7:00 PM Saturday time slot, Cox left the station when the WSAZ management chose Dean Sturm, a staff announcer, to emcee the program instead of him. He resurfaced later as a country deejay on WHTN radio before departing from Huntington again.[3]

The other early group on local television made less impact locally but in the long run a considerably larger one nationally. The Stanley brothers, Carter and Ralph, natives of Dickinson County, Virginia, ranked second only to Bill Monroe as a pioneer bluegrass band. They had already established themselves on radio at WCYB Bristol's popular "Farm and Fun Time" and recorded for Rich-R-Tone and Columbia records when they came to Huntington. In addition to Carter's guitar and lead vocal and Ralph's hard-driving banjo, the Clinch Mountain Boys included fiddler Lester Woody and Pee Wee Lambert on mandolin and tenor vocal. The Stanleys did a daily half-hour show in the early evening for about six months. Despite the quality music and the effort, the show seemed a bit ahead of its time. Not enough people had television sets as yet and the Stanleys left Huntington for the "Louisiana Hayride" in Shreveport and shortly returned to Bristol.[4]

One other live television show graced Huntington's studios in the earlier days. Little recollection of the program exists but, like the Stanleys', it may have been on the scene a little too early. The Rainbow Trail Gang remained for about two years and included musicians associated with other Huntington bands. At various times they had quarter-hour programs in the early and late afternoons.[5]

In 1952 and 1953 two country groups came to WSAZ-TV that soon rivaled Richard Cox's Harvesters. Odey Crabtree and the Western Pioneers also had two quarter-hour shows weekly. Crabtree and his sister Retha Neal gained local renown by winning a contest that led to their appearance on "The Horace Heidt Show" over the CBS Network. Other Western Pioneers included fiddler Eddie King and guitarists Ken Farley and Bill Rhodes. The third group, Gene McKnight and the Happy Valley Boys, featured its bass fiddle playing leader and Jackie "Butterball" Starr on electric lead guitar, Paul "Pappy" Thornton, once associated with Cincinnati's famed Ernie Lee, on steel, and Glen Ferguson, a long-time Huntington fiddler who had long associations with both Bobby Cook and Hawkshaw Hawkins to his credit.

These three groups minus Cox formed the initial nucleus of the jamboree when it moved to the Saturday night slot. Without Cox, Ralph Shannon came to the forefront as a vocalist and he and Crabtree became the show's singing stars. Both Retha Neal and Margie Shannon appeared on some of the earlier "Saturday Night Jamborees," but Ralph and Odey became virtual fixtures. Dean Porter, a lead guitar picker of considerable skill from Scioto County, Ohio, who had been a sideman with Little Jimmy Dickens, shared the instrumental spotlight with fiddlers Keaton and Ferguson. Dubbed the "Mayor of Bear Creek" by announcer Sturm, Porter and his successor Bob Baker both won acclaim. Some personnel changes occurred over the years; Thornton gave way to Buddy Gearhart on steel and Keaton missed some shows because of work conflicts. Girl vocalists also changed as Retha Neal and Margie Shannon gave way to Phyllis Noel and Norma Hoople, who in turn found themselves supplanted by Connie Smith. By 1965, Connie became a top figure in Nashville and a "Grand Ole Opry" star.

For more than a decade WSAZ-TV's "Saturday Night Jamboree" did exceedingly well. It was sponsored by Red Top Beer in its first year, but Ashland Oil took over sponsorship in 1954 and continued to support the show for the next ten years. By 1956 it ranked as the ninth most popular show in the region, receiving higher ratings than such NBC network programs as Groucho Marx's "You Bet Your Life" and everything on CBS except "Lassie." By 1960 expenses had climbed to $756.00 per show (from $385.00 in 1952) of which $345.00 went to the performers. Emcee Sturm received $25.00, the square dancers $7.50 each, and the musicians approximately $20.00 per show. Keaton, one of the few artists who held a regular job, recalls that most of the others earned their entire income from music. A half-hour local weekly television program provided sufficient exposure for a dozen or so musicians to make ends meet, although as much of it tended to be in bars and clubs as in school auditoriums. The "Saturday Night

Jamboree" continued as a popular feature until early 1964 when WSAZ-TV changed ownership. The syndicated "Porter Wagoner Show" took over the 7:00 PM position.[6]

The second live show to be a major success at WSAZ-TV really constituted part of a larger whole. In 1955 Martha White Mills set up a series of five television shows featuring Lester Flatt, Earl Scruggs, and the Foggy Mountain Boys, who already appeared on an early morning radio show at WSM. Each weekday evening the band appeared on a 6:00 PM live program, generally played a show in the station's listening area, then moved to the next location. The circuit included Chattanooga on Monday, Knoxville on Tuesday, Bluefield on Wednesday, and Huntington on Thursday, while the Friday location varied between Wheeling, Parkersburg, and Clarksburg. Since the band returned to Nashville on Saturday night for the "Grand Ole Opry," they stayed on the road a great deal of the time and managed to squeeze in time for record sessions and for transcribing their early morning WSM shows. The work made Flatt and Scruggs highly popular in West Virginia and environs, guaranteed their prosperity when other bluegrass bands found their futures threatened, paved the way for their national stardom in the 1960s, and sold countless tons of "the good Martha White Flour with Hot Rize, and Corn Meal Mix."

The Flatt and Scruggs show contained features that made it extremely appealing to Appalachian adults—good banjo and fiddle work as exemplified by Scruggs and Paul Warren, respectively, a blend of old and new songs, and old-time comedy featuring Charles Elza, known as Kentucky Slim the Little Darling, Uncle Josh Graves, and Jake Tullock. Finally the inclusion of a hymn every week also contributed to the show's popularity. At times the group would do an entire program of sacred material. Furthermore, Roy Crockett recalls that on showdates they never got above their audience. Lester and Earl would be as humble to a man in worn bib overalls as to the wearer of a stylish business suit.[7]

So successful did the system become that Martha White emulated it elsewhere, organizing a circuit featuring Jim and Jesse McReynolds in Georgia and Alabama, and Hylo Brown and the Timberliners in west Tennessee and Mississippi. Later in 1958 Brown, who had earlier worked as a featured vocalist on the Appalachian circuit, switched places with Flatt and Scruggs. Brown's group became almost as popular as his mentors' had been. Hylo, from near Paintsville, Kentucky, developed a sizable following in the WSAZ listening area and his Capitol recordings compare with those of Flatt and Scruggs as classic bluegrass. When scientists perfected video tape, however, the Flatt and Scruggs shows became syndicated and Brown was displaced, an event from which in a sense he never recovered commercially.[8]

No other country television shows in Huntington ever matched the success of the "Saturday Night Jamboree" or Flatt and Scruggs although a few others did exist. The Lonesome Pine Fiddlers played a half-hour weekly show for several months in 1958. In addition to Ezra's bass and Curly Ray's fiddle, Charlie Cline and his wife Lee Barnett rounded out the band. Abandoning bluegrass for what they hoped would be a more commercial mainstream country, the Fiddlers still found the influence of rock and roll too strong for them at the time. Gospel quartets, somewhat on the fringe of country music, also had regular shows. In 1952 the Huntington Harmonaires had the first regular program, but from 1954 the Gospel Harmony Boys had the most success, continuing in demand for church song fests into the 1980s, years after their programs ended.[9]

On October 2, 1955, Huntington acquired a second station in the form of WHTN-TV. The earlier station had built up a large audience, however, and since ABC lagged behind the other two networks, the WHTN-TV management found the competition challenging in the early years. Nonetheless, some musicians made valiant efforts. Everett Lilly, who worked with Flatt and Scruggs in 1958 as mandolin player, observed their local success and urged Charlie Monroe (once quite popular but then in retirement) to form a band with him. Roy Crockett, who had been a popular guest on Lester and Earl's show, also came into the group. Crockett recalls that despite some good music they just could not make it. Another talented bluegrass band from Ashland, the Bluegrass Playboys, had some able musicians in their group, including fiddler Paul Mullins and Thurman Endicott, and introduced such songs as the now standard "Katy Daley" to the idiom, but their program on Channel 13 had only fair success in enhancing their reputation with local audiences. Not until late 1966 did WHTN-TV obtain a popular live country show when they enticed Buddy Starcher away from Charleston. But that daily show had only a thirteen-week duration, largely because the success of his hit recitation song "History Repeats Itself" lured Starcher to Nashville. Several years later Starcher's successor, Sleepy Jeffers, also had thirty-nine weekly programs on the station, but by that time local live entertainment had pretty much become an anachronism.[10]

Television development in Charleston witnessed a virtual reversal of the situation in Huntington. The initial station in the state capital, WKNA-TV, began in 1953 as Channel 49 on UHF, which placed it at something of a disadvantage to WSAZ-TV, whose signals blanketed the same geographic region. Slim Clere, former partner of T. Texas Tyler and a time salesman at WKNA radio, approached WKNA program director Don Hayes about a live country program. Early in 1954 "Music Mountain Style" went on the air with Slim Clere and the Mountain Melody Boys from 6:15 to 6:30 on weekday evenings. The group also had a quarter-hour show at noon on the radio. Slim had a guest on each program and recalls meeting a youngster named Bobby Bare at the Jackson County Fair in Wellston, Ohio, in July who made a particularly strong impression. He invited the youth to guest on his program and Bare later filled in for a week in early October during Slim's brief illness. Despite a promising beginning, WKNA-TV ran into serious difficulties after August 15, 1954, when WCHS-TV Channel 8 hit the airwaves. Within weeks the station lost most of its advertising to the stronger rival and by the end of the year ceased operation.[11]

Country music in Charleston made a dramatic comeback in 1960 with the inauguration of the "Buddy Starcher Show." Starcher returned to WCHS after a twenty-three-year absence and virtually took up where he had left off previously. His daily early morning TV show ran for six years and varied from one to two hours in length. Buddy himself clearly emerged as the program's star although he usually did only one or two songs or recitations per show. His wife Mary Ann also sang and, as with the "All-Star Roundup" in earlier years, other musicians got ample air exposure. Steel player Herman Yarbrough doubled as Roscoe Swerps, a zany character who wore bermuda shorts and a baseball cap twisted sideways. Electric bassist Chester "Butch" Lester performed rockabilly material, and drummer Dorsey Ray "Pudgey" Parsons also did more modern country stylings. Instrumental stars included Norm Chapman on electric guitar and for substantial portions of the series Wick Craig on autoharp and Ralph "Joe" Meadows on fiddle. Eventually Sleepy Jeffers and the no-longer-child-stars Davis Twins also joined the cast, with Jeffers portraying his comic character, the oversized child Little Willie. For much of its run the show held a number-three rating in the Tri-State region, exceeded only by two popular network programs, one of them the "Beverly Hillbillies." The Starcher artists kept busy on personal appearances during most of their stay at WCHS-TV.

In 1966 Buddy had a national hit with "History Repeats Itself" and also opted for a lucrative and less demanding program at Huntington's WHTN-TV. Sleepy Jeffers took over the early morning show at WCHS-TV and, although a little less popular than Buddy had been, still maintained a large and loyal following. Many of the old Starcher musicians remained with the show and helped foster continuity. In addition, popular guests augmented the program's appeal, such as bluegrass banjo picker Lowell Varney from Crum and the Goins Brothers after their reforming in 1969. Varney, along with Jim Horn, had his own program for a time.[12]

Besides the continuingly popular Roscoe Swerps and the Davis Twins, the "Sleepy Jeffers Show" saw some newer performers advance to the forefront. Brady Withrow did some vocals and played electric bass. Harry Griffith performed in a modern style but had musical roots that went back to playing locally with Billy Cox. More importantly, Lori Lee Bowles, a Charleston native born in 1956 who had guested in the Starcher days, became a regular while maturing from child prodigy to an attractive young lady performing primarily country gospel songs. So too did the five years younger and more petite Little Linda, the daughter of Sleepy and Honey. The show terminated only on April 27, 1973, by which time CBS officials had decided to institute a more serious rivalry with the "Today Show" on NBC, and new WCHS manager Curtis Butler dropped most of the local programs.[13]

One other live country program flourished briefly at WCHS-TV. The "Ralph Shannon Show" starred the one-time WSAZ performer for a thirteen-week series in the summer of 1969. Sponsored by an insurance firm, Shannon utilized a country band from Charleston led by organist George Hall for instrumental backing. Although the once-popular "Saturday Night Jamboree" had been off the air for four years, the Wayne County Whippoorwill continued to maintain a high visibility, both as a performer and in politics, having unsuccessfully sought a congressional seat in the fall of 1968. The show proved to be only a transition for Shannon from his earlier popularity at WSAZ to his later success in Sarasota, Florida, as owner-vocalist of a quality restaurant/night club appropriately called Shannon's Way.[14]

While the "Buddy Starcher Show" established a high in popularity for local daytime country music television, the team of Cecil Surratt and Smitty Smith set the record for longevity. WHIS-TV in Bluefield went into operation on July 31, 1955, and their show ran from the station's early days until 1969. For the first two years the program ran for an hour in the early afternoon, but later from 5:00 to 5:30 PM. Surratt, born at Coalwood in 1926, had gained his earlier experience at Welch and Pineville, and later did some deejay work at WHIS concurrently with his television performing. King Edward Smith, born at Saltville, Virginia, in 1929 had varied experience on Virginia stations including WCYB Bristol and television in Roanoke. As a duo,

Surratt and Smith performed both country and folk material with skill and could also do bluegrass if the occasion demanded. They recorded extensively and, while not scoring any major hits, their records sold well, some doing surprisingly well in Germany. Numerous other musicians also worked as regulars on the program from time to time, including bluegrass stalwarts Billy Edwards, Melvin Goins, and Ray Goins, along with Buddy Pennington, a steel player. Boots Collins worked as a girl vocalist and Darnell Miller gained regional fame there prior to and concurrently with his membership at the WWVA Jamboree. Gordon Jennings also joined as a regular on the daily program, having earlier been associated with the Saturday-only "Country Jamboree." Finally, Mel Street, whom Surratt had first known during his radio days in Welch, worked on the program before getting his own show sponsored by Hill's Department Store.[15]

In the early 1970s Street made the transition from regional favorite to national star. A hit song entitled "Borrowed Angel," followed by an even more popular "Lovin' on Back Streets," proved to be the vehicle which brought Street to the forefront. As an interpreter of the honky-tonk "cheatin'" brand of hard-country vocal, Street had few if any equals in the early 1970s. Yet he also became virtually stereotyped in this brand of lyric, with only the nostalgic "Smoky Mountain Memories" as an exception to the pattern. He died by his own hand at the age of forty-two on October 21, 1978. Nonetheless, his fifteen chart-makers in a six-year career in the limelight marked him as a major, albeit tragic, figure in the 1972-1978 era.[16]

Bluefield television probably featured a wider variety of live programs than any other West Virginia station. Rex and Eleanor Parker had programs, and daughters Conizene and Rexana helped transform the group into the Parker Family. From 1959 they did almost totally country gospel. Lester Flatt and Earl Scruggs did about as well at WHIS-TV on Wednesday as they did in Huntington on Thursday, and Hylo Brown's Timberliners followed in a similar pattern after the Foggy Mountain Boys went to the western circuit. Another duo of East Tennessee origin, Bonnie Lou and Buster, also developed a series of shows for Morris Homes on different stations that included WHIS-TV. Buster Moore, a native of Cocke County, Tennessee, born in 1920, had performed on daily radio regularly from 1939 (except for service in World War II), and Margaret "Bonnie Lou" Bell, born in Asheville in 1927, also did radio work from the time of their marriage in 1945. The Moores had a successful daily show at WJHL-TV Johnson City for several years from 1953 before developing their circuit. Although not completely bluegrass, the Moores performed in a hard-country style reminescent of older Mountain State duos like Wilma Lee and Stoney Cooper or Molly O'Day and Lynn Davis without imitating either. In addition, Bonnie's brother Lloyd Bell sang newer country songs and Buster's comedy character, Humphammer, also augmented the show's appeal. Fiddler Benny Sims and banjoist Buddy Rose gave them a strong bluegrass touch. After three years their live shows, too, gave way to videotaping and a new sponsor. Their "Jim Walter Jubilee" continued as a syndicated show right into the 1980s, one of the few not based in Nashville, but originating from WATE-TV Knoxville.[17]

The Bluefield Saturday show "Country Jamboree" rivaled Huntington's "Saturday Night Jamboree" as a weekly regional favorite for a decade. Originally called the "Hillbilly Jamboree," its length varied from sixty to ninety minutes and included all of the station's live entertainers although the circuit travelers like Brown, Flatt and Scruggs, and the Moores generally had other commitments. Gordon Jennings, Surratt and Smith, Mel Street, and Don Whitt were the mainstays, but the cast tended to be broader than that heard on the daytime show.[18]

A fourth southern West Virginia center of live country music on television developed at WOAY-TV Oak Hill. Although a town of only 4,518, Oak Hill managed to have a VHF station on the air over Channel 4 in December 1954, making it one of the state's older stations. Furthermore, the signal reached portions of south-central West Virginia that found it difficult to tune in the broadcasts from larger cities. Rex and Eleanor Parker were the most successful and longest-running country act on the station with their weekly "Songs for Salvation" program. The oldest Parker daughter Conizene eventually married and moved to Indiana, but younger daughter Rexana Champ remained with the program after marrying and the Parkers maintained a faithful following and continued to work in area churches.[19]

In earlier periods, however, other acts had programs at WOAY-TV. Billie Jean and Red Lydick and their Dixie Drifters with Speedy Krise did television as well as radio in the mid-1950s. Later in the decade Marshall Pack, well-known in country-gospel circles, headquartered there. Bluegrass made its appearance with Bill Duncan and his Harmony Mountain Boys. This band featured not only Duncan but also Don Sowards, an excellent songwriter, tenor singer, and mandolin picker. A little later the Lilly Brothers came back from Boston and, together with Bill Pack on banjo and Joe Meadows on fiddle, had another all West Virginia group of considerable skill. In 1970-1971, Everett Lilly, returning permanently from New England, put together another band, but Bea's attachment to Boston made the show one of short duration and Everett's young son Mark began coming more to the forefront. Crum's Lowell Varney also had a Thursday evening program at WOAY-TV in the mid-1960s and the Stanley Brothers did frequent guesting on many of these programs.[20]

Live country music never flourished on northern West Virginia television with quite the vigor that it did in the southern parts of the state. In part this stemmed from the fact that all the southern stations tended to be offshoots of radio stations that had previous experience with the idiom. Neither WWVA nor WMMN ever went into television, and the stations that did had less background in country music. Nonetheless, the four northern West Virginia cities with commercial television outlets all programmed some live country shows.

The first television station in the north, WTAP-TV Parkersburg, began operation on October 8, 1953, on Channel 15. Although its area of dominant influence covered only Wood County, it also beamed its signals to adjacent counties on both sides of the Ohio River. Eddie Bailes, a local recording artist and mainstream country singer, had the initial program on WTAP-TV in the mid-1950s. Bailes has long been a popular regional performer and his recording "West Virginia" attracted attention at the time of the American Bicentennial celebrations. Flatt and Scruggs played their live Friday show there for a time, as did Hylo Brown. After Brown's connection with Martha White Mills terminated, the local management even made an early effort at syndicating his show, apparently with little success.

Parkersburg's major live program, however, lasted for nearly a decade. Local viewers first heard the "Big Red Jubilee" on November 21, 1963. The term "Big Red" derived from the Big Red Supermarkets which served as the program's primary sponsor, although the phrase has a broader identification with the city in also being the nickname of the local high school athletic teams. Denny Deever, a WTAP-TV announcer, conceived the show and served as the first emcee. After Deever left Parkersburg in 1965, Carl Lipps, a Big Red official, took over and ran the program for the next eight years. On August 6, 1964, the show expanded from thirty to sixty minutes and so remained until its termination on May 31, 1973. The "Big Red Jubilee" came to an end not because of sliding ratings or station management policy but because the main sponsor went out of existence. Nonetheless, the show outlasted any other country music studio presentation in the state other than Rex and Eleanor Parker's and Sleepy Jeffers's programs at WHTN-TV.

When the "Big Red Jubilee" premiered, the regular cast consisted of Ron Rader and the Night Raiders, a gospel trio known as the Temple Ettes, and vocalists Sue Williams and Connie Smith. To the extent that the show had a star, Connie Smith soon emerged in that role. But after Bill Anderson met and heard her performing at Frontier Ranch the following spring, Connie's days in Warner, Ohio, and WTAP-TV Parkersburg were numbered. She left the program a few weeks after her initial RCA Victor session of July 17, 1964, which resulted in "Once a Day." This Anderson song gave the petite twenty-three-year-old housewife a number-one hit which remained on the charts for twenty-eight weeks and helped propel her to Grand Ole Opry membership in June 1965. By the end of the 1960s she had a dozen more top-ten hits. She let her career taper off somewhat in the 1970s to devote more time to religious activity, but has remained a prominent figure on the national country scene and an Opry regular. The significance of her "discovery" by Anderson cannot be underestimated, but it obscures her training through experience via two West Virginia television programs and numerous appearances in the Ohio Valley.

Needless to say, no other "Big Red Jubilee" performers equalled or surpassed Smith in ascending the ladder of success. But some other artists did become popular regionally, such as Fran Bowen of Wheelersburg, Ohio, and Kay Fouss of Beverly, Ohio. Among male vocalists, veteran performer Bobby Cook often appeared in the later 1960s while doubling as a deejay and salesman at WPAR radio. Switching into radio station management, Cook moved on to Eminence, Kentucky, where he died several years later. Junior Norman also played regularly before gaining a wide following at "Jamboree U.S.A." After the "Jubilee" expanded to an hour, guest vocalists appeared nearly every week, including such known Mountain State performers as Keith Anderson, Dale Brooks, Harry Gorrell, and Ralph Shannon. On occasion nationally renowned artists even guested, such as Guy and Ralna, the popular duo with the "Lawrence Welk Show." Staff band members included steel player Buddy Gearhart, bass player Paul Elrod, and lead guitarists Bob Baker, Jerry and Pat Deer, and Max Farley, of whom all but the last had also been on the staff band of WSAZ-TV's "Saturday Night Jamboree." Overall, the "Big Red Jubilee" provided WTAP-TV viewers with quality country music by regional favorites for nearly a decade although, in the opinion of one local fan whose own experience extended from old-time radio to technicolor films, the local station lacked the facilities and engineering know-how to present the program in its best light.[21]

In the northern panhandle, WTRF-TV Wheeling began its programming only a few days after the Parkersburg station. As a VHF outlet on Channel 7, WTRF-TV had advantages that WTAP-TV lacked, yet its nearness to Pittsburgh placed some limits on the size of its hinterland. Doc Williams and the Border Riders did thirteen weeks of programs in 1957 and the popular WWVA Jamboree act Abbie Neal and her Ranch Girls also had a program of their own. Flatt and Scruggs spent several months there prior to switching southward.

The most popular country show in WTRF-TV's live programs was probably Slim Bryant and his Wildcats. A one-time associate of Clayton McMichen and his Georgia Wildcat band, and author of the Jimmie Rodgers song "Mother, the Queen of My Heart," Hoyt Bryant had become a virtual fixture at KDKA Pittsburgh from 1940. In addition to singers like Slim and brother Raymond, or "Loppy," the band included a hot fiddle, an accordion, and an electric guitar. Hardly a pure country band, the Wildcats absorbed influences of western swing, jazz, polka, and mainstream pop over the years. Still, they possessed enough of their original roots to retain their country audience appeal while also attracting fans from other types of music. Since Bryant already had a wide following in the region familiar with his radio and television programs from KDKA, his work at WTRF-TV simply augmented an existing popularity for Slim and the Wildcats in the upper Ohio Valley during the 1959-1960 season that he appeared there.[22]

At Clarksburg, WBOY-TV took to the air on November 17, 1957. One of its earliest local shows, the "Big Boy Frolics," featured a variety of live country artists. Dale Brooks probably constituted the program's major figure during its two-year life. Brooks, a young deejay and country artist born in 1933, did extensive personal appearance work throughout northern West Virginia. Since he first deejayed and then combined his country music work with radio station management and ownership, he had a rather broad audience. At one time or another he headquartered at Keyser, New Martinsville, Spencer, Buckhannon, Berkeley Springs, and nearby Oakland, Maryland. In a sense Brooks represented something of a transitional figure between near old-timers, such as Dusty Shaver and Hank Stanford, and a new generation of West Virginians such as Penny DeHaven and Sandy Rucker, who would identify with the modern Nashville sound. Brooks himself played accordion as well as guitar and not only could perform well but also wrote well in such varying styles as honky-tonk, western, rockabilly, and gospel. He left West Virginia for North Carolina after nearly twenty years of steady performing on radio, television, and stage. Not content with music only, Brooks also wrote a syndicated column of rural philosophy that appeared in numerous weekly papers and a few dailies.

In addition to Dale Brooks, several other musicians appeared on the "Big Boy Frolics," some of them veterans of radio days at WMMN and WPDX. Lawrence Calhoun, known as Plain Slim, a native of Rowlesburg, played guitar and did some singing. Bill and Ronny Huffman, guitarist Johnnie Lane, mandolin picker Boogie Bill Boggs, and fiddler Shorty Brooks all made contributions to the show's success.[23]

One other television station flourished in northern West Virginia. It began as WJPB-TV Channel 35 in Fairmont, but in 1960 relocated at Weston, subsequently becoming Channel 5 and taking the call letters WDTV. At least five live country shows thrived on the station at various times during the 1960s. Reverend Robert Robinson had a gospel music program, as did radio veterans John and Lucy Bava. "Happy-Go-Lucky" Joe Barker had one of the first shows, often performing as a solo artist with occasional guests. Barker continued to work as a deejay and salesman at WBUC Buckhannon. The Piney Mountain Boys led by Red Goldsmith had a show which also featured the talents of such musicians as Earl Radcliff and Charlie Messenger.[24]

By far, however, the "Bar 5 Ranch" comprised the most popular live program at Weston. The group consisted largely of Stanley Odell and his three daughters, Judy, Linda, and Kay. Odell, a veteran fiddler and radio performer, had been born in Roane County on October 15, 1919. He had played quite a bit with groups at WPAR in the 1940s and then switched to Huntington. There he worked in the Rainbow Trail group on WSAZ-TV, on WHTN, and with Lonnie Lucas at WJEH in Gallipolis, Ohio. After some years of relative inactivity, Odell and his daughters guested on Barker's program and their popularity led to their own show early in 1962. They initially did three half-hour programs on Monday, Wednesday, and Friday, but as time passed, first the Friday and then the Monday spots were phased out. Nonetheless the Odells remained quite popular and by Stanley's account the girls were the major attraction. One by one they married and left the show, and Stanley finally gave up the program in late 1965 as the rigors of show business had become more tiring. His children, including a couple of sons, have continued as leaders or members of country bands in an area extending from Ohio to Virginia right up to the present.[25]

A pair of noncommercial stations, WMUL-TV Huntington and WNPB-TV Morgantown, have shown some interest in country music. The former station, connected with Marshall University, has twice put together hour-long reunion programs of performers from the old WSAZ Jamboree, largely through the efforts of Dean Sturm. As a result, in 1976 and 1981 Tri-State fans had renewed, if brief, opportunities to see again old favorites such as Ralph Shannon, Dean Porter, Big Foot Keaton, and Curley Wellman. The former West Virginia University station, largely through the influence of Carl Fleischhauer, later with the Library of Congress's American Folklife Center, has given television viewers opportunities to see many of the state's traditional performers and also paid some attention to commercial performers by producing some programs by "Jamboree U.S.A." legend Doc Williams. Producer Bill Jaker has also given some thought to a television recreation of WMMN's once famed "Sagebrush Round-up."[26]

The residents of several West Virginia counties had an opportunity to see live country music on television shows originating from stations outside the state. In the southeastern counties, WDBJ-TV Roanoke broadcast the "Top O' the Mornin' Show" with Don Reno, Red Smiley, and the Tennessee Cutups for a decade, and after 1965, when Reno withdrew, Smiley and his Bluegrass Cutup band carried on with the show until its termination in 1969. Reno and Smiley also broadcast weekly from WSVA-TV Harrisonburg for a time, as did the Valley Four and Linda, and Buddy Starcher had a daily television program in the late 1950s prior to his return to Charleston. Blaine Smith, quite popular on radio in Wheeling, Fairmont, and Harrisonburg, settled permanently in the Shenandoah Valley city where he had a twice-weekly television show for several years. Eastern panhandle residents could tune in to shows from Washington, D.C., from the late 1940s and see programs produced by Connie B. Gay which featured future Nashville stars such as Jimmie Dean, the Stonemans, and Roy Clark along with the late bluegrass fiddler of renown, Buck Ryan.[27]

Looking back at the era of live-television country music, Herman Yarbrough, who worked extensively at Charleston and for briefer periods in Harrisonburg and Huntington for more than fifteen years, offered some interesting perspectives. Through the early and mid-1960s local stations could and did offer decent regional entertainment and built up successful followings from their fans. But by the end of the 1960s an increasing number of country shows on the networks, exemplified by Johnny Cash and "Hee Haw," along with syndicated programs from Nashville (pioneered by Flatt and Scruggs, Porter Wagoner, the Stonemans, and "Stars of the Grand Ole Opry," now often seen as "Classic Country" on PBS stations) began to take their toll. Although the quality of talent on these shows may have been no better, the local programs found it increasingly difficult to compete with the more lavish productions featuring guest artists constantly turning out hit records. The local popularity of shows like that of Sleepy Jeffers at Charleston caused him to survive into the mid-1970s, and the Parkers at Oak Hill held on until the end of the decade. But except for news and related activity, together with an occasional show for kids, locally produced entertainment vanished from the airwaves. Like the village opera house, vaudeville, silent films, and live radio, it became another casualty of the changing times and technology that have periodically altered the format of American popular entertainment.[28]

7. The Renaissance of Folk and the Rise of Bluegrass

As country sounds moved increasingly in the direction of mainstream popular music after the beginnings of the rockabilly era, not only in West Virginia but in the United States as a whole, movements soon appeared that looked toward more tradition-rooted styles. Although the manifestations of this trend became obvious at the end of the 1950s, its origins went back a great deal further. The folk revival essentially evolved from the interests and studies of urban intellectuals and scholarly folklorists, whereas bluegrass emerged from commercial country music as a sort of reactionary yet innovative styling. While neither movement originated in the Mountain State as such, West Virginia, known for its rich musical traditions, soon became fruitful ground in the development of both folk and bluegrass.

Scholars trace the roots of the contemporary folk music revival back to the Library of Congress field recording efforts during the Great Depression. Highly knowledgeable and dedicated collectors such as George Korson went into the hills of West Virginia and other Appalachian states and gathered from blacks and whites not only the old ballads and fiddle tunes but Victorian popular material absorbed into oral tradition and newer songs associated with industrialization, particularly coal mining. In fact, one of Korson's more interesting discoveries in West Virginia was Orville Jenks, purported to be the original composer of "The Dying Mine Brakeman," a song that had already found its way onto phonograph records at least four times. Jenks, of Welsh background, had migrated to southern West Virginia from another coalfield in Jackson County, Ohio. He sang and played a rather simple guitar style not unlike that of contemporary hillbilly singers on radio. He also recorded for Korson another ballad entitled "Sprinkle Coal Dust on My Grave," a realistic lyric of coal miner life generally which parodied the recently popular "Maple on the Hill" in tune and style. Not all of Korson's folksingers possessed the talent or relative polish exhibited by Jenks. Two, George Sizemore and Archie Conway, suffered physically from the effects of their work, being victims of silicosis and a slate fall, respectively. Conway sang "A Coal Miner's Goodbye" from his deathbed at Man in 1940. Jerrel Stanley of Braeholm also showed commercial hillbilly influence with his Jimmie Rodgers-styled "Coal Diggin' Blues." Fiddler Charles Underwood demonstrated slick techniques on his instrument that suggested he had more than a little familiarity with radio musicians. A few, such as G.C. Gartin, vocalized in the older style of the archaic balladeers with "The Hard Working Miner." Overall, while West Virginia miners generated less excitement with their folk compositions and performances than their Eastern Kentucky counterparts, they still displayed some interesting skill in interpreting their work experience.[1]

Following the era of heavy song gathering by the Library of Congress in the years just prior to World War II, Professor Patrick Gainer of West Virginia University expended considerable effort in the study of Mountain State folksongs. Born at Parkersburg in 1904, Gainer grew up in Gilmer County where he attended Glenville Normal School (now Glenville State College) and came under the influence of Carey Woofter. Later he moved to Morgantown, where he studied with John Harrington Cox and Louis W. Chappell. In Missouri Gainer earned a doctorate in English at St. Louis University and for a time directed the St. Louis Glee Club. In 1946 he returned to West Virginia where he expended his academic energy studying folksongs and other folk music. Although he accomplished a great deal, Gainer consistently clung to the notion that no connection existed between what he termed "hillbillyism" and true folk music. Since few if any radio and recording artists came from Gilmer County and since Gainer, to judge from his writings, made little attempt to understand or explore the roots of the music he criticized, his attitude becomes somewhat explainable. He did a great deal of ballad collecting and sang and recorded some himself in a stilted manner not unlike that of John Jacob Niles. Most significantly of all, he organized the West Virginia Folk Festival at Glenville State College.[2]

Gainer began the festivals in 1950 and retained a guiding hand throughout that decade, after which Fern Rollyson exercised the main influence. From the beginning commercialism was kept at low key. The committee stated recently that "the core of the festival must remain with the native, rural, nonprofessional, traditional musician." Yet, at the same time, the directors of the festival acknowledged "that traditional music is a difficult word to define." The emphasis has been on fiddle and banjo tunes, square dancing, old hymns, and ballads. Held on the third weekend in June, the festival attracts crowds generally estimated in the low thousands. Glenville, a town somewhat lacking in relatively level space, likely could not handle many more.

In recent times the formal concert portions of the festival have included such events as two banjo and fiddle contests (senior and junior), folk music programs, square dances, and such nonmusical events as a muzzle loader shoot, craft displays, and activities involving the folk festival belles (ladies over seventy representing various counties who exemplify "true pioneer mountain spirit"). In spite of the emphasis on countering "hillbillyism," some of the performers, such as frequent fiddling-contest participant Woody Simmons, have extensive backgrounds as radio artists from the earlier days. Other fiddlers, such as Clay County's Wilson Douglas and Braxton County's Melvin Wine, have been recorded by companies that specialize in commercial folk, bluegrass, and old-time country music. Hammered dulcimer expert Worley Gardner of Morgantown gives mini-concerts for those who pass by and sells his long-playing record albums. All of this suggests that some degree of professionalism has crept into the festival and the directors concede that "things are a little more liberal now than they used to be."

Jam sessions play a significant role in creating the atmosphere of any festival. At Glenville, "the Folk Festival Committee has no control over what kind of music is played on the streets and makes no attempt to control it." Therefore, a great deal of music can be heard at Glenville that remains outside the formal structure of the festival. Much of that tends toward material of commercial hillbilly origin, whether of old-time country, bluegrass, or western swing. Groups of musicians congregate and the small throngs that gather around request songs such as "Roll in My Sweet Baby's Arms," "Little Cabin Home On the Hill," "Faded Love," "Sunnyside of the Mountain," and "Love Please Come Home," all originated and popularized by professional country musicians despite their more nearly traditional sound. In one sense, Dr. Gainer's fears that forms of "hillbilly music becoming popular in the mountains were sounding the death knell for the traditional music" are being realized, but in another sense we are simply watching the folk process at work. The current generation absorbs these songs into tradition just as a prior one took "The Letter Edged in Black" and "Put My Little Shoes Away" into tradition.[3]

Except for the festival at Glenville, most folk music events in the Mountain State came into existence following the "hootenanny" fad in American colleges. Prior to 1958, the national urban folk crowd was a relatively small but dedicated one and many of those within it had a tendency to identify with leftist political causes. Pete Seeger became the leading figure for this group, and authentic folk figures such as Oklahoman Woody Guthrie and Kentuckian Aunt Molly Jackson, who had become alienated from the mainstream of American society, found themselves accepted as true spokespersons for the downtrodden proletariat. For the most part the masses rejected or ignored the radicalism of these folk poets although they did accept some of their more moderate songs advocating trade unionism, such as "Union Maid" or "Hard Times in Coleman's Mines." For a period after the Kingston Trio's exceedingly popular song "Tom Dooley," urban folk material dominated the music market and had an immense impact on the college campus. Like most fads, the folk movement has now subsided, but the loyalists to the movement since 1958 greatly outnumber those of the early years. Many also came out of the movement still enthralled by the music but less interested in its contemporary political overtones, which soon became involved in the civil rights movement, attempts to abolish poverty, and antiwar activism. However, those deeply concerned with musical roots, whether apolitical or activist, soon found fertile ground in West Virginia for harvesting traditional musicians.[4]

Kenneth Davidson, a young Charleston resident, brought several folk performers of real quality into the public eye. In Clay County he made contact with French Carpenter, an excellent old-time fiddler who possessed a repertory of highly uncommon tunes bearing such archaic titles as "Shelvin' Rock," "Camp Chase," and "Yew Piney Mountain." Davidson also found Jenes Cottrell, an old-time banjo picker and singer who maintained a lifestyle in harmony with his music. In 1963 he took Cottrell to the Newport Folk Festival in Rhode Island and later to banjo and fiddle conventions in western Virginia and North Carolina. In the Calhoun County community of Orma he located Phoeba Parsons, a ballad singer and clawhammer banjo player, and aged ladies such as Maude Altizer, Holly Schartiger, and Sara Schoolcraft, who sang ancient ballads unaccompanied by any instruments, as well as numerous other local folk performers. A younger musician in the Bluefield area, Franklin George, displayed amazing abilities on the fiddle, banjo, dulcimer, and even the bagpipe. Davidson also sought out commercial musicians from the early days of phonograph records such as Clark Kessinger and Bill Cox, and introduced them to new audiences. Davidson started a small record firm for his discoveries, Folk Promotions, which he later renamed

Kanawha. Although neither a trained folklorist nor an expert at the record business (his company was short-lived), Ken Davidson deserves credit for his musical activities on behalf of some excellent and significant figures.[5]

These early efforts resulted in other traditional pickers and singers being brought to public attention. Billy Edd Wheeler, born in 1932 in Highcoal in Boone County and the natural son of a coal miner, was educated at Warren Wilson College in North Carolina and at Berea College in Kentucky. He won acclaim both as a singer and as a gifted composer of folklike material. As early as 1959 Wheeler wrote a song which became a chartmaker for Pat Boone, and a little later wrote one of the Kingston Trio's bigger hits, "The Reverend Mr. Black." Performing at the Mountain State Arts and Crafts Fair at Ripley in 1963, Billy Edd recorded a humorous piece of nostalgia about outdoor privies entitled "Ode to the Little Brown Shack out Back" which subsequently reached the number-four spot on the *Billboard* charts. Wheeler's "Jackson" became a number-one hit for Johnny Cash and June Carter. Because he found acceptance both from the academic folk scholars and as a country songwriter in Nashville, Wheeler was never a one-dimensional figure. He wrote numerous other songs, plays, poems, and the noted outdoor musical drama "Hatfields and McCoys." Perhaps Wheeler won applause from the academics because of his formal education. One suspects that "Ode to the Little Brown Shack" would have been ignored or scoffed at by them had it emerged from the pen of Roscoe Swerps, Lonzo and Oscar, or Homer and Jethro, yet these untrained hillbillies composed similar material with regularity. Based in the Asheville, North Carolina, area for several years, Wheeler continues his creative activities although his material (the 1979 Kenny Rogers hit "Coward of the County" excepted) has not been so much in the commercial mainstream as it was in the mid-1960s. Nonetheless, Billy Edd Wheeler proved that the gap between academic folk and commercial country could be bridged.[6]

Wheeler also helped introduce fully traditional performers to broader audiences. Among West Virginians, none have been aided more than Aunt Jenny Wilson of Logan County, an old-time banjoist, singer, and storyteller. Aunt Jenny's music goes back at least to the days of Frank Hutchison and Dick Justice. Since the mid-1960s her music has livened numerous folk festivals through the Appalachian states. Her grandson Roger Bryant has also followed in her footsteps, albeit in a more modern vein. Some of Bryant's material of a satirical nature has been particularly effective, a song entitled "Daytime Television" being a case in point.[7]

Other traditional musicians abounded in the Mountain State.

The Hammons Family of Pocahontas County—Maggie, Burl, and Sherman—together with a couple of neighbors, Lee Hammons and Mose Coffman (from Greenbrier County), had a fine repertory of old-time songs and stories which folklorists began to explore in 1969. Subsequently Rounder Records and the Library of Congress issued recordings featuring these various individuals (they are not a family band). Rounder also waxed an album by the father-son fiddle band of Oscar and Eugene Wright, a pair of old-time musicians from near Bluefield. Two additional members of the Hammons family, Currence and Minnie, resided in Randolph County, as did a fine guitarist named Blackie Cool. Mason County could boast of fiddler Bernard Connolly, somewhat country-oriented in style and always interested in helping with contests. An older performer from the same area, Walden Roush, played not only fiddle but also hammered dulcimer. In the eastern panhandle lived such musicians as Sloan Staggs, the Welch Brothers, and the Whiteacre Family. Most noted of all in this region, Andy Boarman of Hedgesville played an old-time banjo in a folk style akin to the classic pickers of the turn of the century, and a fine autoharp as well. A highly skilled craftsman, Boarman held equal fame for the quality of banjos he made. More recently a somewhat younger fiddler, John Johnson, has attracted considerable attention, as has Elmer Bird, the Banjo Man from Turkey Creek. A farmer from near Hurricane, Bird has developed a somewhat jazzed-up style of clawhammer banjo that has kept him in demand at festivals. Like some of the other performers, Bird had a brief career as a radio hillbilly, at WCMI Ashland, Kentucky, which ended when he entered the service in World War II.[8]

Although folksongs of social protest comprise but a minor part of a broad tradition, they have received excessive attention from some segments of the academic community, perhaps because such lyrics reflect their own tastes. In West Virginia, where the rough terrain and dependence on coal have often made a livelihood for the common man fraught with danger, the songs have indeed played a significant role. As revived interest in folk music evolved, the chief authentic performer to reflect this aspect of Mountaineer culture was the octogenarian retired coal miner from Chattaroy, Nimrod Workman. An activist in both the Black Lung Crusade and the Miners for Democracy, which helped elect the reform-minded West Virginian Arnold Miller president of the United Mine Workers, the one-time Mingo Countian sang his own compositions, such as "Mother Jones' Will," along with older songs learned through oral tradition. Younger musicians such as Mike Kline, who moved to West Virginia to work in antipoverty programs, and Richard Kirby specialized in songs that highlighted the dangers of coal mining to life, limb, and environment. The most musically talented in this tradition include Workman's daughter, Phyllis Boyens, who recorded both with her father and more recently on her own. She also made a name for herself as an actress playing the role of Loretta Lynn's mother in the popular film *Coal Miner's Daughter*. Overshadowing all the others in significance, however, has been Hazel Dickens, who generally performs in bluegrass style and often as a duet with Alice Gerrard. The daughter of a Mercer County miner and preacher, she also frequently reflects a strong feminist viewpoint in her songs, such as the beautiful but bitter lament "Disaster in the Mannington Mine."

After several years of relative inactivity, field recording activity at West Virginia University resumed with vigor in the 1970s. Thomas Brown, a young music professor from the Midwest, spearheaded the efforts following a meeting with Jenes Cottrell and his sister Sylvia O'Brien in 1970. In addition to some of the previously recorded Mountain State folk performers, Brown taped material by such artists as Harvey Sampson of Calhoun County, Gus McGee of Huttonsville, Oval Cogar of Webster County, and the former tent-show-playing Boserman Sisters of Randolph County. Other evidence of the renewed interest of West Virginians in their heritage includes the publication of Michael E. Bush's small multivolume series *Folk Songs of Central West Virginia* and Patrick Gainer's most nearly definitive work, *Folk Songs from the West Virginia Hills*, with its now almost ritualistic denunciation of "hillbilly."[9]

From the early 1960s folk music has spread via the festival route to many parts of West Virginia. Although music is subordinate to crafts, the Mountain State Arts and Crafts Fair at Cedar Lakes near Ripley has always featured a generous proportion of folk performers, including Cottrell, who also operated a wood lathe and sold his products at the fair. Russell Fluharty of Mannington, a hammered dulcimer player, had some hillbilly professionalism in his background, as did Paul Crane of Fairmont, who sometimes played rhythm guitar and vocalized a bit. Patrick Gainer had an influence in the proceedings at Ripley, too, and one wonders how he felt about a song recorded there that reached hit status on the country charts, since he considered "country" only a dignified form of hillbilly.

Another West Virginia folk festival that merits attention has been held annually since 1966 in August at Don West's Appalachian South Folklife Center near Pipestem in Summers County. West, a Georgian who generally describes himself as a poet and preacher, includes not only traditional West Virginia performers but those from other Appalachian states and outsiders as well. He also covers a wide range of both black and white folk and folk-derived styles. Artists at his 1982 festival, for instance, ranged from commercial folksinger Pete Seeger to the late guitar stylist Merle Travis, a Country Music Hall of Fame member. Fiddle experts included the traditional, Clay County's Wilson Douglas, and bluegrass, Mercer County's Joe Meadows. West, who has been embroiled in controversy partly because he tends to oversimplify complex issues, has generally impressed those who disagree with his philosophy with his sincere approach to preservation of all aspects of mountain culture.

Another southern West Virginia event, the John Henry Folk Festival, has taken place since 1973 at Athens. It features traditional musicians from the area, including adjacent parts of Virginia. Banjo picker Uncle Homer Walker of Glyn Lyn, Virginia, has often been a favorite. Although not segregated, a major purpose of the John Henry Festival has been to "celebrate West Virginia's black cultural heritage."

In central West Virginia several noted events have taken place. From 1969 to 1973, two younger musicians interested in traditional music, John and Dave Morris, held what they termed "back porch" festivals at their family farm near Ivydale in Clay County. The Morrises themselves performed although they tended to add an increasing proportion of their own creations to their tradition-rooted style. Ira Mullins and Lee Triplett, two more local old fiddlers, attended, as did many other area pickers and singers. In 1980 a film, *The Morris Family Old Time Music Festival*, using footage from 1972, premiered at the state culture center. In Elkins the Augusta Heritage Workshops featured generous amounts of music, although it did not dominate the program.[10]

Perhaps most significant of all, the West Virginia Department of Culture and History headed by Norman Fagan inaugurated its Vandalia Gathering in 1976. Both black and white traditional musicians as well as bluegrass bands have been featured. Fiddle and banjo contests have attracted most of the musicians discussed here as well as other entertainers from radio days, such as fiddlers Mike Humphreys and French Mitchell, banjoist Tex McGuire, and even the "Grand Ole Opry's" Wilma Lee Cooper. In 1979 Vandalia organizers recognized the relationship between older forms of country music and folk music and had workshops and four hours of concerts that featured two quarter-hour performances by such veterans of the "Old Farm Hour" as the Bailes Brothers and Ernest Ferguson, Rex Parker (and Eleanor),

Slim Clere, and Buddy Starcher, along with WWVA old-timers like Silver Yodelin' Bill Jones and Doc and Chickie Williams. For good measure, Lee Moore and the Lilly Brothers, who had been in the casts of both shows, played and the Currence Brothers, a bluegrass band who grew up listening to the others, rounded out the event. One suspects that perhaps somewhere the ghost of Frank Welling smiled while that of Patrick Gainer shuddered. A group of hillbillies literally took over the state capital.[11]

The revived interest in traditional music led not only to a search for and performances by both amateur and once-professional old-timers, but also to the adoption of the older styles by younger persons, both rural and urban, West Virginia-born and immigrants. In the early 1970s, for instance, the Morgantown-based Wild Turkey String Band and the eastern panhandle's Hickory Wind began to play music based largely on the styles of the string bands of the 1920s. Many learned their tunes from reissued editions of the old phonograph records or visited old masters like the Hammons Family or Jenes Cottrell so they could be taught directly. Some became interested in reverting to older life styles, learned skilled crafts, and resettled in rural areas. They are exemplified by the Booger Hole Revival based in the community of Walton in Roane County.

Perhaps the most noted of the recent revival groups has been Trapezoid, an Elkins-based band who essentially built their sound around the hammered dulcimer, from the shape of which they derived their name. Originally Sam Rizetta on the dulcimer and Paul Reisler on guitar formed the nucleus of the group. After 1978, however, Rizetta left and Reisler restructured the group around the talents of violinist Freyda Epstein and Loraine Duiset, who carries much of the vocal load while playing mandola, mandolin, and bowed psaltery. The dulcimer remains prominent but no longer dominates the sound. Unlike most revival bands, Trapezoid's members have been largely trained musicians. Bassist-celloist Ralph Gordon studied at the Manhattan School of Music and Reisler holds a B.A. in music from George Washington University. Not limiting themselves to Appalachian sounds, Trapezoid incorporates Irish, classical, ragtime, and various European traditions.[12]

The other type of old-style music—bluegrass—evolved directly from professional hillbillies. In essence bluegrass is an acoustic up-tempo form of the older string band music augmented by a three-finger banjo and rather piercing vocal solos and harmonies. Bill Monroe, a Western Kentucky native and veteran of the mandolin-guitar duet, was the principal architect of bluegrass, and most of the early band members came from the piedmont or mountain sections of North Carolina, East Tennessee, and southwestern Virginia. In the late 1940s, from those southern mountain sections and from Nashville's "Grand Ole Opry," where Monroe worked, bluegrass spread into other Appalachian regions and the midwestern cities that housed large numbers of Appalachian migrants.[13]

The Lilly Brothers already played in styles near enough to bluegrass that a three-finger banjo and bass fiddle could complete their unit. But the Lonesome Pine Fiddlers became the first West Virginia bluegrass band when Bob Osborne and Larry Richardson joined the outfit at Bluefield late in 1949. Northern West Virginia's exposure to the full sound came when the Bailey Brothers joined the Wheeling Jamboree. Although not bluegrass, the bands of Rex and Eleanor Parker and Cecil Surratt contained strong elements of the styling. The television programs of Lester Flatt and Earl Scruggs and later those of Hylo Brown probably did more than anything else to popularize the music in the Mountain State, particularly at a time when other tradition-oriented performers found the economic going difficult. Ironically, while non-West Virginians did a great deal to spread bluegrass locally, the Lilly Brothers with fellow Raleigh County native Don Stover picking a high-powered banjo, gave New Englanders similar doses of the music from Boston radio programs and nightly appearances at a bar known as the Hillbilly Ranch.[14]

Relatively few bands, however, formed in West Virginia on the prosperous coattails of the Foggy Mountain Boys. The unsuccessful attempts of Everett Lilly and Charlie Monroe to emulate their former boss and sideman illustrate that not all could win fan following with bluegrass. Bill Duncan and his Harmony Mountain Boys did somewhat better for a brief time. Duncan, a lead-singing, guitar-strumming native of Putnam County born in 1929, along with banjo player Denver Jackson and the mandolinist tenor singer Don Sowards (who also wrote some good songs) did thirty-nine weeks of television at WOAY-TV and recorded a fine album of original material for King records on April 4, 1961, but broke up soon afterward. The team of Bill Rogers and Ed Lackey from Cameron in Marshall County recorded a half-dozen sides for Cozy in the late 1950s. A little later Roy Crockett put together a good part-time band, the Pleasant Valley Boys, that won a following in the Huntington area, but for most of the 1960s bluegrass did not prosper in the Mountain State.[15]

In fact, nationally, other than Flatt and Scruggs, many of the top bands had trouble surviving except for a spurt of popularity during the hootenanny era. Bill Monroe had the Opry, Don Reno and Red

Smiley had their daily television show, and the Stanley Brothers, Carl Story, and Jimmy Martin managed to get by, while Jim and Jesse, the Osborne Brothers, and Mac Wiseman made some accommodations to modern country. Most country radio station managers considered the sound too archaic for airplay. David Freeman, a specialist in old-time and bluegrass records by mail order, made reference about 1966 to "the sad dying days of bluegrass." But the ground was being laid for a comeback that in many respects made bluegrass more popular than it had ever been in spite of continued rejection by most of the mass media. In 1965 promoter Carlton Haney held the first bluegrass festival at Fincastle near Roanoke, Virginia. A modest crowd attended that first event, but in the next three years more festivals began and in the next decade they sprang up nearly everywhere in the eastern states and some in the far west. Most remained small and many failed financially, yet those few that really made it encouraged pickers, bands, and potential promoters over wide areas. To a greater degree than folk festivals, bluegrass festivals attract a broad cross-section of the populace. This illustrates the music's universal appeal, but in a few instances it created potential difficulties among extreme representatives of varying lifestyles.

Bluegrass festivals arrived somewhat more slowly in West Virginia than in such neighboring Appalachian states as Virginia and North Carolina. The Goins Brothers, Melvin and Ray, Mountain State natives and Lonesome Pine Fiddler veterans, but more recently residents of Eastern Kentucky, apparently sponsored the first one in the state on August 20, 21, and 22, 1971, at Lake Stephens near Beckley. Fans heard the sounds of Ralph Stanley, Don Reno and Red Smiley, Jim and Jesse, and Carl Story's Rambling Mountaineers, in addition to the Goins' band and several local groups. Since the weekend sometimes conflicted with the State Fair at Lewisburg, Melvin later moved the festival to the third weekend of June. Unfortunately, when the event began to reach its potential in drawing power in 1975, some minor confrontations between local police and a rowdy youth element led the park owners to withdraw the location from future use. Melvin moved the festival to Pipestem for a season, but thereafter concentrated his efforts in Scioto Furnace, Ohio, until his recent involvement with Twelvepole Creek.[16]

No bluegrass festival in West Virginia has yet reached the proportions of those in McClure, Virginia, Camp Springs, North Carolina, Beanblossom, Indiana, or Hugo, Oklahoma, in terms of gate receipts or prestige although several very good ones have flourished. The Skyline Festival at Ronceverte has done quite well and several large ones have been held at Stumptown near Glenville, despite some murmurings about the rowdiness of some of the crowd. The Butler Brothers held several festivals in varied locations, their better ones being held at Sutton and the Spring Festival at Cox's Field near Parkersburg.

The Summer Festival at Cox's Field in Wood County, promoted by John Cox, has probably been the most consistent festival in quality since the initial one in 1975. Possessing good shade trees and located only a few miles from an interstate highway, the event has featured good entertainment by name acts such as the Lewis Family, Bill Harrell's Virginians, Larry Sparks, the Boys from Indiana, and on occasion such giants of the genre as Ralph Stanley, the Osborne Brothers, and Jim and Jesse McReynolds. Numerous regional West Virginia bands have also been on the schedule. Rain has curtailed the audience size in a couple of years, but those attending generally rank among the most nearly satisfied customers on the circuit.[17]

Many other bluegrass festivals are held in various parts of the Mountain State. These include Potomac Highlands at Moorefield, Locust Grove near Morgantown, Pickin' on Twelvepole Creek near Huntington, and the Summersville Festival. Cecil Surratt and J.C. Parks in 1973 revived the fiddlers' convention at Glenwood Park that Joe Woods and Leslie Keith had found so exciting in the late 1930s. Several other fiddle contests are held in various parts of the state, often as part of such local festivals as the Forest Festival at Elkins or the Pioneer Days at Marlinton.[18]

West Virginia bluegrass bands in the last decade and a half have ranked in a category somewhat like the festivals. Many good bands have been formed, but except for the pioneer efforts of the Lillys and the Lonesome Pine Fiddlers none have really joined the ranks of the all-time greats. The Goins Brothers, residents of Kentucky since 1953, could still in many respects be termed the most outstanding and longest-lasting band since their reorganization in 1969. Like most groups they have changed sidemen frequently, but Melvin and Ray have by and large retained a consistent sound built around that of the Lonesome Pine Fiddlers and the early years of Flatt and Scruggs. A major group by any reckoning, the Goinses have long been in the shadow of the Stanleys, the Osbornes, and the other front-runners without being quite their equal.

Among other bluegrass aggregations, several have thrived although at times their duration has been brief. The Black Mountain Bluegrass Boys of Pocahontas County had a good band and several original songs in the early and mid-1970s. Two band members,

Dwight Diller and Wayne Erbsen, also made some contributions to folk music scholarship, Diller participating in the work involving the Hammons Family, while Erbsen wrote some good biographical articles and edited a pair of song collections. Roy Crockett's Pleasant Valley Boys thrived through the mid-1970s in the Huntington area, sometimes sharing personnel with the Teays Valley Boys, a band based in that increasingly suburban section of Putnam County. Homer and Jerry Butler, natives of Nicholas County, although separated in residence by the Ohio River and over a hundred miles, maintained a vigorous weekend schedule, recorded often, and promoted many small festivals, mostly from a sincere love of the music. Toward the east, the Currence Brothers in Randolph County played a lot of good bluegrass and had a half-dozen quality albums to their credit. At the southern end of the state Clayton Hale and his Bluegrass Mountaineers performed similarly. Elsewhere, Parkersburg has the McCumbers Brothers, Buckhannon the Country Travelers, and Harrisville the Richie County Grass.

In an area that once had few bands, the number of new groups seems endless. Don Sowards, after several years of relative inactivity, organized the Laurel Mountain Boys in 1974 and briefly even reunited with Bill Duncan. Through the later 1970s and into the 1980s Sowards maintained an interesting group although veering increasingly away from his original traditional orientation toward a more progressive styling. More recently the group has become the Laurel Mountain Band. Another newer group based in the Big Sandy country, the Riverside Grass, combines the talents of two veteran performers. Lowell Varney of Crum, a banjo picker in the Scruggs tradition, has joined with Landon Messer of Kermit, a high lonesome singer along the order of Ralph Stanley but if anything higher and more lonesome.

Several bluegrass groups work within the framework of the family structure. Such include the Griffins of Summersville, the Cochrans of Webster County, and two Sissonville area bands, Hillbreed composed largely of Harrisons, and the Sons of Bluegrass made up primarily of Chapmans but including a daughter-in-law. In recent years the Outdoor Plumbing Company, once made up of both Kentucky and West Virginia residents, has become a one-family group—Jim and Ada McCown and their two sons of Lavelette.

In addition to those groups remaining resident in the Mountain State, out-migrants have contributed much to bluegrass in other regions. Many bands in the Akron/Canton/Warren, Ohio, area, for instance, contain numerous musicians of West Virginia origin. The duo of Bill and Ed relocated (in New Jersey) at a relatively early date, as did the obscure duet of Howard Knight and Ronnie Westfall, who recorded as the West Virginia Boys. The Detroit area has received Curley Dan and Wilma Ann Holcomb, natives of Clay County, and Wendy Smith, leader of the smooth-singing Blue Velvet. After Everett Lilly returned to West Virginia in 1970, Don Stover remained to lead the White Oak Mountain Boys for several years and then relocated in Maryland where he worked with Bill Clifton and Red Rector. West Virginians became prominent on the Washington bluegrass scene, helping to make it the bluegrass center of the nation. Cliff Waldron, a McDowell County native born in 1941, led pioneer groups in popularizing the so-called newgrass sound. As leader of the New Shades of Grass, first with Bill Emerson and then by himself, Waldron took the lead in making such songs of rock origin as "Proud Mary" and "Fox on the Run" into bluegrass standards. Hazel Dickens, both by herself and in association with Alice Gerrard, ranks as one of the female pioneers of the music. Dickens has also bridged the gap between the urban folk artist's social activism and the relatively apolitical bluegrass idiom and retained admirers in both areas.

In the mid-1970s the Marshall Family, made up of Wayne Countians relocated near Columbus, Ohio, exercised a profound impact on bluegrass gospel circles. Membership fluctuated in the stage group, which occasionally included family patriarch Chester "Pop" Marshall, but generally consisted of some four or five of his eleven talented children. Daughter Judy made an especially deep impression on many critics as both a composer and a vocalist. She had a knack for bridging the broad gap between the more archaic traditional styles of her mountain heritage and contemporary sacred music. To a lesser degree the skills of the other Marshalls followed suit. Ralph Stanley, long a potent force in traditional bluegrass circles, called them "out of this world" and did much to help the Marshalls in 1974 and 1975. By 1977 the Marshall Family had five albums to their credit, three of them influential releases on Rebel, but thereafter some family members who had always had reservations about commercialization of their music played relatively seldom in public. Meanwhile, banjo picker David Marshall waxed three albums on his own which included a few secular songs, and mandolin-lead guitar player Danny Marshall served a stint as a sideman with Stanley's Clinch Mountain Boys.[19]

Mountain Staters also made their contribution to traditional bluegrass in the D.C. area. Benny and Vallie Cain, both reared in Berkeley Springs, have more than a quarter-century of club work to their credit. Although their festival appearances tend to be minimal, the Cains became widely known to bluegrass devotees through their

Rebel recordings. The duo's harmony has a unique sound and they choose their material well. More recently the Johnson Mountain Boys, led by Scheer, West Virginia, native Dudley Connell, have made a greater impression on traditional bluegrass fans than any other group since the days of the genre's founding fathers. By combining a tasteful number of Connell's original songs on traditional themes with some largely-forgotten classics, along with near musical perfection, the band has received much acclaim in an amazingly short time. Somewhat less spectacular, Whetstone Run, based in Pennsylvania but popular in Washington and elsewhere, has built its traditional sound with a slightly progressive touch around the strong smooth lead voice of Parkersburg-born Mike Gorrell, who cut his musical teeth in the shadow of older brother Harry back in the middle and late 1960s.[20]

In song lyrics nearly all of the out-migrant bluegrass musicians from West Virginia have one characteristic in common—they have penned some outstanding nostalgic tributes to their native state. These range from Bill and Ed's "My West Virginia Rose" and "When the Sun Sets in West Virginia" to Curly Dan Holcomb's "South on 23" (among several) and from Howard and Ronnie's "West Virginia, I Love You" to Hazel Dickens's powerful "West Virginia My Home." The old saying that absence makes the heart grow fonder certainly seems to apply when Mountaineers celebrate their native state. Dallas Corey wrote several West Virginia songs and had them recorded in a Stoneman Family album. Only neighboring Kentucky seems to match West Virginia in this area.

If West Virginia has not matched neighboring states to the south in great bluegrass bands, it has certainly produced a fair share of super-sidemen. Pee Wee Lambert, mandolin player and tenor singer in the original Stanley Brothers' band and a native of Mingo County, played a key role in this group's development. Since 1966 former Lonesome Pine Fiddler Curly Ray Cline has played a major part in maintaining the Stanley sound. His brother Charlie spent many years as Bill Monroe's all-around band member, playing everything but mandolin for the Father of Bluegrass. Joe Meadows did some great fiddle work for the Stanleys in the mid-1950s and with Jim and Jesse from 1974 to 1979. Banjoist Don Stover filled in an important spot in the Lilly Brothers' sound for some fifteen years. In fact, Everett Lilly himself played mandolin in the Flatt and Scruggs band on two significant occasions, first in 1951-1952 and again in 1958-1959. Among the younger set of "superpickers," dobroist Jerry Douglas originated in the northeast Ohio-West Virginia migrant community, his father being John Douglas of the West Virginia Travelers.[21]

Both bluegrass and old-time music have managed to thrive despite the fact that the mass media have generally ignored them. They tend to be heard, but seldom on commercial television or even on the country radio stations. Only public television and radio, watched and heard by only a small minority, give these musical styles their just share of airplay, and some evidence suggests that playing it has substantially increased the clientele of the public stations. Only financially troubled WZTQ radio in Hurricane ever attempted a heavy programming format that featured generous amounts of bluegrass, gospel, and traditionally-oriented country airplay. Veteran musician Slim Clere instituted this format when he became station manager in the spring of 1981. The station changed ownership in the summer of 1982, Clere departed, and how long the experiment will continue remains to be seen. Preliminary examination suggests that the new use of the old format seemingly brought some increase in listeners but only partial relief from the economic woes. If WZTQ continues its 1981-82 programming it will bear watching.[22]

The popularity of traditional folk and bluegrass music through the weekend festival has been one of the more significant social developments of the last fifteen years. It has certainly led to a boom in the music that has increased the numbers of fans, musicians, and bands several times over. Whether or not the phenomena will persist remains to be seen. It would appear that some fans may tire of weekend festival-running after a few years, but others take their places and the movement has endured thus far. Upward and downward shifts in the economy have affected some individual festivals, but through 1983 the activity of the past decade appears to be holding steady. This leads one to conclude that the most traditional forms of country music will manage to endure.

8. West Virginia and the National Country Scene

When the Bailes Brothers left WSAZ Huntington for WSM Nashville in October 1944, they represented part of what would become a trend in country music circles—that many of the stronger acts in the trade would become affiliated with the "Grand Ole Opry." As events began to unravel in the coming years, some of the Mountain Staters who gained the widest recognition were those gravitating toward the southern metropolis soon to be called Music City U.S.A.[1]

The Bailes Brothers may have blazed the trail to Nashville for West Virginia musicians but, somewhat ironically, Homer, Johnnie, Kyle, and Walter did not remain there permanently. By the end of 1946 they had moved on to Shreveport, and Jimmy Walker, the Roy Acuff replacement, had temporarily become the Mountain State's Opry star. From the Baileses onward, however, West Virginians maintained a steady presence in the emerging country music capital as one by one Little Jimmy Dickens, Hawkshaw Hawkins, and the Coopers took their places among the ranks of Opry regulars.[2]

Eventually performers began to come to Nashville from West Virginia who had obtained only minimal fame during their apprenticeships in the Mountain State. For instance, Lloyd "Cowboy" Copas, the Adams County, Ohio, farmboy, had toiled a great deal around WSAZ and WCHS, among other places, with fiddle-contest promoter Larry Sunbrock and with artists like Jake Taylor, Rusty Gabbard, and Natchee the Indian, but really began to ascend toward the ranks of stardom only after he replaced Eddy Arnold as featured vocalist for Pee Wee King's Golden West Cowboys, a headline act on the Opry. During the last months of World War II Copas encountered former Mountain Melody Boy Bob Shortridge, then an army officer. Shortridge recalls that Cope told him "You quit too soon; now we don't have to starve anymore." Wartime prosperity had accomplished what talent could not always guarantee for struggling hillbilly musicians in the Depression years. Like his predecessor, Cowboy Copas soon struck out on his own and, although he never attained the success of Eddy Arnold, he too took his place among the ranks of a new generation of country stars. While Copas had struggled during his West Virginia days, he could still claim that his education there made his later attainments possible. His first big hit, "Filipino Baby," constituted but a slight revision of Bill Cox's old number, and fifteen years later "Alabam," a renaming of Frank Hutchison's "Coney Isle," rejuvenated his career when traditional country music began to recover from the rockabilly era. Copas died in the same plane crash that took the lives of Patsy Cline, Hawkshaw Hawkins, and his own son-in-law, Randy Hughes.[3]

Another West Virginia performer who eventually found commercial success in Nashville accomplished it by a route that went through Montgomery, Alabama, and Shreveport, Louisiana. Woodrow Wilson "Red" Sovine, born at Charleston on July 17, 1918, worked on radio with Johnnie Bailes, Billy Cox (his first cousin once removed), and others around the "Old Farm Hour." With the monetary rewards so meager in the late 1930s, Red finally opted for a factory job at a hosiery mill established as part of a New Deal project in Eleanor, West Virginia. During the years of wartime prosperity he rose through the ranks to a middle-level management position. At the same time Red kept his acquaintance with musician friends like the Bailes Brothers, who would visit Charleston on their vacations from Nashville and Shreveport. As he recalls, Johnnie always had a new car and plenty of money. By 1948 he had lured Red back into the music business in Shreveport, which seemed logical since Radio Dot and Smokey, Harmie Smith, and the Baileses had all prospered there. Red got a band together called the Echo Valley Boys, purchased a house trailer, and took off for Louisiana.

Sovine found the path to stardom a difficult one, particularly in the early months. When he arrived at KWKH in early August, a coalition of the other musicians, the Bailes Brothers excepted, opposed his working at the station by not letting him join the union. Finally the station manager worked out a compromise, but Red's show came on so early in the morning, 5:30 AM, that he attracted few listeners and even fewer showdates. By Christmas Red's life savings had been used, his band had received their lay-off notices, and his wife and kids had been sent back to West Virginia by bus. Then Hank Williams came to his rescue and helped him secure a job at his old station, WFSA in Montgomery, Alabama. Red did well enough in Alabama so that within a few weeks his family rejoined him and he recruited three more West Virginia musicians, Tommy Cantrell and Charles and Honey Miller, for a new band. Hank's mother, Mrs. W.W. Stone, acted as his booking agent and the lanky Williams helped him get a contract with MGM records. When Hank received his call to Nashville and the "Grand Ole Opry" in June, Red Sovine became his replacement on the daily spots at KWKH and the "Louisiana Hayride."

Back in Shreveport, Red had a much more successful stay in his second experience. His most lucrative daily show, "Johnny Fair Syrup Time," did even more for him than it had for Williams, and sales of the product increased by a phenomenal 280 percent. He also became one of the Hayride's premier performers and attracted good crowds on his showdates. Floyd Cramer, who eventually became country music's best known piano player, worked in his band for a time. Sovine also appeared often on personal appearances with Ray "Groovy Boy" Bartlett, a young KWKH deejay who made use of a pseudo-Negro accent to win a wide following among youth of both races in the Ark-La-Tex region. Red even had a song about him on MGM entitled "Groovy Boy." Red spent five years in Shreveport and had a well-received television show on KTBS in addition to his radio stardom at KWKH. The only field of endeavor where he had limited success was recording. In retrospect Red decided after twenty-eight sides on MGM that the company promoted only the sales of Hank Williams records and neglected their other country artists.

In the meantime, another "Louisiana Hayride" star, Webb Pierce, had a hit record on Decca and followed the trail to Nashville that Hank Williams had blazed earlier. In the fall of 1954 Pierce enticed Sovine to Nashville as his front man on showdates and also helped him get a contract with Decca. Soon the pair had a number-one chart-maker with their duet version of the early George Jones song "Why Baby Why." They repeated this success with "Little Rosa," a classic tearjerker with Red doing a recitation. The song related a sad tale of a poor Italian immigrant laborer's difficulties in obtaining a rose to place on the grave of his little daughter, who had been run over by a train. On the strength of those two hits and a somewhat lesser one of "Are You Mine" with Goldie Hill, Red joined the Opry and went on his own.

For a man who had essentially the talents of a straight country vocalist, Red's timing left something to be desired, for it corresponded to the heyday of rockabilly influence on the idiom. Sovine managed to survive and did a few rockabilly numbers like "Juke Joint Johnny," but generally found the going tough until late 1956 when he signed on for thirteen weeks with the Philip Morris Caravan, which guaranteed him three months of steady employment but forced him to sever connections with the Opry. Fortunately he continued with the tobacco company's mammoth road show for a total of sixteen months and by the time it terminated in the spring of 1958, his $600.00 weekly salary had risen to $800.00. By the time the show ended the national economy had entered a slump, but Red managed to survive by playing clubs—sometimes two simultaneously on staggered schedules—until better times returned.

In the early 1960s Red Sovine had established himself as a durable figure on the Nashville scene but, except for his duet numbers with Pierce, still lacked a hit song that fans could identify with his image. This came in 1965 with a number that marked him as the master of the sentimental truck driver recitation. Like numerous other West Virginians, Red had been influenced by Frank Welling, who had recorded recitations and read a great many sentimental and humorous poems over the air. "Giddy-Up Go" narrated the story of a truck driver's reunion with a long-lost son. It remained on the charts for twenty-two weeks, reaching number one. The song became so identified with trucker culture that bumper stickers bearing the phrase could often be spotted on the rear of trucks for the next four to five years. He followed this up with "Phantom 309," an eerie narration about a hitchhiker who received a ride from the ghostly "Big Joe" who had perished in a wreck to avoid crashing into a school bus loaded with children. Both songs did a great deal to develop the image of the truck driver as a modern hero in the fashion of the pony express rider and the brave engineer.

Like Little Jimmy Dickens, Red Sovine also gained a reputation as a musician who would go out of his way to help others. Through his association in Shreveport with "Groovy Boy," Red had pleasant experiences with black audiences in Louisiana and this apparently made him something of a racial liberal as country musicians generally went. In 1963 he met a young black singer named Charley Pride at a show in Great Falls, Montana. He not only suggested that Pride try his luck in Nashville but subsequently introduced him to the folks at Cedarwood. From that chance meeting young Charlie Pride went on to become one of country music's major superstars. Sovine's son Roger also pursued a singing career for a time with his father's help and had a couple of chartmakers, but eventually opted for work in the business side of the industry.

Red Sovine continued to place songs and recitations on the country charts through the later 1960s and early 1970s, but did not have another major success until 1976, when another nostalgic truck driver recitation surpassed all of his previous efforts. "Teddy Bear" combined a truck driver theme with a crippled child and the current CB radio fad to produce a number that not only topped the country charts but sold a million records and even made the top forty in the pop field. If nothing else, Red Sovine and "Teddy Bear" proved that with a few modern trappings old fashioned sentimentality could still thrive in contemporary Nashville. Red continued to record with moderate success until April 4, 1980, when he perished in an auto crash. At the time of his death he had recorded more songs (over 300) and placed more of them on the *Billboard* charts than any other West Virginia performer.[4]

Not all the West Virginia performers who found national success in the postwar country music world did so in Nashville. T. Texas Tyler, for example, made his mark on the west coast and via the smaller but well-distributed Four Star label. Only in 1958 with his fame declining did Tyler base himself in Nashville and the "Grand Ole Opry." Jimmy Walker, despite his year at the Opry and two stints in Wheeling, also made his major contributions to country music during his three sojourns in California. Albeit less-known than Tyler, he too played a significant role as a honky-tonk, western-swing vocalist in the company of such musicians as Tex Atchison, Noel Boggs, and Speedy West. For Lynn Davis and Molly O'Day, the "Mid-Day Merry-Go-Round" at WNOX Knoxville happened to be their base at the time their Columbia recordings of songs like "Tramp on the Street" and "Teardrops Falling in the Snow" hit the market. Uncomfortable with fame, Molly and Lynn found consolation in religion and evangelism from 1950. More often than not Huntington or its suburbs has been their home and since 1974 they have had a program called "Hymns from the Hills" on WEMM-FM radio which features country gospel records and inspirational talk.[5]

For some West Virginia expatriate musicians, acclaim has remained regionally limited. Back in the 1930s a few Mountaineers found radio success in areas outside the state. Smilin' Bill Waters performed extensively on radio in Akron, Ohio, for several years, playing largely for audiences of West Virginia migrants, and then relocated in New England. In Pittsburgh, Dick Hartman of Hampshire County and Harry Blair of Wetzel County put together a band called the Tennessee Ramblers. Cecil Campbell, a Carolinian, also became a key member. The Tennessee Ramblers worked on radio in several locations including Rochester, New York, but mostly at WBT Charlotte, North Carolina. They also worked in two Gene Autry films, *Ride Ranger Ride* and *The Yodelin' Kid from Pine Ridge*, and recorded for

Bluebird. Although transcending regionalism in some respects, their fame still rested primarily on radio. Hartman returned to West Virginia in 1939 and worked in the lumber mill at Luke, Maryland, until retirement in 1960 and death in 1962. Blair remained with the Tennessee Ramblers for several more years, eventually retiring to Murrell's Point, South Carolina. Campbell took over the band after Hartman's departure and kept it going into the 1960s, becoming especially known for his Hawaiian guitar work. Another West Virginian, Walden Whytsell, using the stage name Don White, also worked at WBT Charlotte with Fred Kirby, with the Briarhoppers, and with the Tennessee Ramblers. A smooth western-style vocalist despite his apprenticeship with mountain performers like Frank Hutchison and Arnold Williamson, White also worked nationally as he headed the WLS Sage Riders in Chicago for four years, but remained well-known primarily in the Carolinas. Earl Songer, purely regional in his appeal, became one of the major figures in the Detroit-Toledo area for a decade after the war as a honky-tonk singer. Still his West Virginia background remained prominent as Songer popularized locally some of the lesser-known songs of Billy Cox.[6]

Cincinnati proved to be the locale where Charlie Gore achieved his fame. Born in Chapmanville on October 4, 1930, he was among the wartime performers at WLOG Logan. After finishing high school Gore made brief stops at WSAZ Huntington and WRFD Worthington, Ohio, before moving to 50,000-watt WLW, where he quickly became a star on the "Midwestern Hayride" and also recorded for King. Charlie managed to benefit from both radio and television in Indianapolis as well as the Queen City. He returned to Logan in 1959 as a deejay and later entered politics. As one reviewer recently expressed it, Charlie never had the one big hit needed to catapult him to national stardom, but remained suspended somewhat above the category of a regional performer. Although out of the limelight for several years, Gore retained a sufficient following to have an album of his original recordings reissued in Germany.[7]

Moving into the rockabilly era, no West Virginians gained wide fame with this musical style although several excellent performers of the genre appeared on the local level. These included Keith Anderson of Paden City, who did deejay work at both Moundsville and New Martinsville, Bruce Lambert of Franklin, who did similar labor at WELD in Fisher, and the Vandergrift Brothers of Fairmont, who later joined the WWVA Jamboree for a time. Previously known stars like Jimmy Dickens, Hawkshaw Hawkins, and Red Sovine did some material in this vein, as did the Jamboree's Bob Gallion and even straight country singers like Hank the Cowhand, Dale Brooks, and Sleepy Jeffers. Overall, however, West Virginians made relatively minimal contributions to this phase of country music's development.

Wilma Lee and Stoney Cooper's fame had pretty much hit its zenith prior to the duo's departure from Wheeling in 1957 although it continued through their early years on the "Grand Ole Opry." But the interest in bluegrass led to a resurgence full of benefits. Since Stoney's death Wilma Lee has continued pretty much with a straight bluegrass sound augmented with veteran musicians like fiddler Tater Tate and youngsters such as Gene Wooten on dobro. Having been recently dubbed the "First Lady of Bluegrass," Wilma Lee's place in history seems secure at least among traditionalists.[8]

The years immediately following Wilma Lee and Stoney Cooper's arrival at the "Grand Ole Opry" saw no major new figures from West Virginia making a lasting impact on the country scene. Billy Edd Wheeler had a major hit with "Little Brown Shack" in 1964, and Buddy Starcher with his "History Repeats Itself" in 1966, but both of these incidents represented somewhat special cases rather than the arrival of new national stars. Of course, Hawkins (until his death), Dickens, and Sovine all hit peaks in the 1960s, but all had made themselves heard and seen much earlier. Not until the latter part of the decade did some major new figures appear in the personages of Penny DeHaven, Charlie McCoy, Mayf Nutter, and a group known as the Four Guys.

Penny DeHaven, although born Charlotte DeHaven in Winchester, Virginia, on May 17, 1948, lived from 1956 in Berkeley Springs, West Virginia, and was graduated from high school there in 1966. Long before then she had performed on shows with local performers like Dale Brooks and Dusty Shaver, using the stage name Penny Starr. Under that pseudonym she joined "Jamboree U.S.A." in the spring of 1966 and experienced her first minor hit with "Grain of Salt" on the Band Box label in January 1967. By mid-1967 she reverted to the more correct sobriquet of Penny DeHaven and became one of the first female country singers to entertain troops in Vietnam. She enjoyed the prestige of several chartmakers on the Imperial, United Artists, and Mercury labels. Country versions of Joe South's "Down in the Boondocks" and the Beatles hit "I Feel Fine" ranked among the more prominent. She also waxed some duets with Buddy Cagle and Del Reeves. More recently she has sung "Bayou Lullaby" on the soundtrack of Clint Eastwood's film *Bronco Billy* and recorded a duet, "We Made Memories," with Boxcar Willie.

Penny's stage presence and determination have helped to keep her among the most active country artists in recent years. One critic referred to the dynamic character of her show as a "happiness explosion" and she has maintained her enthusiasm despite being on the road most of the time. In addition to a heavy personal appearance schedule, she appeared on Johnny Cash's CBS Network Special in 1981, played a dramatic role in Clint Eastwood's 1982 movie *Honkytonk Man*, guested on "Hee Haw" early in 1983, and highlighted her summer touring by performing at Jamboree in the Hills. Still, Penny needs that one giant hit to put her over the top. As she told an interviewer in 1978, "I've had sixteen chart records, but never the big one." Although she is hardly a superstar threatening to displace Loretta Lynn, Barbara Mandrell, or Dolly Parton, Penny DeHaven has established herself as a durable figure on the contemporary Nashville scene.[9]

Charlie McCoy has probably received the most widespread acclaim among contemporary West Virginia artists in Nashville. Born at Oak Hill in Fayette County on March 28, 1941, McCoy moved to Florida in his youth. He attended college for a time and acquired some formal musical training, then worked as a sideman for Opry star Stonewall Jackson. As early as 1960 he made recordings on the Cadence label under his own name but they attracted little attention. Meanwhile McCoy began to gain a reputation as a session musician. Roy Orbison's pop hit "Candy Man" in 1961, featuring Charlie's harmonica, ushered in a revival for a nearly forgotten country instrument. Soon he began appearing on recordings ranging from those of bluegrassers Lester Flatt and Earl Scruggs to such pop stars as Ann-Margret, Brook Benton, and Perry Como and even folkniks like Joan Baez and Bob Dylan. McCoy also signed with Orbison's label, Monument, to record on his own. Although none of his initial efforts made much of an impact, company head Fred Foster continued to produce Charlie's waxings.

In the early 1970s Charlie McCoy began to be spoken of increasingly as something more than a quality session man. A string of instrumental album releases and occasional chartmaking singles put him in the lamplight as a musician in the same sense that Chet Atkins, Floyd Cramer, or Pete Drake became known as masters of their respective instruments. In both 1972 and 1973 the Country Music Association chose him as Instrumentalist of the Year. By the end of the decade Charlie had more than a dozen albums to his credit, several of which had been on the best seller listings. He also began to broaden his image by doing more vocals and exhibiting skills on other instruments such as vibraphone, piano, guitar, and even horn.

A 1979 album entitled *Appalachian Fever* not only displayed McCoy as a competent singer but also allowed him to pay tribute to his West Virginia heritage. He also became music director for the popular syndicated television show "Hee Haw" and recorded some duets with vocalist Laney Hicks.[10]

Mayf Nutter of Jane Lew, West Virginia, has probably maintained more of his Mountain State identity than the other younger country performers and also exhibited more diversity in his talents. Born on October 19, 1941, Nutter began playing music in his teens, first guested on radio with Cherokee Sue and John Graham, and held down a part-time job at WBOY-TV prior to his graduation from Bridgeport High School in 1959. His parents had both been semiprofessional country musicians, but Mayf first worked with various television stations in Michigan and other states. He lived in Atlanta in 1966 when he had his first record on the Vault label. He also had some releases on Starday and Reprise in the late 1960s and then shifted to California, which has since been his main base.

On the west coast Mayf Nutter became a featured vocalist on the "Buck Owens Ranch" television series. Several of his songs such as "Simpson Creek" and "Goin' Skinny Dippin'" have had West Virginia themes. Beginning in 1970 with "Hey There Johnny," Nutter has had eight songs on the national country charts. He has toured extensively and also manifested an interest in acting and directing, with dramatic roles in television shows and narrations for Walt Disney Studios. In March 1982 Nutter toured mainland China and became the first American country singer on Chinese video. In all, Mayf Nutter has shown himself to be an extremely versatile performer.[11]

A West Virginia group—the Four Guys—has made out well in Nashville and at the "Grand Ole Opry" and seems to have accomplished a great deal in Music City without really making a major national impact. Comprised of vocalists from the industrial towns north of Wheeling, on both sides of the Ohio River, the country quartet has included in their number Sam Wellington, Richard Garratt, Brent Burkett, and Berl Lyons, the last followed by Gary Buck, Glen Bates, Laddie Cain, and John Frost. Wellington and Garratt both worked at radio station WEIR in Weirton as manager and program director, respectively. In 1966 they worked the WWVA Jamboree and came to Nashville guesting on Ralph Emery's television show and the Opry. They signed as "Grand Ole Opry" regulars in April 1967, becoming the only act in recent times, other than Stonewall Jackson, invited to the select circle without a prior hit record. Although they have recorded some, the Guys still have not had a major hit. Some of their sessions have resulted in interesting lyrics, such as "Streakin' with My Baby" at the height of the 1974 "streaking" fad, and more recently "Made in the U.S.A.," which defends home industry in opposition to foreign products and carries a strong "buy American" theme. Often considered the Opry's answer to the Statler Brothers, the Four Guys toured extensively with Charlie Pride in the early 1970s. Laura Eipper, columnist for the *Tennessean*, probably described the Four Guys best when she said that they "have earned a reputation for versatility that combines a little country, a little pop-music, and even a bit of soft-edged western music into a unique sound." Since 1975 they have concentrated their appearances at their Harmony House Supper Club near Opryland, where they also entertain almost daily in the summer.[12]

In the 1970s Mel Street led the list of West Virginians to win national fame in Music City. Moving from local television at Bluefield to Nashville came relatively easy for Street in 1972, but his earlier apprenticeship had been a lengthy one, going back to radio performances at WELC Welch in the early 1950s. Through six years and fifteen songs on the charts, Street's songs like "Borrowed Angel" made him one of the more prominent new figures in country music during the decade. Yet happiness and satisfaction apparently eluded the man, for he took his own life on October 21, 1978.[13]

After Street, no new Mountain Staters made it that high. Sandra Rucker, a Logan native who moved to Cumberland, Maryland, played in the eastern panhandle. She had some good songs including "When You're Number Two," but no major hits. She recorded for Monument, Royal American, and United Artists. Beverly Heckel went from Wheeling to Nashville with husband Johnny Russell, waxed a single with RCA, but from there her progress slowed. One fellow who did considerably better although submerged in a group—Ray Benson—helped lead the resurgence in Texas-style western swing music. Benson, from Paw Paw, and two fellows from nearby Pennsylvania started the group known as Asleep at the Wheel. Together with such vocal stars as Willie Nelson and Waylon Jennings, this band has had much influence in the development of Austin, Texas, as a music center over the last ten years.[14]

Somewhat in a category of his own, Jimmy Wolford ranks as a performer who is hard to classify. Born in Mingo County in 1934, Wolford sings in a country style, but much of his material resembles that of contemporary folk singers. Wolford, a loyal devotee of Minnesota senator and presidential aspirant Hubert Humphrey, gained much of his fame through participation in his idol's campaigns for president and vice president in 1960, 1964, 1968, and 1972. Wolford's songs, however, range over a much wider spectrum than politics, including more conventional country material, general social commentary, and an album of Hatfield-McCoy feud compositions. Wolford's career as a singer actually preceded his association with Humphrey since he recorded on the Four Star label as early as 1957 and worked in radio at WHJC Matewan, although apparently more in sales than as a deejay or singer. Wolford's work in the Humphrey campaigns added sufficient color to his efforts to merit discussion in Theodore White's *The Making of the President, 1960.*[15]

Another difficult performer to classify, Cecil Null, gained considerable renown as an autoharpist in the 1960s. Born in East War, McDowell County, on April 26, 1927, Null had a variety of country music experiences prior to 1958. In that year he and a man named Semie Moseley built an electric autoharp which Null later improved. Something of a folk-country crossover, he got considerable national television exposure through the mid-1960s and recorded for Briar, Epic, and Decca, having a pleasant gospel instrumental album for the latter firm in 1968. Null's wife Annette augmented his harp work with her vocals. While fans found their music appealing, they never quite got the hit record they needed to make them top stars.[16]

Country music has, of course, been a great deal more than those who write and record the hits or sing them on stage at Opryland or "Jamboree U.S.A." The local musicians who play in the clubs and bars or make their joyful noises unto the Lord at the brush arbors and church reunion picnics make up part of the scene, too. The fans who see the shows, buy the tickets, tune in the radio stations, and purchase the records remain the backbone of the whole commercial system, whether in West Virginia or elsewhere. And although a thorough survey of country music activity on the local scene does not seem either practical or desirable, a few examples of continued down-home activity in an era of virtually nationalized country music seems a necessity.

The days of live radio and apparently even live television have pretty much become a thing of the past. Yet on the local level country music as a medium for social entertainment flourishes in a manner that might be described as a technologically updated version of what travelers observed in the nineteenth century. For instance, the Liberty Mountaineers, who hail from a hamlet near the Putnam-Jackson County border, are musicians whose activities go back to the late 1930s. Harrell Bailey and Tom Bonnett learned to play fiddle and guitar, respectively, before World War II, and following their military service decided to "form a little band and entertain around at the local school houses." On Saturday afternoons they had a show on WTIP radio in Charleston and occasionally also broadcast over WKNA from a small jamboree held in Dunbar. After a few years the Mountaineers, all working full-time jobs in industry, drifted apart, but in 1967 they reorganized with some new members. As fiddler Bailey wrote, they mostly wished to enjoy themselves and entertain others a bit with "no aspirations about gaining notoriety." They play a variety of "bluegrass, country, light rock, etc." No doubt, the Liberty Mountaineers typify many bands throughout West Virginia who differ only in the range of music they play and their aspirations.[17]

For musicians and fans who prefer a place to play and listen morally situated somewhere between the extremes of saloon and church, the little country jamboree shows often have much to offer. Several of these thrive throughout the state. Sometimes big-name artists appear at them, but rising fees seem to be making such visits an increasing rarity. Typical of these is the Country Store Opry House at Pansy in Grant County near the Virginia border. Unlike most local jamborees, this one can also be heard via live broadcast over WELD Fisher, whose manager, Zag Pennel, has some appreciation for live radio, having experienced fifteen years of it as an artist himself. At Milton, near Huntington, the Mountaineer Opry House has thrived for several years on a format oriented toward half country and half bluegrass. Since bluegrass bands tend to charge more moderate fees, name bands have appeared there, including the late Charlie Moore and his Dixie Pardners (his last show) and the Lewis Family.[18]

A look at some West Virginia counties, even less populated ones, can often reveal a great deal of local activity. Some residents of Morgan County in the eastern panhandle, for example, have exhibited much musical aptitude. From the 1940s on local bands have included those led by Elwood Liggett, Sammy Moss, and the McCumbee Family. Liggett worked on radio out of Hagerstown for years and a son has a band regionally popular in the area. Sammy Moss had a band in the area for years which once included Patsy Cline of nearby Winchester, later a Hall of Famer. Moss also does deejay work at the local country station, WCST Berkeley Springs. Various members of the McCumbee Family worked for both Liggett and Moss at times as well as with people like Hank the Cowhand, Bud Messner, Jimmy Mahue, and with groups at powerful stations like WWVA and WRVA.

In later years popular bands in the area included Gib Sage and the Country Seasons; the Zephyrs, whose orientation veered more in the direction of folk and folk-rock; and She and the He's, who performed both country and rock material and shared some personnel with the Seasons. For good measure, a pair of minister-gospel singers lived in the county; Raymond Jones and Dave Kidwell, both of whom made recordings, the latter of whom also runs a Christian Academy. Finally, an old-time revivalist group based in the village of Paw Paw, the Critton Hollow String Band, played and recorded in the area, and the once-local couple Benny and Vallie Cain worked as major figures on the Washington, D.C., bluegrass scene for some twenty-five years. A teenage singer, Lisa Kirk, has recently cut her first record and some local folks think she may soon become a bigger star than any of Morgan County's existing stable of artists.[19]

Another Berkeley Springs musician pursues a country music career in California, combining it with work in drug abuse programs. Charlie Frederick, born about 1939, went on to college, eventually obtaining a Ph.D. from the University of Iowa in 1974. In addition to songs opposing drug usage, Frederick has another message lyric entitled "The Hating Game," which urges toleration of such diverse unpopular groups (depending upon your own circle) as hippies, Indians, and rednecks.[20]

If Berkeley Springs and Morgan County do not already have a high degree of recognition as a cradle of musicians ranging from turn-of-the-century archaic fiddler Harvey VanGoshen to contemporary Nashville songstress Penny DeHaven, it should come soon. Thus far the most noteworthy Mountain State product to emerge in the 1980s also comes from there. Theresa Ann "Terry" Gregory, born on April 30, 1956, in Washington, D.C., moved first to Maryland and then to her mother's hometown of Berkeley Springs, where she graduated from high school in 1973. She subsequently went to Montgomery County Junior College in Rockville, Maryland, for a year. She also entered the National Country Music Championships in Warrenton, Virginia, placing runner-up in the vocalist category. This led to personal appearances with such stars as Crash Craddock and Dolly Parton.

After some experience in rock music, Terry made a favorable impression on west coast publisher Al Gallico and signed with Handshake records. Her initial release in May 1981, "Just Like Me," became a top-twenty hit, and at least four other songs have made the charts to date. Somewhat indicative of the trend toward the mingling of older pop styles with contemporary country, Terry Gregory counts such middle-of-the-road vocalists of the 1960s as Janet Lennon and Connie Francis among her early influences. A serious-minded young lady with strong religious convictions, Terry found her faith reaffirmed when her father suffered through a fatal illness, and dedicated her first album to him. Two album releases to date, the second with such personnel as Buddy Emmons on steel, Phil Baugh on lead guitar, and Hargus Robbins on piano, suggest something of the prestige accorded her sessions.[21]

Somewhat ironically, the best known West Virginia country musician in recent times has been a good, albeit part-time, fiddler whose major impact has been in Washington rather than Nashville or Wheeling. Robert Byrd, the Democratic leader in the United States Senate and a Raleigh County resident since infancy, has always fiddled and sung in his political campaigns, and since recording an album for County records in 1978 has even guested on the "Grand Ole Opry." Byrd's stylings date back to his childhood when he listened to and learned from the Brunswick discs of the Kessinger Brothers. In the early 1940s he worked briefly with a hillbilly band at WJLS Beckley, and his nationwide prestige has been beneficial to the music. The writer who labeled Byrd the best fiddler of all time no doubt let flattery interfere with his judgment. But Fiddlin' Bob Byrd ranks as a figure of consequence in West Virginia musical development as much as he does in its political history.

Other newer Mountain Staters have advanced more slowly. John Henry Alger of Jefferson County, a former Virginia champion fiddler, had a group in 1977 called the Steel Drivers. Johnny Paycheck picked up one of his songs entitled "I'm the Only Hell My Mama Ever Raised." Alger subsequently formed a new group in 1981 called Country Kotton which has worked extensively throughout eastern West Virginia, Maryland, and adjacent parts of Virginia, but his accomplishments have lagged considerably behind those of Byrd and Gregory.[22]

The deaths of nationally prominent figures in recent years, such as Mel Street and Red Sovine, have left something of a void in the numbers of current West Virginia stars. Yet others will doubtless take their place. Mountain State performers have never dominated Nashville and the national country scene. Yet their numbers have been adequate to attract attention. Wilma Lee Cooper and Jimmy Dickens, the old pros, command considerable respect. Established veterans like Charlie McCoy, the Four Guys, and Penny DeHaven have likewise paid their dues. Relative newcomers like Terry Gregory will bear watching in the future. In a sense, West Virginians in Nashville seem to be a great deal like the fellow in the Little Jimmy Dickens song, "I'm Little But I'm Loud." They have been and will be heard.

9. Retrospect

A look back over a half-century of commercial country music in the Mountain State covers a wide range of time, territory, and style. It extends from the time when Philip Tweedy first set his talented sons up on the back of a flatbed truck to Terry Gregory singing her latest hit, "I'm Taking a Heartbreak." The economics may vary from a penny placed in a tin cup for a blind singer like John Unger, Alfred Reed, or David Miller to the six-figure gate receipts of a huge festival like Jamboree in the Hills. The locale could be anyplace from a square dance in the remote Elk River country to a primitive radio studio in Fairmont or Bluefield, or the stage at the Capital Music Hall. Surveying this broad spectrum of activity, one might ask: Is West Virginia different in its musical products? If so, in what way?

A quick answer to such queries invites either oversimplification or qualifications on the original question with regard to time or style. Certainly modern commercial country instrumentation tends to be an amalgam of sounds associated with Nashville. One can look at the back of a recent primarily instrumental album by Charlie McCoy and quickly learn that the work of thirty musicians plus three choral voices went into the album besides the featured harmonica of the star. Since McCoy left West Virginia before he was fully grown, one might ask how much "West Virginiaess" is displayed in this music. One obviously concludes that it is limited and integrated into the whole.

In earlier times, different conditions prevailed. When Charlie and Harry Tweedy first entered the Gennett studios, the only music for the session came from their piano and fiddle. Similarly when David Miller followed the Tweedys a few months later, only his own guitar and the banjo of Cecil Adkins accompanied his vocal on that primitive recording. More than two decades later things had not changed much. In 1945, when the Bailes Brothers had their initial Columbia session, besides Johnnie and Walter the recordings featured bass player Evy Thomas from Paden City and Del Heck of Huntington. The only non-

West Virginian in the band, Ernest Ferguson, had up to that time played about as much at WCHS Charleston and at WHIS Bluefield as anyplace else in his professional career. When the Lonesome Pine Fiddlers recorded for Victor in 1952 they had spent virtually their entire lives in southern West Virginia, except for Paul Williams of nearby Wythe County, Virginia, a similar socioeconomic area. Although a movement toward musical mixing began early, only in the post-rockabilly era did it become the dominant trend.

An examination of West Virginia in the pre-1960 era for distinctiveness in style and sound reveals a few loosely defined characteristics. The social commentary found in early lyrics contains some of the more acute observations of the era. Blind Alfred Reed's criticisms of modernization and materialism rank as among the best ever made in poetic form by a representative of the common man. The best of those by Bill Cox, John McGhee, and Frank Welling come not far behind. Yet their accomplishments stand as the products of individual genius more than of their local environment. Nevertheless, the harsh nature of the industrialization process in a state with rough terrain and the peculiar characteristics of lumbering, mining, and railroading may have been contributing factors in molding their minds.

Within the music itself, two or three developments seem particularly West Virginian. First the state, especially Wheeling and Fairmont, serves as a meeting place and melting pot for northern, southern, and even western styles. The widespread incorporation of the accordion in bands perhaps symbolized this characteristic. Yet the real reason may have stemmed from a conscious or unconscious knowledge that a heavily Caucasian yet ethnically diverse audience existed out there in "radio-land." The early members of Doc Williams's Border Riders—Curley Sims, the WASP from Ohio's Hocking Valley; Doc and Cy, Slovaks from near Kittanning, Pennsylvania; Sunflower Calvas, the Italian-American girl from Thomas, West Virginia; one southerner, Rawhide Fincher from Anniston, Alabama, an industrial town on the fringe of Appalachia; and later Marion Martin, the Polish-American from Moundsville—were a diverse group playing hillbilly music to entertain the even more diverse audience in WWVA's hinterland. The Williams group stands only as the most obvious example. Many of the other successful acts in the region, such as Slim Bryant, Big Slim, Curley Miller, and Blaine Smith, made room for the instrument in their bands. The accordion has almost vanished from country music, but because of the status accorded it in the Upper Ohio-Monongahela Valley (and also by Pee

Wee King, originally located in ethnically diverse Wisconsin), it once held sufficient attraction for traditionalists like Roy Acuff and Bill Monroe to integrate it into their sounds (not too successfully one might add). Skilled practitioners of the instrument, such as Martin, Al Azzaro, Sonny Day, Flash Meshinsky, Buddy Ross, and Phyllis McCumbee, often enjoyed a featured status like that enjoyed by the top fiddlers and banjo pickers in contemporary bluegrass.

The recitation within a song and the recitation as a country song seem to be peculiarly West Virginian. From 1928, when Frank Welling's "Too Many Parties and Too Many Pals" appeared, the recitation has come and gone repeatedly in country music. Welling, of course, recorded other recitations and did many more on radio. Many if not most of the later recitation specialists tended to be West Virginia performers—Buddy Starcher, Doc Williams, Chickie Williams, Red Sovine, Charlie Arnett, Blaine Smith, and finally T. Texas Tyler, who one might say matured as an artist in his West Virginia years. Unrecorded recitationists of note included Murrell Poor and Smilin' Dale Roseberry. Other than Hank Williams (as Luke the Drifter), Red Foley, and Tex Ritter (a known admirer of Buddy Starcher), few recitation experts can be found (even if one includes Senator Everett Dirksen) who can match this list of Mountain State specialists. Although the tradition established by Welling had much influence on the movement in West Virginia, the nearness of Mary Jean Shurtz, the housewife, homespun poet, and pioneer country music journalist, constituted a strong catalyst. Residing in Newcomerstown, Ohio, and a regular listener to many daytime country shows, Mrs. Shurtz provided plenty of material for her hillbilly radio friends. A 1942 edition of her poems included a list of hillbilly singers and announcers who had read her works over the air—in addition to those already mentioned, Cliff Allen, Joe Edison, Al Hendershot, Big Slim, Bobby Cook, Grandpa Jones, Rusty Hiser, Howard Wolfe, Cowboy Loye, and Lew Childre. Numerous artists included her poems in their songbooks. At one time Wheeling Records had a radio mail order special of her recitations by John Corrigan, Chickie, and Doc Williams on a set of four extended-play records. Oddly enough, only one of her recitations—"Daddy Gave My Dog Away"—ever reached standard status, while two of her songs became hits, one of them, "There Stands the Glass," being among the all-time classics. With Welling initiating the genre, Shurtz furnishing original poems, and a whole host of experts, it is little wonder that West Virginians led the field in recitations.[1]

The wide range of radio activity in West Virginia may have been unique in its intensiveness. Unfortunately, insufficient material currently exists for comparative purposes. Most previous studies of early country music have focused on recordings, which in essence are like preserved documents. In contrast, the live radio show, generally conceded as more significant, vanished except in the mind and memory of the listener. Only a small fragment of the transcribed shows seems to have been preserved, and most of these come from the 1940s and early 1950s. Various national listings exist of country radio acts in the 1944-1956 period, but when closely analyzed some prove to be incomplete, contain obsolete information, fail to distinguish live from transcribed programs, or do not differentiate performers, disc jockeys, and announcers. Considerable work needs to be done in the history of live country music on radio. It seems safe to conclude, however, that WWVA Wheeling and probably WMMN Fairmont, at least between 1935 and 1950, ranked among the major outlets for live country programming. Not far behind came Bluefield's WHIS and Charleston's WCHS, both of which played important roles over a long period of years. Huntington's stations held considerable talent during the Mike Layman-Flem Evans era. The other stations generally played secondary roles, although a few ranked high for brief periods.

As a state, West Virginia boasts fewer people than any other southern or border state except Delaware. Yet the role of its musicians and radio stations has been a significant one. As both a repository and a conveyor of the traditions that have made country music a major mode of entertainment for the common man, and indeed for much of what has been termed "Middle America," the Mountaineers and their melodies have more than done their part.

Afterword

In the dozen years that have elapsed since the original publication of *Mountaineer Jamboree*, both continuity and change have characterized the country music scene. For instance, "Jamboree U.S.A." has moved into its seventh decade—utilizing the same format that it has had since the early eighties. Doc and Chickie Williams appear on the same show once or twice a year with a few other older performers, and there is also an annual bluegrass night in the winter months. The rest of the time, guest stars dominate the stage, with their summer extravaganza Jamboree in the Hills as the number one attraction. Buddy Starcher, in his ninetieth year, still lives in Harrisonburg, Virginia.

In Nashville, veteran stalwarts such as Little Jimmy Dickens and Wilma Lee Cooper still grace the stage of the "Grand Ole Opry." Chester "Butch" Lester, former country and rockabilly performer on the WCHS-TV "Buddy Starcher Show," is a songwriter who has had some moderate success, including the Johnny Cash hit "Goin' by the Book" in 1990. Grandpa Jones, who got much of his earlier experience at WWVA and WMMN, remained on "Hee Haw" through 1992 and is also heard regularly on the Opry. The West Virginia–born harmonica player Charlie McCoy also remained with "Hee Haw" until its demise. Penny DeHaven continues to sing in dynamic fashion, still searching for the big hit.

Within the Mountain State, a few worthy performers from past years who were inadvertently omitted from the first edition have been identified or located. Cecil Vaughn, who recorded for Columbia and Gennett, was found to have been a Calhoun County resident. The careful research of the late Guthrie Meade identified an "old time sacred singing" father and son duo from Kanawha County as M. Homer and Hugh Cummings. This pair recorded five sides for Champion in mid-August 1934, four of them released in both the 16,000 and 45,000 series. After years of searching, labor lore scholar Archie Green located the singers Charlie and Bonnie Barley, who waxed the fine coal mining songs "John L.'s Contract Time" and "Miner's Welfare Fund" as well as a pair of sacred numbers for Bullet in 1949.

Residents of the Beckley area, the Barleys performed their lyrics at United Mine Workers rallies throughout Appalachia for a time. Some years later Bonnie resurfaced in Meigs County, Ohio, where she and her second husband, George Ingles, operated a tavern near the town of Pomeroy.

Two brothers from Harrison County, Martin and Neal Bland— known as Slim and Steve respectively—had some interesting experiences in radio during the mid-thirties at WMMN Fairmont, WWVA Wheeling, WBLK Clarksburg, and locales outside the state from St. Louis to Philadelphia. The Bland Brothers usually worked as part of larger groups such as the Shady Valley Folks and the Sleepy Hollow Ranch Gang. Like many radio acts, they recorded sparingly; they cut four sides for the Rainbow label in New York late in 1947 and some more songs for an even more obscure company called Quaker. From the early fifties the Blands worked separately with various groups or as solo musicians, eventually moving back to West Virginia in the late seventies. Martin died in 1991, a few months short of his seventy-fifth birthday. Neal, however, still cuts brush and raises a vegetable garden in retirement.

Within the last decade, four younger West Virginia artists have gained some attention in Nashville, one becoming a star of major proportions. One might conclude that 1959 constituted a vintage year for Mountain State musical figures, since three of these newer figures were born then. Vicky Bird, however, came along four years earlier in Bird's Hollow and grew to become well known for her winning personality and attractive features. Bird was a "Hee Haw" regular for some time, and in frequent appearances on Nashville Network interview shows she struck a responsive chord with country fans who delighted in her down-home accent. Her pronunciation of such words as "Miz-zory" (for Missouri) seemed more memorable than her four placings on the country charts, as her strongest offering, "A Little Bit of Lovin,'" peaked at number sixty-one in Spring 1988.

Of the "fifty-niners," Jeff Stevens led a country-rock trio called the Bullets that recorded for Atlantic in the late eighties. Born in Charleston and reared in Alum Creek, Stevens grew up the son of a Johnny Cash fan. Having learned to play guitar at an early age, Jeff and his brother Warren won a talent contest as the Stevens Brothers in 1968. The duo played at numerous local entertainments and added cousin Terry Dotson about 1975, when they became the Bullets. By this time they expanded their audiences by becoming an opening act for well known country stars. Jeff and Terry wrote a pair of top ten hits for the Georgia-based group Atlanta. As a result the Bullets moved to Nashville in 1986 and contracted with Atlantic Records. They subsequently had four chartmakers with the top one, "Geronimo's Cadillac," reaching the fifty-first spot on the *Billboard* listings in 1987. Never quite able to score the big hit that would elevate them to stardom, the Bullets disbanded in 1990. Warren and Terry returned to West Virginia. Jeff remained in Nashville and has done well as a songwriter, coauthoring hits for both John Anderson and Alabama in 1993.

Lionel Cartwright tasted even more success than the Stevens brothers did in Music City after serving an apprenticeship in Wheeling. Born in Gallipolis, Ohio, on February 10, 1959, Cartwright spent his early childhood in the river town of Mason, West Virginia, and went to high school in Moundsville. He developed an amazing degree of musical proficiency on at least ten instruments, ranging from keyboards to Dobro, and worked for a time at the WMNI Country Cavalcade in Columbus, Ohio, before leading the staff band at "Jamboree, U.S.A." During this time, Cartwright not only cut his first album with the band under the name New Generation Express but also earned a degree in business at Wheeling Jesuit College. In 1983, he left WWVA and took a job with the newly opened Nashville Network. Cartwright worked as an arranger, musical director, and performer closely identified with the programs "I 40 Paradise" and "Pickin' at the Paradise."

These experiences brought Cartwright to the attention of MCA Records, which signed him to a contract in 1987. His first single made the charts late in 1988, and "Give Me His Last Chance" peaked at the third spot in mid-1989. In 1990 the nostalgic "I Watched It All on My Radio" and "My Heart Is Set on You" both made the top ten. His "Leap of Faith" reached number one in September 1991. However, three chartmakers in 1992 placed no higher than fifty, and MCA dropped him. Cartwright's career seems on the wane in the mid-nineties, but the youth's talent and skill still hold considerable potential.

The last of this threesome with the same birth year could well eclipse all her fellow West Virginians in musical achievement. Kathy Mattea was born in Cross Lanes, near Charleston, on July 21, 1959, and showed more interest in rock and folk music than in country during her youth. As a student at West Virginia University in the late seventies, she sang in a local bluegrass band called Pennsboro and left school before graduation to try her luck in Nashville. After supporting herself at various jobs, including a stint as tourguide at the Country Music Hall of Fame, Mattea began recording demos and in 1983 signed a contract with Mercury Records. Her first chartmaker,

"Street Talk," appeared that same year, and several more moderate successes debuted over the next two years. In 1986 "Love at the Five and Dime" and "Walk the Way the Wind Blows" both made the top ten. The latter song came from the pen of Tim O'Brien, a Wheeling native, who had made a name for himself as a member of the Colorado-based bluegrass band Hot Rize (and its alter-ego Red Knuckles and the Trail Blazers). O'Brien subsequently wrote "Untold Stories" (another Mattea hit) and recorded solos as well as duets with his sister Molly. His only chart success, however, came in a duet with Mattea in 1990, titled "The Battle Hymn of Love," which reached number nine.

Meanwhile, Mattea recorded a series of songs that went to the very top, beginning with "Goin' Gone" in late 1987 and continuing with "Eighteen Wheels and a Dozen Roses," "Come from the Heart," and "Burnin' Old Memories." Nine more songs made the top ten between 1987 and 1991. The Country Music Association recognized her achievements by naming her the Female Vocalist of the Year in both 1989 and 1990. Furthermore, her biggest hit, "Eighteen Wheels and a Dozen Roses," won the CMA Single of the Year Award in 1988.

On the personal side, Mattea married songwriter Jon Vezner on February 14, 1988, and did some charity work for the American Federation for AIDS Research. After nearly a decade with Allen Reynolds as her producer at Mercury, she switched to Brent Maher in 1992. Her best song that year, "Lonesome Standard Time," peaked at the eleventh spot. Mattea had experienced some problems with her vocal chords and subsequently underwent delicate surgery at Vanderbilt University Hospital. In 1994, she came back with another major hit in "Walking Away a Winner." In fact, this title would appear to be a brief description of her own life. As of early 1996, it appears that Mattea may well be the Mountain State's all-time ranking country star with more than thirty charted hits to her credit.

With the country music scene in a state of constant change, it is difficult to predict whose star may rise or fall next on the Nashville horizon. For instance, in 1992 Billy Ray Cyrus, a native of Flatwoods, Kentucky, came out of the obscurity of a five-year stint at the Ragtime Lounge in Huntington with a giant hit on Mercury Records. "Achy Breaky Heart" spent five weeks at number one and showed crossover strength as well, peaking at four on the pop listings. This success put Cyrus in the difficult position of having a hard act to follow. However, four more songs in the top ten by the end of 1993 proved that Cyrus was not a one-hit wonder. When the editors of *Country America* magazine picked their top ten new stars for 1996, they also included West Virginian Jeff Copley. His initial single, "Evergreen," looks promising, but only time will tell whether or not true stardom will follow.

While no new West Virginia figures have gained major attention in the bluegrass music field other than Tim O'Brien, the Ceredo-based Perry Sisters have won acclaim in the realm of Southern Gospel. Molly O'Day at WEMM-FM radio dubbed them the "sweetest singers this side of heaven" because of their pleasing three-part harmonies, and their reputations soon spread beyond the Tri-State area. Sweet harmony notwithstanding, the Perrys can also belt out raw primitive songs such as Brother Claude Ely's "Ain't No Grave Gonna Hold My Body Down" with as much fervor as the original. A series of albums produced by Nashville's Eddy Crook brought the Perrys considerable fame during the 1980s and 1990s.

Unfortunately, the passing of time also witnessed illnesses and deaths of numerous veteran performers. Cousin Ezra Cline, who founded West Virginia's pioneer bluegrass group, the Lonesome Pine Fiddlers, died on July 11, 1984. His cousin Curly Ray Cline, the longtime band fiddler who went on to work some twenty-seven years with Ralph Stanley's Clinch Mountain Boys, retired in the spring of 1993 and is currently in poor health at his home in Rock House, Kentucky. Frank Dudgeon, the West Virginia Mountain Boy, went to his reward on March 16, 1987, in Pittsburgh, unaware that scholarly interest had developed in his music. Molly O'Day continued as a familiar voice on WEMM-FM radio in Huntington until she was diagnosed with cancer. She "went home to be with the Lord" on December 4, 1987, and Lynn Davis has continued their radio ministry alone. Flip Strickland retired to Alabama in 1979 after a thirty-three-year residence in Indiana. He remained in good health until the last year of his life but suffered a stroke some months before his death on July 21, 1988. His widow brought his remains back to Gallipolis, Ohio, for burial. Johnnie Bailes passed away in Georgia in December 1989, and his brother Kyle in Alabama in 1996; only Walter and Homer survive from this legendary harmony team. Ernest "Jimmy" Walker died in the Huntington V.A. hospital in June 1990. Arthur "Rusty" Gabbard, the Kentucky native who toiled on WMMN and other West Virginia radio stations in the tough pre–World War II years with Cowboy Copas, Billy Stallard, and Natchee the Indian before he worked as a front man for the Texas Troubadours, died on July 23, 1990.

In addition to Jimmy Walker, several artists associated with the Wheeling Jamboree have died. These include Joe Barker, Milly Wayne, Marion Martin, and Ray Myers. Little Shirley Barker, who appeared at many reunion concerts, and trucker favorite Dick Curless passed on in January and May 1995, respectively. George "Sleepy" Jeffers, who had early experiences on the Jamboree before going on lengthy radio and television work in Charleston, went to his reward in the same late November week in 1992 when Roy Acuff died in Nashville. In the Mountain State and elsewhere, many older musicians passed on—Bernice Coleman and Ernest Branch among them—with little notice outside their home communities.

The popularity of American country music has seemingly reached great heights in recent years. New stars capture the public's attention and replace the ranking favorites of the recent past. Garth Brooks or Alan Jackson comes upon the scene and relegates Ricky Skaggs and Randy Travis to secondary positions. Meanwhile, the careers of singers like George Jones, George Strait, or Little Jimmy Dickens seem to advance with little or no interruption. Kathy Mattea may or may not sustain a career at the top for several more years. Jeff Copley could be the next West Virginian star, but, then again, it might be someone else. New stars will appear; some will be from West Virginia and more will come from other states with large populations of Appalachian, southern, and working-class folk. The music will change while retaining strong elements from the past, and many West Virginians will continue identifying with the culture and listening to sounds of this down-home music. Certainly country fans from throughout the nation will continue to enjoy music played and influenced by pickers and singers from the Mountain State.

Notes

Abbreviations Used

BU	Bluegrass Unlimited	JEMFQ	John Edwards Memorial
CMR	Country Music Report		Foundation Quarterly
CSR	Country Song Roundup	MBPR	Mountain Broadcast & Prairie
CWJ	Country & Western Jamboree		Recorder
DB	The Devil's Box	ME	Musical Echoes
GS	Goldenseal	NHN	National Hillbilly News
JAF	Journal of American	OTM	Old Time Music
	Folklore	WF	The Wheeling Feeling
JCM	Journal of Country Music	WVR	West Virginia Review

1. The Mountaineer Folk Music Heritage

1. Anna Davis Richardson, "Old Songs from Clarksburg, W.Va., 1918," *JAF* 32 (1919):497-99.

2. Joseph Doddridge, *Notes on the Settlement and Indian Wars . . . 1824* (Pittsburgh: Ritenour and Lindsey, 1912), p. 104.

3. William Alexander MacCorkle, *Recollections of Fifty Years of West Virginia* (New York: Putnam's, 1928), pp. 217-18.

4. Ibid., pp. 218-21.

5. Charles K. Wolfe, "The Tweedy Brothers," *DB* 13, no. 3 (Sept. 1979):53; Ted Green, "The Champion of Greenbrier Valley," *GS* 4, no. 23 (April-Sept. 1978):39-42; Sam Rizetta, "'Whoop It Up a Little Bit': The Life and Music of Blackie Cool," *GS* 7, no. 3 (Fall 1981):51-64; Michael Kline, "A Pretty Good Thing All the Way Around," *GS* 7, no. 4 (Winter 1981):9-51, 17-24; *Morgan Messenger* (Berkeley Springs), Mar. 17, 1982, p. 15; Randolph E. Spencer, *A West Virginian's View of Musical Life Yesterday and Today* (Smithtown, N.Y.: Exposition Press, 1982), p. 150; Buddy E. Starcher, personal interview, Craigsville, W.Va., May 14, 1978; James (Carson) Roberts, personal interview, Lexington, Ky., Apr. 29, 1979; Jessie Wanda Smik (Chickie Williams), personal interview, Wheeling, W.Va., June 4, 1980; Harry Tweedy, personal interview, Columbus, Ohio, June 12, 1980.

6. Melvin N. Artley, "The West Virginia Country Fiddler: An Aspect of the Folk Music Tradition of the United States," Ph.D. diss., Chicago Musical College, 1955, pp. 38-61; Bill C. Malone, *Southern Music/American Music* (Lexington: Univ. Press of Kentucky, 1979), pp. 8-13.

7. Doddridge, *Notes*, p. 125, quoted in Otis K. Rice, *The Allegheny Frontier: West Virginia Beginnings, 1730-1830* (Lexington: Univ. Press of Kentucky, 1970), p. 176.

8. See Malone, *Southern Music*, pp. 20ff, for further elaboration on this theme.

9. Patrick Gainer, ed., *West Virginia Centennial Book of One Hundred Songs* (Morgantown: West Virginia Centennial Committee, 1963), no. 4; see also no. 11.

10. Malone, *Southern Music*, pp. 28-32; see also Bill C. Malone, *Country Music USA* (Austin: Univ. of Texas Press, 1968), pp. 6-7.

11. Malone, *Country Music*, p. 7; Cecil J. Sharp, *English Folk Songs from the Southern Appalachians*, 2 vols. (London: Oxford Univ. Press, 1932), 1:xx-xxvi.

12. Guy B. Johnson, *John Henry: Tracking Down a Negro Legend* (Chapel Hill: Univ. of North Carolina Press, 1929); Louis W. Chappell, *John Henry: A Folk-Lore Study* (Jena, Germany: Walter Biedermann, 1933); John Harrington Cox, *Folk-Songs of the South* (Cambridge: Harvard Univ. Press, 1925), pp. 175-88, 221-30. The first of Cox's confused articles appeared as "John Hardy," *JAF* 32 (1919):505-21. For indication that the identity question persists see MacEdward Leach, "John Henry," in Bruce Jackson, ed., *Folklore and Society* (Hatboro, Pa.: Folklore Associates, 1966), pp. 93-106.

13. Cox, *Folk-Songs*, pp. xv-xvii.

14. Arthur Kyle Davis, Jr., "John Harrington Cox," in John Harrington Cox, *Folk-Songs of the South* (Hatboro, Pa.: Folklore Associates, 1963)), pp. i-ix.

15. Cox, *Folk-Songs*, pp. xxiv-xxx.

16. Josiah H. Combs, *Folk-Songs du Midi des Etats-Unis* (Paris: Presses Universitaires de France, 1925); see also D.K. Wilgus, "Forward," in Josiah H. Combs, *Folk-Songs of the Southern United States* (Austin: Univ. of Texas Press, 1967), pp. ix-xxi; John A. Cuthbert, "A Musicological Look at John Johnson's Fiddling," *GS* 7, no. 4 (Winter 1981):16; John A. Cuthbert, ed., *West Virginia Folk Music: A Descriptive Guide to Field Recordings in the West Virginia and Regional History Collection* (Morgantown: West Virginia Univ. Press, 1982), pp. 1, 44-46, 49-50.

17. Rice, *Allegheny Frontier*, pp. 265-98; Henry Howe, "Life in Western Virginia, 1845," in Maude A. Rucker, *West Virginia: Her Land, Her People, Her Traditions, Her Resources* (New York: Walter Neale, 1930), pp. 50-51. See also the various books of George Pullen Jackson.

18. Combs, *Folk-Songs of the Southern U.S.*, pp. 93-94.

19. Ibid., pp. 92-93.

20. Ibid.; Malone, *Southern Music*, pp. 7-10.

21. Russel B. Nye, *The Unembarrassed Muse: The Popular Arts in America* (New York: Dial, 1970), p. 342; Charles K. Wolfe, *Tennessee Strings: The Story of Country Music in Tennessee* (Knoxville: Univ. of Tennessee Press, 1977), p. vii; John Greenway, "Country-Western: The Music of America," *American West*, 5, no. 6 (Nov. 1968):39, 40; Malone, *Country Music*, p. 3.

22. Malone, *Country Music*, p. vii; Malone, *Southern Music*, p. 63.

23. Gainer, *West Virginia Centennial*, p. 1.

24. Malone, *Southern Music*, p. 62; see also Archie Green, "Hillbilly Music: Source and Symbol," *JAF* 78 (1965):204-28.

25. Artley, "West Virginia Country Fiddler," pp. 18-19; Combs, *Folk-Songs of the Southern U.S.*, pp. 100-101; Ivan M. Tribe and John W. Morris, *Molly O'Day, Lynn Davis, and the Cumberland Mountain Folks: A Bio-Discography* (Los Angeles: John Edwards Memorial Foundation, Univ. of California, 1975), p. 2.

26. Louvada Caplinger, "The Hill Billy," in *Old Time Songs and Mountain Ballads as Featured by Cap, Andy and Flip* (n.c.: n.p., 1934), p. 42.

2. Pioneer Recording Artists

1. Green, "Hillbilly Music." This article remains the best source for the beginnings of recorded country music. After fifteen years only a few small details have been found to add to Green's account.

2. Wolfe, "Tweedy Brothers"; Harry Tweedy, personal interview, Columbus, Ohio, June 12, 1980. A basic source for the Starr Piano Company's recordings is the computerized printout of that firm's ledgers found in the files of the John Edwards Memorial Foundation at UCLA. All subsequent references to Starr recordings (Gennett and Champion labels) draw heavily from this source.

3. Norman Cohen, *Paramount Old Time Tunes* (Los Angeles: John Edwards Memorial Foundation, Univ. of California, 1977), pp. 6, 12; Arthur Satherly Notebooks in the John Edwards Memorial Foundation files; *Gennett Records of Old Time Tunes* (Richmond, Ind.: Starr Piano Co., 1928), reprint by John Edwards Memorial Foundation, 1975, p. 4; Jean, Robert, William C., and David O. Miller, Jr., personal interviews, Huntington, W. Va., Mar. 2, 1981.

4. Tony Russell, "Frank Hutchison: The Pride of West Virginia," *Old Time Music* (Summer 1971), pp. 4-7; (Winter 1973-74), p. 23; Mark Wilson, liner notes for *Frank Hutchison*, Rounder LP 1007; Arnold Williamson, personal interview, Mt. Gay, W. Va., Aug. 26, 1981.

5. Eugene W. Earle and Archie Green, "Interview with Mrs. Roy Harvey," *JEMF Newsletter* 10 (June 1968):74-77; Norman Cohen, "Notes on Some Old Time Musicians from Princeton, West Virginia," *JEMFQ* 8 (1972):94-98, 103; Clifford Kinney Rorrer, *Charlie Poole and the North Carolina Ramblers* (Eden, N.C.: Tar Heel Printing Co., 1968); see also idem, *Rambling Blues: The Life and Songs of Charlie Poole* (London: Old Time Music, 1982), pp. 34-35, 60-62.

6. Rounder Collective (Ken Irwin, Marion Leighton, Bill Nowlin), "The Life of Blind Alfred Reed," *JEMFQ* 7 (1971):113-15; see also their liner notes for *Blind Alfred Reed: How Can a Poor Man Stand Such Times and Live*, Rounder LP 1001.

7. Brian Rust, *The Victor Master Book*, 3 vols. (London: n.p., 1969), 2:144-47.

8. Donald Lee Nelson, "The West Virginia Snake Hunters: John and Emery McClung," *JEMFQ* 10 (1974):68-73; idem, "Cleve Chafin: Carnival Musician," *JEMFQ* 10 (1974):38-40; *Beckley Herald*, Aug. 30, 1950.

9. Cohen, *Old Time Tunes*, pp. 8-9; Satherly Notebooks; Donald Lee Nelson, "The Crime at Quiet Dell," *JEMFQ* 8 (1972):204-6; material in Frank Welling file at John Edwards Memorial Foundation; John Max McGhee and Anna McGhee Schrule, personal interview, Huntington, W. Va., Aug. 28, 1980.

10. Cohen, "Notes on Musicians," pp. 102, 104; Chris Strachwitz, liner notes for *The String Bands #2*, Old Timey LP 101; Bernice Coleman, telephone interview, Princeton, W. Va., Aug. 8, 1983.

11. Warren Caplinger, "A Brief History of the Radio Team of Cap, Andy and Flip," in *Fireside Melodies #2* (Charleston: n.p., 1938), inside front cover; John W. Hevener, "Appalachians in Akron, 1914-1945: The Transfer of Southern Folk Culture," typescript of paper presented at Northern Great Plains History Conference, Grand Forks, North Dakota, Oct. 11, 1975, p. 16; Charles K. Wolfe, "Early Country Music in Knoxville," *OTM* (Spring 1974), p. 26; Kenneth Caplinger, telephone interview, Davis, W. Va., Feb. 28, 1978.

12. Guthrie T. Meade, Jr., liner notes for *The Legend of Clark Kessinger*, Kanawha LP 304; Nancy Dols, liner notes for *The Kessinger Brothers, 1928-1930 Recordings*, County LP 536, 1975; *Charleston Daily Mail*, Aug. 27, 1955, p. 13.

13. William J. Cox, personal interview, Charleston, W. Va., June 2, 1967; Ken-

neth Davidson, liner notes for *Billy Cox: The Dixie Songbird*, Kanawha LP 305; death certificate for William J. Cox, Kanawha County, West Virginia; Kenneth Davidson to Graham Wickham, letter in John Edwards Memorial Foundation files dated Feb. 11, 1967; James A. Haught, "Life's Song Sour for Billy Cox," *Charleston Gazette*, June 30, 1966.

14. Tony Russell, "Back Track: Dick Justice," *OTM* (Winter 1973-74), p. 23; unpublished discography of Reese Jarvis and Dick Justice in John Edwards Memorial Foundation files; Orville Ellis and Ephra Walker, personal interview, Rio Grande, Ohio, Oct. 11, 1980.

15. Cohen, "Notes on Musicians," pp. 98-102, 104; Conza Raines (sister of J.O. Harpold), personal interview, Cottageville, W. Va., Aug. 4, 1981; Bernice Coleman interview, Aug. 8, 1983.

16. "Biography of Richard Cox" in *Greetings from Bert Layne and His Mountaineer Fiddlers with Riley Puckett and Richard Cox* (n.c.: n.p., 1936), p. 3.

17. *NHN* (Apr. 1946), p. 3; *MBPR* (June 1946), pp. 16-17; Mrs. Frank Dudgeon, telephone interview, Cleveland, Ohio, Nov. 30, 1981.

18. Harlan Daniel, "Who Was Who? An Index of Hill Country Recording Pseudonyms," *The American Folk Music Occasional* (New York: Oak Publishers, 1970), p. 67; see also "The Brunswick 100 Series—Songs from Dixie," *JEMFQ* 9 (1973):103-8; Norman Cohen, *Long Steel Rail* (Urbana: Univ. of Illinois Press, 1981), pp. 232-39; John W. Newbraugh, letter to author, Mar. 2, 1982; Mark Wilson and Guthrie T. Meade, Jr., liner notes for *Blind Ed Haley: Parkersburg Landing*, Rounder LP 1010.

3. WWVA and the "World's Original Jamboree"

1. *West Virginia Legislative Hand Book and Manual and Official Register, 1931* (Charleston: State of West Virginia, 1931), p. 798.

2. "WWVA-Wheeling," *WVR* 23, no. 2 (Nov. 1945):20; *WWVA 10th Anniversary Family Album, 1926-1936* (Wheeling: West Virginia Broadcasting Corp., 1936), p. 3.

3. *WWVA 10th Anniversary Album*, p. 4; William Wallace Jones, personal interview, Bridgeport, Ohio, June 4, 1980.

4. William Wallace Jones interview, June 4, 1980; *WWVA Family Album 1936*, pp. 3-4; Harry Tweedy, personal interview, Columbus, Ohio, June 12, 1980; see also Wolfe, "Tweedy Brothers."

5. *WWVA 10th Anniversary Album*, pp. 15-16; Grandpa Jones, "I Remember When," in *Country Music Who's Who* (Denver: Heather Publications, 1966), p. 8:32-33; French Mitchell, personal interview, Buffalo, W. Va., July 15, 1981.

6. French Mitchell interview, July 15, 1981; *WWVA Family Album, 1936*, pp. 16-18; Marshal M. Jones, "Grandpa Jones: The Nice Guy Who Didn't Finish Last," typescript in the Country Music Foundation Library, p. 4; Charles K. Wolfe, "Grandpa and Ramona Jones: Two Lives, One Music," *DB* 14, no. 1 (Mar. 1980):5-10.

7. Ken Griffis, "The Shug Fisher Story," *JEMFQ* 10, no. 2 (Summer 1974):55-61; *Hugh and Shug's Songs and Stories* (n.c.: n.p., 1937), pp. 18-21; *Hugh Cross' Anniversary Song Book* (New York: Peer International, 1944), p. 1.

8. Barbara Kempf, "Meet Doc Williams: Country Music Star, Country Music Legend," *JEMFQ* 10, no. 1 (Spring 1974):1-13; Larry Wilson, "A Man Called Doc," *WF* 1, no. 1 (Oct. 1973):8-9.

9. H.C. McAuliffe, "My Life Story," in *Big Slim—The Lone Cowboy: Favorite Songs* (n.c.: n.p., 1939), inside front cover, pp. 8, 12; *Wheeling Intelligencer*, Oct. 15,

1966, p. 7; Norma Clarke (former president of Big Slim Fan Club), personal interview, Newcomerstown, Ohio, Sept. 3, 1981.

10. *Frankie More's Log Cabin Girls Book of Souvenirs* (n.c.: n.p., 1938), pp. 1-13; *Frankie More's Log Cabin Boys and Girls: Favorite Song Folder* (n.c.: n.p., 1938); *1941 Souvenir Folder of Frankie More and His Log Cabin Boys* (n.c.: n.p., 1940); *Billboard*, Oct. 30, 1948, Feb. 3, 1951, June 30, 1952.

11. *Doc Williams Border Riders Family Album* (n.c.: n.p., 1939), p. 10; *Songs of Mack Jeffers and His Fiddlin' Farmers* (n.c.: n.p., 1940), p. 11. See also Virginia Alderman, "Jamboree History," in *Jamboree U.S.A.* (Steubenville, Ohio: Tri-State Publishing Co., 1972), pp. 5-6; Andrew Smik, Jr. (Doc Williams), letter to author, Aug. 20, 1982.

12. *Jake Taylor and His Railsplitters Log Book* (n.c.: n.p., 1939), pp. 3-12; *Joe Barker and His Chuckwagon Gang: Roundup of Song Hits #1* (New York: Dixie Music, 1943), inside front cover; "Joe Barker/Shirley Barker," captioned WWVA publicity photograph, ca. 1945.

13. John J. Bailes, taped autobiography, Swainsboro, Ga., Aug. 18, 1974 (in author's collection); Andrew Smik, Jr. (Doc Williams), personal interview, Wheeling, W. Va., Dec. 29, 1981; Ivan M. Tribe, "Charlie Monroe," *BU* 10, no. 4 (Oct. 1975):14-15.

14. *WWVA Jamboree 6th Anniversary Good-Will Tour Souvenir*, Apr. 10-16, 1939; Alderman, "Jamboree History," p. 5; Andrew Smik, Jr. (Doc Williams), telephone interview, Wheeling, W. Va., June 9, 1982; Ray Nemic, liner notes for *Blue Grass Roy's Collection of Mountain and Home Songs*, Old Homestead LP OHCS 106, 1977.

15. *Second Annual WWVA Jamboree Good-Will Tour Souvenir*, 1940; *Third Annual WWVA Jamboree Good-Will Tour Souvenir*, 1941; "1942 WWVA Jamboree Good-Will Tour Cast," official photograph, 1942.

16. *WWVA 20th Anniversary Family Album, 1926-1946* (Wheeling: n.p., 1946), pp. 2, 24; Kempf, "Meet Doc Williams," p. 6.

17. *Billboard*, Oct. 3, 1942, p. 69; *Joe Barker Song Hits #1*, pp. 2-3, 8-9; *Smilie Sutter's Roundup of Song Hits #1* (New York: Dixie Music, 1943), pp. 4-5, 24-25; *Chuck Wagon Gang's #1 Roundup of Song Hits* (New York: Dixie Music, 1944), rear covers.

18. *Millie Wayne's Collection of Old Time Hymns and Gospel Songs* (Wheeling: Rangerette Publishing Co., n.d.), inside front cover; Bonnie Baldwin, letters to author, Apr. 8, Apr. 21, 1982; Flavil Miller, letter to author, May 15, 1982; Gay Schwing, letter to author, May 25, 1982; *Gay Schwing and His Boys from the Hills* (Davis, W. Va.: John Bava Publishers, 1947), rear cover; *Introducing Tony Stroud and His Hill Billy Song Hits* (Wheeling: n.p., 1944), inside rear cover. See also Peter V. Kuykendall, "Tony Stroud: One of Bluegrass Music's Originals," *BU* 16, no. 9 (Mar. 1982):34-39.

19. *WWVA 20th Anniversary Album*, pp. 1, 15-17.

20. *NHN* (July-Aug. 1947), p. 2; Margie Shannon, personal interview, Huntington, W. Va., July 22, 1981; Wilma Lee Cooper, personal interview, Brentwood, Tenn., March 4, 1983; James C. Dickens, personal interview, Brentwood, Tenn., March 4, 1983. See also Linnell Gentry, *A History and Encyclopedia of Country, Western, and Gospel Music*, 2nd ed. (Nashville: Clairmont, 1969), pp. 440-41.

21. Wilma Lee Cooper interview, Mar. 4, 1983; Robert Cogswell, "We Made Our Name in the Days of Radio: A Look at the Careers of Wilma Lee and Stoney Cooper," *JEMFQ* 11, no. 2 (Summer 1975):67-79; *Billboard*, Mar. 16, 1957. See also Wayne W. Daniel, "Wilma Lee Cooper: America's Most Authentic Mountain Singer," *BU* 16, no. 8 (Feb. 1982):12-15.

22. Walter LeRoy Moore, personal interview, Wheeling, W. Va., Oct. 12, 1980; Everett Lilly, personal interview, Clear Creek, W. Va., Dec. 26, 1973; Buddy Starcher, "Red Belcher," *MBPR* (June 1945), pp. 11-12.

23. Don Kidwell, personal interview, Wheeling, W. Va., Oct. 10, 1981; John Graham, personal interview, Wheeling, W. Va., Oct. 11, 1981; Ernest E. "Jimmy" Walker, telephone interview, Point Pleasant, W. Va., Nov. 12, 1982; *NHN* (Nov.-Dec. 1947), p. 22; Gentry, *History and Encyclopedia*, p. 529.

24. Ruth Lee Miller, "Hank, the Singing Ranger," *MBPR* (June 1945), p. 17; Marshall Fallwell, "Hank Snow Moves on in the Old Tradition," *The Best of Country Music II* (New York: KBO Publishers, 1975), pp. 11-12; Alderman, "Jamboree History," p. 15; Norma Clarke interview, Sept. 3, 1981; Walter LeRoy Moore, personal interview, Wheeling, W. Va., Oct. 11, 1981.

25. James (Carson) Roberts, personal interview, Lexington, Ky., Apr. 29, 1979; Roy Scott, personal interview, Wheeling, W. Va., Oct. 7, 1979.

26. Alderman, "Jamboree History," p. 7; *Billboard*, May 15, 1948; *NHN* (July-Aug. 1947), p. 19.

27. Gentry, *History and Encyclopedia*, pp. 378, 434-35, 509; *Skeeter Bonn Souvenir Photo and Song Album* (n.c.: n.p., 1957), p. 1; *WWVA Jamboree Souvenir Album, 1955* (Wheeling: Storer Broadcasting Co., 1955), pp. 7, 10.

28. *WWVA Jamboree Album, 1955*, pp. 2-3; Norman E. Messner, letter to author, Apr. 13, 1982; *Bud Messner and the Skyline Boys* (n.c.: n.p., n.d.), pp. 2-3; *CWJ* 2, no. 10 (Jan. 1957):47.

29. *WWVA Jamboree Album, 1955*, p. 6; *WWVA Jamboree Souvenir Album, 1953* (Wheeling: Storer Broadcasting Co., 1953); *WWVA Jamboree Souvenir Album, 1954* (Wheeling: Storer Broadcasting Co., 1954).

30. *WWVA Jamboree Album, 1954*, Gary A. Henderson and Walter V. Saunders, "The Bailey Brothers," *BU* 5, no. 8 (Feb. 1971):5-6.

31. Nelson Sears, *Jim and Jesse: Appalachia to the Grand Ole Opry* (n.c.: n.p., 1976), pp. 90-96; Frank (Hylo) Brown, personal interview, Jackson, Ohio, Feb. 11, 1974; Neil V. Rosenburg, "The Osborne Brothers: Getting It Off," *BU* 6, no. 8 (Feb. 1972):5-8.

32. *Billboard*, Oct. 9, 1954; Doc Williams interview, June 9, 1982.

33. Gentry, *History and Encyclopedia*, p. 426; Bill Millar, liner notes for *The MGM Rockabilly Collection*, MGM LP 2315394 (Great Britain), ca. 1979; liner notes for *The Island Recordings*, White Label LP 8814; Nick Tosches, "Rockabilly!" in Patrick Carr, ed., *The Illustrated History of Country Music* (New York: Doubleday, 1980), p. 223; Alderman, "Jamboree History," p. 26.

34. Alderman, "Jamboree History," pp. 10-11; Doc Williams interview, June 9, 1982.

35. Doc Williams interview, June 9, 1982; Walter LeRoy Moore interview, Oct. 12, 1980; *WWVA Jamboree Newsletter*, Nov. 15, 1966, pp. 1-5.

36. See Alderman, "Jamboree History," pp. 11-13.

37. Ibid., pp. 26-38; Thomas Gray, personal interview, Logan, Ohio, May 30, 1982.

38. Andrew Smik, Jr. (Doc Williams), personal interviews, Wheeling, W. Va., Oct. 10, Dec. 29, 1981. The opinions expressed here are all mine, not those of Doc Williams.

39. Alderman, "Jamboree History," pp. 26-32. See also Gentry, *History and Encyclopedia*, pp. 426, 492.

40. Gentry, *History and Encyclopedia*, p. 407; "Delightful Kathy Dee," in *Country Music Report*, p. 18 (from undated clipping in Country Music Foundation Library, Vertical file D445); Alderman, "Jamboree History," p. 28, 29, 38; see also *Official Jamboree History/Picture Book* (Wheeling: Jamboree U.S.A., 1979); *WF* 1, no. 1 (Oct. 1973):7.

41. *Official Jamboree History/Picture Book* (1979), pp. 23, 26; Alderman, "Jamboree History," pp. 26, 28, 31-32.

42. Alderman, "Jamboree History," p. 25; Louise Fox, "Blue Ridge Quartet Comes

Home," *Wheeling News-Register*, Apr. 1, 1979; *WF* 1, no. 2 (Nov. 1973):12. See also Ivan M. Tribe, "The Bailes Brothers," *BU* 9, no. 8 (Feb. 1975):8-13.

43. *WF* 1, no. 1 (Oct. 1973):4-5; Alderman, "Jamboree History," pp. 18-22.

44. *Official Jamboree History/Picture Book* (1979), pp. 35-37; *Louisville Courier-Journal & Times*, July 17, 1977; *Wheeling News-Register*, July 17, 1978; *Marietta Times*, July 26, 1979; *Warren Tribune Chronicle*, Feb. 22, 1980.

45. *WWVA Jamboree Newsletter*, Nov. 1967.

4. Tune In: Radio to 1942

1. *West Virginia Legislative Hand Book, 1931*, p. 798; Stephen Buell, "The History and Development of WSAZ-TV Channel 3, Huntington, West Virginia," Ph.D. diss., Ohio State Univ., 1962, pp. 1-4.

2. John Max McGhee and Anna McGhee Schrule, personal interview, Huntington, W. Va., Aug. 28, 1980; Virginia Miller Day, personal interview, Cheasapeake, Ohio, Mar. 2, 1981; Robert, Jean, William C., and David O. Miller, Jr., personal interviews, Huntington, W. Va., Mar. 2, 1981.

3. *Huntington Herald-Dispatch*, July 1, 2, and 3, 1930; Charles Keaton, taped personal interview, Argillite, Ky., Aug. 7, 1981 (in author's collection); *Jack and Little Jackie Present Songs You Love to Hear* (Sioux Falls, S.D.: Radio KSOH, n.d.), inside front cover.

4. Clarence C. Clere, personal interview, Hurricane, W. Va., July 21, 1981; Robert Shortridge, personal interview, Catlettsburg, Ky., Aug. 18, 1981. For a brief sketch of Smith, see *MBPR* (Dec. 1945), p. 6.

5. Clarence C. Clere, telephone interview, South Charleston, W. Va., Aug. 3, 1982; David O. Miller, Jr., interview, March 2, 1981; *MBPR* (Apr. 1941), p. 2; (Sept. 1941), p. 14.

6. *Huntington Herald-Dispatch*, May 1, 1933; Clarence C. Clere interview, July 21, 1981; Edward K. Nesbitt, letter to author, undated (ca. mid-Apr. 1982).

7. Clarence C. Clere interview, July 21, 1981; Charles Keaton interview, Aug. 7, 1981; Robert Shortridge interview, Aug. 18, 1981. See also photographs and other material in the collections of Clere and Shortridge (copies in author's collection).

8. Robert Shortridge interview, Aug. 18, 1981; Margie Shannon interview, July 22, 1981.

9. Margie Shannon interview, July 22, 1981; *NHN* (Jan. 1946), p. 3. See also Charles K. Wolfe, "The Legend of Riley Puckett," in *Riley Puckett (1894-1946)* (Bremen, Germany: Archiv fur Populare Musik, 1977), pp. 12-13.

10. Clarence C. Clere interview, July 21, 1981; Margie Shannon interview, July 22, 1981.

11. Margie Shannon interview, July 22, 1981; *MBPR* (July 1942), p. 2; *Radio Station WSAZ Huntington, West Virginia and the West Virginia Network* (n.c.: n.p., 1940), p. 17; *West Virginia Legislative Handbook, 1931*, p. 798.

12. William J. Cox, personal interview, Charleston, W. Va., June 2, 1967; Walter Bailes and Ernest Ferguson, personal interview, Beanblossom, Ind., June 20, 1982. See also Nancy Dols, liner notes for *The Kessinger Brothers, 1928-1930 Recordings*, County LP 536, 1975.

13. Buddy E. Starcher, personal interview, Craigsville, W. Va., May 14, 1978; Walter Bailes and Ernest Ferguson interview, June 20, 1982; Walter Bailes letter to author, Dec. 31, 1976.

14. Buddy E. Starcher interview, May 14, 1978; Buddy E. Starcher, "The Story

of My Life, Part Two," in *Starcher's Buddies: The Official Publication of the Buddy Starcher Fan Club* (Dec. 1944, Jan.-Feb. 1945), pp. 2-4; Marion R. Goddard, *Bless Your Little Heart: The Story of Buddy Starcher* (n.c.: n.p., 1948), pp. 3-28; Buddy Starcher, letter to author, Aug. 19, 1983.

15. *Frank's Own Song Book: Frank Welling, the Pow-A-Tan Old-Timer* (n.c.: n.p., ca. 1938); *Radio Station WSAZ*, p. 18.

16. *Charleston Daily-Mail*, Oct. 16, 1937; *Souvenir Program of Larry Sunbrock's Official West Virginia Championship Contests for 1937* (in Shortridge collection; copy in author's collection).

17. Walter LeRoy Moore, personal interview, Wheeling, W. Va., Oct. 12, 1980; Clarence C. Clere interview, July 21, 1981.

18. Clarence C. Clere interview, July 21, 1981; Alton Delmore, *Truth Is Stranger Than Publicity* (Nashville: Country Music Foundation Press, 1977), pp. 152-55.

19. Delmore, *Truth Is Stranger*, pp. 152-55; Clarence C. Clere interview, July 21, 1981.

20. *Radio Station WSAZ*, pp. 18-20.

21. *Souvenir Program of the Old Farm Hour Roadshow*, East Bank High School, June 15 [1940] (in Clere collection; copy in author's collection).

22. "WMMN," *WVR* 23, no. 2 (Nov. 1945):21; N.L. Royster, comp. and ed., *WMMN Family Album—1941* (Fairmont: Storer Broadcasting Co., 1941), pp. 13, 31; French Mitchell, personal interview, Buffalo, W. Va., July 15, 1981.

23. Gentry, *History and Encyclopedia*, p. 593; D. "Hoss" Williams, letter to Thomas Screven, Jan. 25, 1979 (copy in author's collection); *Fairmont City Directory, 1933*, p. 359; Charles Satterfield, personal interviews, Fairmont, W. Va., Sept. 1, 1981, Aug. 20, 1982.

24. *Memory Album of Al Hendershot's Dixie Ramblers* (Huntington: Poster Print Co., 1948).

25. Starcher, "The Story of My Life, Part Two," p. 4; *Fairmont Times*, Dec. 31, 1935; Program Log, Radio Station WMMN, Fairmont, W. Va., week of May 31, 1936. Three volumes of these logs spanning the period May 31, 1936, to June 21, 1941, are in the private collection of Bill Jaker, Morgantown, W. Va. Subsequent time and date references for specific programs at WMMN through this time span come from these logs.

26. Charles Satterfield interview, Sept. 1, 1981; Mrs. Frank Dudgeon, telephone interview, Cleveland, Ohio, Nov. 30, 1981.

27. Blaine Smith, personal interview, Wheeling, W. Va., Oct. 7, 1979; Artie and Thelma Mayse (widows of Budge and Fudge), personal interviews, Clarksburg, W. Va., June 5, 1980; Royster, *WMMN Family Album—1941*, p. 27.

28. French Mitchell interview, July 15, 1981; Buddy Starcher interview, May 14, 1978; Andrew Smik, Jr. (Doc Williams) personal interview, Wheeling, W. Va., July 6, 1982; Royster, *WMMN Family Album—1941*, p. 22; data in Cowboy Loye File in John Edwards Memorial Foundation, Los Angeles, Ca.

29. Ray R. Myers, personal interview, Wheeling, W. Va., Oct. 7, 1979; *Ray R. Myers, World's Famous Armless Musician: His Life Story as Told in Words and Pictures* (n.c.: n.p., ca. 1941).

30. Gentry, *History and Encyclopedia*, pp. 560-61; Wetzel County, W. Va., Delayed Birth Records 1, sec. H; John Graham, personal interview, Clarksburg, W. Va., June 5, 1980; Earl Northrup interview with William Shaver, Oakland, Md., May 21, 1982 (in author's collection). Transcriptions of two Radio Dot programs from Nov. 1937 are in the Country Music Foundation Library, Nashville, Tenn. (copies in author's collection).

31. John Graham interview, June 5, 1980; *Fairmont Times*, June 5, 1939; *NHN* (Dec. 1945), p. 5.

32. Buddy Starcher interview, May 14, 1978; Buddy E. Starcher, "The Story of My Life, Part Three," in *Starcher's Buddies* (Mar., Apr., May 1945), pp. 3, 6.

33. Royster, *WMMN Family Album—1941*, p. 20.

34. Ibid., pp. 14-15, 29; Charles Keaton interview, Aug. 7, 1981. A transcription of one and a half hours of the "Sagebrush Roundup" from ca. Oct. 28, 1939, is in the Country Music Foundation Library (copy in author's collection).

35. Daily Program Sheet, WMMN (Bill Jaker Collection, Morgantown, W. Va., copy in author's collection). This particular sheet is somewhat more useful than the traffic log, which has some hillbilly shows concealed, the sponsor's product being the name of the program.

36. Jack Dunigan, personal interview, Wheeling, W. Va., Oct. 10, 1981; Nolan Porterfield, "A Conversation with Jack Dunigan," *JCM* 7, no. 2 (May 1978):102-10; *Songs of Mack Jeffers and His Fiddlin' Farmers* (n.c.: n.p., 1940); Royster, *WMMN Family Album—1941*, pp. 24-25.

37. John Graham interview, June 5, 1980; Artie and Thelma Mayse interview, June 5, 1980; Arthur Gabbard, telephone interview, Annville, Ky., Nov. 10, 1981.

38. Starcher, "Story of My Life, Part Three," pp. 3, 6; Walter LeRoy Moore interview, Oct. 12, 1980.

39. "WHIS," *WVR* 23, no. 2 (Nov. 1945):24-25; Douglas Kirke Gordon and Roy Burke, III, "Gordon Jennings: Country Music in Bluefield," *JCM* 9, no. 1 (1981):87-93; *Radio Bi-Tone News*, ca. 1937; Gentry, *History and Encyclopedia*, p. 454.

40. Bob Sayers, "Black Mountain Odyssey: Leslie Keith," *BU* 11, no. 6 (Dec. 1976):13-17; Ray Cline, personal interview, Prestonsburg, Ky., July 10, 1982.

41. Ray Cline interview, July 10, 1982; James (Carson) Roberts, personal interview, Lexington, Ky., Apr. 29, 1979.

42. *Radio Bi-Tone News*, ca. 1937; Molly O'Day and Lynn Davis, personal interview, Huntington, W. Va., May 18, 1974; Ezra Cline, personal interview, Gilbert, W. Va., Feb. 10, 1974.

43. Walter LeRoy Moore interview, Oct. 12, 1980; *Bluefield Daily Telegraph*, Nov. 19, 1939.

44. *Bluefield Daily Telegraph*, Nov. 19, 1939; Walter LeRoy Moore interview, Oct. 12, 1980.

45. *Bluefield Daily Telegraph*, Mar. 30, Oct. 19, 1941; Ray Cline interview, July 10, 1982.

46. Wayne W. Daniel, "Roots of Bluegrass: The Holden Brothers," *BU* 16, no. 5 (Nov. 1981):24-29.

47. Walter LeRoy Moore interview, Oct. 12, 1980; *Bluefield Daily Telegraph*, Sept. 15, 1941; Bob Roseberry, *Life Story of Smiling Dale Roseberry* (n.c.: n.p., ca. 1943), pp. 3-5.

48. Molly O'Day and Lynn Davis interview, May 18, 1974; *Bluefield Daily Telegraph*, Jan. 23, 1942.

49. Roseberry, *Life Story*, pp. 3-4; John Morris, taped interview with Cecil "Skeets" Williamson, Brighton, Mich., May 27, 1974 (copy in author's collection); *Old Fashioned Songs as Sung by the Buskirk Family* (Parkersburg: Scholl Printing Co., 1939), pp. 5, 7; Wood County Marriages, 24:127; Wood County Births, 3: 25-26; vol. 4: 24.

50. *NHN* (July 1945), p. 2; (Jan.-Feb. 1948), p. 2; Wood County Births, vol. 3:42; *Parkersburg Sentinel*, Nov. 29, 1968, p. 13.

51. *Radio Station WSAZ*, p. 30.

52. Ibid., pp. 40-41; Charles K. Wolfe and Carl Fleischhauer, "Foggy Valley: The Story of Ellis Hall," *DB* 13, no. 2 (June 1, 1979):21.

53. John J. Bailes, taped autobiography, Swainsboro, Ga., Aug. 18, 1974 (in author's collection); Walter Bailes letter, Dec. 13, 1976; George Krise, personal interview, Akron, Ohio, Aug. 24, 1974; Molly O'Day and Lynn Davis interview, May 18, 1974; Rex and Eleanor Parker, personal interview, Lake Stephens, W. Va., June 22, 1975.

54. John J. Bailes tape, Aug. 18, 1974; Don Dean taped interview with Mel Steele, Syracuse, Ohio, ca. 1968 (copy in author's collection); James C. Dickens, taped personal interview, Brentwood, Tenn., March 4, 1983.

55. John J. Bailes tape, Aug. 18, 1974; John Morris with Cecil "Skeets" Williamson, May 27, 1974; Clarence C. Clere interview, July 21, 1981; Kyle O. Bailes, telephone interview, Birmingham, Ala., ca. Dec. 1975.

56. Jane Chambers Tyler, personal interview, Fairmont, W. Va., Aug. 31, 1981.

57. Quoted by Jim Comstock in *West Virginia Songbag* (Richwood, W. Va.: Jim Comstock, 1974), p. 525.

58. *Bluefield Daily Telegraph*, Apr. 18, Apr. 21, 1937.

5. Stay Tuned: Radio after 1942

1. John J. Bailes tape; *Favorite Hill-Billy and Mountain Ballads as Sung by the Bailes Brothers* (Huntington: Poster Printing Co., 1944), p. 2.

2. Charles K. Wolfe, "Fiddler's Dream: The Arthur Smith Story," *DB* 11, no. 4 (Dec. 1, 1977):48-49; *Songs from the Hills of Tennessee as Composed and Sung by Arthur Smith* (Huntington: Poster Printing Co., 1943).

3. *WSAZ, Radio at War* (Huntington: n.p., ca. 1944), p. 19; *NHN* (July 1945), p. 2; (Aug. 1945), p. 5.

4. *NHN* (June 1946), p. 1; (May-June 1947), p. 31.

5. Clarence C. Clere, personal interview, Hurricane, W. Va., July 21, 1981; Margie Shannon, personal interview, Huntington, W. Va., July 22, 1981.

6. *NHN* (Sept.-Oct. 1949), pp. 18-19.

7. Jimmie Skinner, personal interview, Blue Creek, Ohio, Oct. 11, 1975.

8. Ray Anderson, personal interview, Richmond Dale, Ohio, Jan. 2, 1970.

9. *NHN* (July 1946), pp. 12-13; (Nov.-Dec. 1947), p. 3; (Jan.-Feb. 1948), pp. 2, 8.

10. Ibid. (May-June 1948), p. 2; *Huntington Herald-Dispatch*, Mar. 1, 1948; *CSR* (Dec. 1950), p. 33; Margie Shannon, telephone interview, Huntington, W. Va., Aug. 10, 1982.

11. Milton Patterson, telephone interview, Harriman, Tenn., Dec. 6, 1981; Kenneth Caplinger, telephone interview, Davis, W. Va., Dec. 15, 1977; *Charleston Daily Mail*, Nov. 20, 1950; July 8, 1957; *Charleston Gazette*, July 8, 1957.

12. *MBPR* (Sept. 1945), p. 16; *Charleston Daily Mail*, Jan. 24, 1957; Thelma Welling, telephone interview, Burbank, Cal., Aug. 29, 1981.

13. Walter LeRoy Moore, personal interview, Wheeling, W. Va., Oct. 12, 1980; Daniel Pennel, personal interview, Fisher, W. Va., Aug. 15, 1981; Ernest Ferguson, personal interview, Beanblossom, Ind., June 20, 1982; Sears, *Jim and Jesse*, pp. 30-33; A.C. Dunkleberger, *Queen of Country Music: The Life Story of Kitty Wells* (Nashville: Ambrose Printing Co., 1977), pp. 29-37.

14. *CSR* (July-Aug. 1949), p. 33; (Dec. 1950), p. 33; (July 1954), p. 45; Clarence C. Clere, telephone interview, South Charleston, W. Va., Aug. 3, 1982.

15. *MBPR* (Sept. 1944), p. 17; (Mar. 1946), p. 14.

16. Ibid. (Sept. 1944), p. 17; French Mitchell, personal interview, Buffalo, W. Va., July 15, 1981.

17. *MBPR* (Sept. 1944), p. 17.

18. Walter LeRoy Moore interview, Oct. 12, 1980; Cogswell, "We Made Our Name in the Days of Radio," pp. 70-72.

19. *Fairmont Times*, Jan. 3, 1946; *MBPR* (Mar. 1946), pp. 24-25, 34.

20. *MBPR* (Dec. 1945), pp. 23, 33; Earl Northrup interview with William Shaver, Oakland, Md., May 21, 1982 (in author's collection); Ruth Stanford, telephone interview, Mt. Savage, Md., June 6, 1982.

21. Ruth Stanford interview, June 6, 1982; *WMMN Family Album, 1948 Edition* (Fairmont: Storer Broadcasting Co., 1948), pp. 8-9; *WMSG Family Album* (Oakland, Md.: Oakland Radio Station Corp., 1966), pp. 7-9; *Hank the Cowhand and the Foggy Mountain Boys, Folio No. 1* (Davis, W. Va.: Musical Melody Publishers, 1947).

22. *Fairmont Times*, Jan. 1, 1947; Hancock County Birth Records, 2:4; *Old Brother Charlie and Daisy Mae* (Tampa: n.p., 1949); *MBPR* (Nov. 1946), p. 20; *ME* (Mar. 1947), p. 2.

23. *ME* (Mar. 1947), p. 14; *WMMN Family Album, 1948*, pp. 8-10; *MBPR* (Nov. 1946), p. 23.

24. *MBPR* (Sept. 1946), pp. 14-15; *Fairmont Times*, Oct. 1, 1948; Apr. 2, 1951; Norma Clarke, personal interview, Newcomerstown, Ohio, Sept. 3, 1981; John Bava, telephone interview, Davis, W. Va., June 6, 1982.

25. Wolfe and Fleischhauer, "Foggy Valley."

26. *Fairmont Times*, July 1, 1947; March 31, 1949; July 1, 1949; Jan. 5, 1952; May 1, 1954; Sept. 1, 1955; *CSR* (Dec. 1950); *West Virginia Mountain Ballads and Sacred Songs* (Fairmont: John Bava's Music, 1955), inside front cover; John Bava, personal interview, Davis, W. Va., Aug. 14, 1981.

27. Marion County Death Records, 12:93; Marion County Marriage Records, 35:110; Rick Toothman, letter to author, Aug. 29, 1978.

28. Ezra Cline, personal interview, Gilbert, W. Va., Feb. 10, 1974; Melvin Goins, personal interview, Prestonsburg, Ky., Feb. 3, 1974; Peter V. Kuykendall interview with Melvin Goins, Glasgow, Del., Sept. 2, 1973 (tape in author's collection). See also Neil Rosenberg, "The Osborne Brothers, Part One," *BU* 6, no. 3 (Sept. 1971):5-10; Russ Cheatham, "Charlie and Lee Cline," *BU* 14, no. 8 (Feb. 1980):18-22.

29. Rex and Eleanor Parker, personal interview, Lake Stephens, W. Va., June 22, 1975; Garland Hess, personal interview, Charleston, W. Va., Aug. 8, 1982.

30. Garland Hess interview, Aug. 8, 1982; William Edwards, personal interview, Salem, Ohio, June 1, 1974; *NHN* (Dec. 1945), p. 5; (Jan. 1946), p. 6; (Apr. 1946), p. 25; *Bluefield Daily Telegraph*, Oct. 17, 1946; May 17, 1947; Bud Kurtz, telephone interview, Lakeland, Fla., Oct. 15, 1982.

31. Ralph Meadows, personal interview, Point Pleasant, W. Va., Feb. 3, 1978; *CSR* (Dec. 1950), p. 33; *NHN* (July 1945), p. 12; *Bluefield Daily Telegraph*, Mar. 19, 1946; anecdote told by Melvin Goins on stage at Scioto Furnace, Ohio, Dec. 4, 1976. For a sketch of the Korn Kobblers see *MBPR* (Dec. 1945), pp. 3-7.

32. *Bluefield Daily Telegraph*, Mar. 16, 1948; Mar. 1, 1949; *CSR* (June 1956), p. 29; Gordon and Burke, "Gordon Jennings."

33. Everett Lilly, personal interview, Clear Creek, W. Va., Dec. 26, 1973; Molly O'Day and Lynn Davis, personal interview, Huntington, W. Va., May 18, 1974; George Krise, personal interview, Akron, Ohio, Aug. 24, 1974; *CSR* (July-Aug. 1949), p. 33.

34. *CSR* (July-Aug. 1949), p. 33; Gentry, *History and Encyclopedia*, p. 552.

35. *The Billboard 1944 Music Year Book* (New York: Billboard Magazine, 1944), p. 360; John J. Bailes tape, Aug. 18, 1974.

36. *CSR* (Dec. 1949), p. 33; John Bava interview, Aug. 14, 1981.

37. *CSR* (Feb. 1950), p. 33; *The Speedy Krise Song and Picture Folder* (n.c.: n.p.,

ca. 1955); George Krise interview, Aug. 24, 1974; Dewey Duvall interview with Bill Carpenter, Webster Springs, W. Va., June 26, 1982 (tape copy in author's collection); John Morris, liner notes for *Bill Carpenter: Meeting in the Air*, Jessup LP MB 105, ca. 1971.

38. Perry and Ruby Scott, letter to author, June 7, 1982; Cecil Surratt, telephone interview, Bluewell, W. Va., Aug. 2, 1982; *CSR* (June 1950), p. 33; Ruby Scott, personal interview, North Wilkesboro, N.C., Aug. 5, 1983.

39. *MBPR* (Dec. 1941), pp. 14-15; Richard Boring, personal interview, Scioto Furnace, Ohio, May 15, 1982; *CSR* (July-Aug. 1949), p. 33.

40. Buddy Starcher, personal interview, Craigsville, W. Va., May 14, 1978; John Graham, personal interview, Clarksburg, W. Va., June 5, 1980; Artie and Thelma Mayse (widows of Budge and Fudge), personal interview, Clarksburg, W. Va., June 5, 1980; Earl Northup interview with Shaver, May 21, 1982; *Fairmont Times*, March 30, 1948; July 1, 1948; July 3, 1950; *CMR* (Dec. 1951), p. 6.

41. Dewey Duvall interview with Carpenter, June 26, 1982; Morris, liner notes for *Bill Carpenter*; Michael Kline, "Woody Simmons: Recollections of a Randolph County Fiddler," *GS* 5, no. 3 (July-Sept. 1979):5-12, 61-68.

42. John Bava interview, Aug. 14, 1981. See also John Bava, *My Life Story* (Davis, W. Va.: John Bava's Music, n.d.).

43. *CSR* (July 1954), p. 45.

44. John Newbraugh, letter to author, Mar. 29, 1982. Mr. Newbraugh conducted interviews with Elwood Liggett and other musicians of note from the eastern panhandle.

45. *NHN* (Apr. 1946), p. 23; Ned Guthrie, letter to author, ca. Oct. 1979.

46. Dale Brooks, telephone interview, St. Pauls, N.C., Nov. 25, 1981.

47. *Broadcasting-Cable Yearbook, 1981* (Tenafly, N.J.: Bonneville Broadcast Consultants, 1981), pp. C255-58.

6. Country Comes to Television

1. Stephen Buell, "The History and Development of WSAZ-TV Channel 3, Huntington, West Virginia," Ph.D. diss., Ohio State Univ., 1962, pp. 5-6.

2. *NHN* (Mar.-Apr. 1950), p. 2; Clarence C. Clere, telephone interview, Charleston, W. Va., Aug. 3, 1982.

3. *Huntington Herald-Advertiser*, Aug. 24, 1953, p. 30; *CWJ* (Jan. 1957), p. 68; Charles Keaton, taped interview, Argillite, Ky., Aug. 7, 1981 (in author's collection).

4. Ralph Stanley, personal interview, Greenwich, Ohio, Aug. 14, 1982; Frank Godbey, "Pee Wee Lambert," *BU* 13, no. 7 (Jan. 1979):14-15; Wayne Erbsen, "Lester Woodie: Coming up the Hard Road," *BU* 14, no. 9 (Mar. 1980):42-48.

5. Stanley O'Dell, telephone interview, Buckhannon, W. Va., Aug. 18, 1982; Buell, "History of WSAZ-TV," pp. 77-79; *Bluefield Daily Telegraph*, Jan. 3, 1955.

6. Buell, "History of WSAZ-TV," pp. 83-84; Charles Keaton interview, Aug. 7, 1981; Margie Shannon, personal interview, Huntington, W. Va., July 22, 1981.

7. The best available surveys of the careers of Flatt and Scruggs are: Neil V. Roseberg, "Lester Flatt and Earl Scruggs," in Bill C. Malone and Judith McCulloh, eds., *Stars of Country Music* (Urbana: Univ. of Illinois Press, 1975), pp. 255-73; Bob Artis, *Bluegrass* (New York: Hawthorn Books, 1975), pp. 42-48. I have also drawn on personal recollections of the program.

8. Frank (Hylo) Brown, personal interview, Jackson, Ohio, Feb. 11, 1974; *Hylo Brown and the Timberliners* (Madison, Tenn.: n.p., 1958).

9. Buell, "History of WSAZ-TV," pp. 77-79; Ezra Cline, personal interview, Gilbert, W. Va., Feb. 10, 1974.

10. Roy Crockett, personal interview, Dickson, W. Va., June 20, 1981; Paul Mullins, personal interview, Lake Stephens, W. Va., June 22, 1975; Buddy Starcher, personal interviews, Craigsville, W. Va., May 14, 1978, and Charleston, W. Va., Aug. 8, 1982. See also Frank and Marty Godbey, "Paul Mullins: Musician, Disc Jockey, and Bluegrass influence," *BU* 10, no. 6 (Dec. 1975):23-24.

11. Clarence C. Clere interview, Aug. 3, 1982; *Charleston Daily Mail*, Apr. 1, 1982.

12. Buddy Starcher interview, May 14, 1978.

13. George and Maxine Jeffers, personal interview, Charleston, W. Va., Aug. 8, 1982; *T.V. Guide* (West Virginia edition), Apr. 21, 1973, p. A66; Lori Lee Bowles, personal interview, Charleston, W. Va., Aug. 14, 1983.

14. Margie Shannon, telephone interview, Huntington, W. Va., Aug. 10, 1982; *Athens Messenger* (Ohio), July 20, July 27, 1969.

15. Cecil W. Surratt, telephone interview, Bluewell, W. Va., Aug. 2, 1982; *Bluefield Daily Telegraph*, Mar. 1, 1956; Mar. 1, 1960.

16. Cecil W. Surratt interview, Aug. 2, 1982.

17. Hubert and Margaret Moore (Bonnie Lou and Buster), personal interviews, Pigeon Forge, Tenn., Mar. 1, 1980; Aug. 23, 1982.

18. Ibid., Mar. 3, 1956; March 1, 1963; Cecil W. Surratt interview, Aug. 2, 1982. See also Gordon and Burke, "Gordon Jennings."

19. Rex and Eleanor Parker, personal interview, Lake Stephens, W. Va., June 22, 1975; *T.V. Guide* (West Virginia edition), Mar. 25, 1978, p. A90.

20. *T.V. Guide*, Mar. 25, 1978, p. A90; Bill Duncan and Don Sowards, personal interview, Little Hocking, Ohio, June 11, 1977; Ralph Meadows, personal interview, Point Pleasant, W. Va., Feb. 3, 1978; Everett Lilly, personal interview, Clear Creek, W. Va., Dec. 26, 1973; Lowell Varney, personal interview, Prestonsburg, Ky., July 10, 1982; *Bluefield Daily Telegraph*, Mar. 3, 1960.

21. Carl Lipps, personal interviews, Kenova, W. Va., Feb. 28, 1981, and Vienna, W. Va., Sept. 1, 1982. Mr. Lipps possesses an excellent collection of documents and photographs to supplement his recollections of the "Big Red Jubilee." Also Wilbert C. Buskirk, personal interview, Parkersburg, W. Va., Sept. 1, 1982.

22. Andrew Smik, Jr. (Doc Williams), personal interview, Wheeling, W. Va., Dec. 29, 1981; see also Gentry, *History and Encyclopedia*, pp. 384, 501, 509, 587.

23. Dale Brooks, telephone interview, St. Pauls, N.C., Nov. 25, 1981; *WBOY-TV The Big Boy Frolics: Songs to Remember* (Davis, W. Va.: John Bava, 1958).

24. Richard Tennent, telephone interview, Weston, W. Va., Aug. 17, 1982. See also *John and Lucy Bava: Songs for Times Like These* (Davis, W. Va.: John Bava, 1962); *Joe Barker: Sacred Songs, Mountain Ballads* (Davis, W. Va.: John Bava, ca. 1961).

25. Stanley O'Dell interview, Aug. 18, 1982.

26. Dean Sturm, personal interview, Huntington, W. Va., Aug. 8, 1981; Bill Jaker, personal interviews, Morgantown, W. Va., June 5, 1980; and Aug. 20, 1982.

27. Blaine Smith, personal interview, Wheeling, W. Va., Oct. 7, 1979; Buddy Starcher interview, May 14, 1978; Don Reno, *The Musical History of Don Reno* (Hyattsville, Md.: Copy-Kate, 1976), pp. 7-8.

28. Herman Yarbrough, personal interview, Charleston, W. Va., Aug. 8, 1982.

7. The Folk Revival and the Rise of Bluegrass

1. George Korson, ed., *Songs and Ballads of the Bituminous Miners from the Archive of Folk Song* (Washington, D.C.: Library of Congress, 1965).

2. Comstock, *West Virginia Songbag*, pp. 234-35.

3. Ibid.; Program of the 1982 West Virginia Folk Festival. Some of my impressions of this festival come from personal observations.

4. For a general overview see R. Serge Denisoff, *Great Day Coming: Folk Music and the American Left* (Urbana: Univ. of Illinois Press, 1971).

5. Kenneth Davidson, personal interview, Charleston, W. Va., June 2, 1967, and numerous subsequent meetings; Sandra Freed, "Folk Artist Gaining Fame" (unidentified news feature, ca. 1966, in author's collection).

6. Comstock, *West Virginia Songbag*, pp. 544-45.

7. Ibid., pp. 549-50; Jennie Wilson and Roger Bryant, personal interviews, Rio Grande, Ohio, Oct. 11, 1980.

8. Carl Fleischhauer and Alan Jabbour, eds., *The Hammons Family: A Study of a West Virginia Family's Traditions* (Washington, D.C.: Library of Congress, 1973); Edward Morris, "Elmer Bird," *BU* 14, no. 10 (Apr. 1980):63; Peggy Jarvis and Dick Kimmel, "Andrew F. Boarman: The Banjo Man from Berkeley County," *GS* 5, no. 1 (Jan.-Mar. 1979):50-57; John A. Cuthbert, "A Musicological Look at John Johnson's Fiddling," *GS* 7, no. 4 (Winter 1981):16-24. See also "West Virginia String Bands," *GS* 4, no. 4 (Oct.-Dec. 1978):12, 64-66.

9. John A. Cuthbert, ed., *West Virginia Folk Music: A Descriptive Guide to Field Recordings in the West Virginia and Regional History Collection* (Morgantown: West Virginia Univ. Press, 1982), pp. 92-93. See also Michael E. Bush, *Folk Songs of Central West Virginia*, 6 vols. (Ravenswood, W. Va.: Custom Printing Co., 1969-1975); Patrick Gainer, *Folk Songs from the West Virginia Hills* (Grantsville, W. Va.: Seneca Books, 1975).

10. Ken Sullivan, "Don West: Poet and Preacher," *GS* 5, no. 4 (Oct.-Dec. 1979):47-56; *GS* 6, no. 3 (June-Sept. 1980): 3; Donna Maynard, "Broomsage Musicians: The Morris Brothers," *BU* 11, no. 3 (Sept. 1976):17-21.

11. "Vandalia Gathering," *GS* 4, nos. 2-3 (Apr.-Sept. 1978): 2-5; "Vandalia Gathering," *GS* 5, no. 2 (Apr.-June 1979):7-10. Joe Wilson of the National Council for the Traditional Arts and I organized and emceed this program.

12. "West Virginia String Bands," pp. 64-66; Paul Reisler, et al., personal interviews, Rio Grande, Ohio, Oct. 17, 1981.

13. For brief overviews of the development of bluegrass, see Bob Artis, *Bluegrass* (New York: Hawthorn Books, 1975), pp. 3-29; Ralph Rinzler, "Bill Monroe," in Malone and McCulloh, *Stars of Country Music*, pp. 202-21.

14. Everett Lilly, personal interview, Clear Creek, Va., Dec. 26, 1973; Mac Martin, "Memories of Blue Grass on WWVA," *Muleskinner News* (Aug. 1972), pp. 12-13, 24-25.

15. Bill Duncan and Don Sowards, personal interview, Little Hocking, Ohio, June 11, 1977; Roy Crockett, personal interview, Dickson, W. Va., June 20, 1981.

16. *Muleskinner Newsletter* (Aug. 1971), p. 4; *BU* 6, no. 2 (Aug. 1971):17, 24; *Bluegrass '76* (Broad Run, Va.: Bluegrass Unlimited, 1976), pp. 41-42.

17. *Bluegrass '76*, p. 42; John Cox, personal interview, Walker, W. Va., Aug. 29, 1982. I have attended most of the Cox's Field Summer events.

18. *BU* 16, no. 10 (Apr. 1982):57-58; Cecil Surratt, telephone interview, Bluewell, W. Va., Aug. 2, 1982.

19. Bill Duncan and Don Sowards interviews, June 11, 1977; Lowell Varney and Landon Messer, personal interviews, Prestonsburg, Ky., July 10, 1982; H. Lloyd Whittaker, "Cliff Waldron and the New Shades of Grass," *BU* 5, no. 10 (Apr. 1971): 5; Everett Lilly interview, Dec. 26, 1973; Glenn Roberts, Jr., "The Marshall Family," *BU* 11, no. 12 (June 1977):16-24.

20. Walter V. Saunders, "Benny and Vallie Cain," *BU* 7, no. 11 (May 1972): 7-12; Don Rhodes, "Band on the Run—The Johnson Mountain Boys," *BU* 16, no. 6 (Dec. 1981):12-17; Mia Boynton, "Whetstone Run: Past and Present," *BU* 13, no. 1 (July 1978): 52-53.

21. Godbey, "Pee Wee Lambert"; Russ Cheatham, "Charlie and Lee Cline," *BU* 14, no. 8 (Feb. 1980): 18-22; Jan Campbell, "Jerry Douglas: They Call Him Flux," *BU* 16, no. 5 (Nov. 1981): 31-32; Ralph Meadows, personal interview, Point Pleasant, W. Va., Feb. 3, 1978; Donna and Patsy Stoneman, personal interviews, Milton, W. Va., Sept. 4, 1982.

22. Clarence C. Clere, personal interview, Hurricane, W. Va., July 21, 1981; and telephone interview, Charleston, W. Va., Aug. 3, 1982.

8. West Virginia and the National Country Scene

1. Homer, Kyle, John, and Walter Bailes and Ernest Ferguson, personal interviews, Swainsboro, Ga., Sept. 4-5, 1977; John J. Bailes, taped autobiography, Swainsboro, Ga., Aug. 18, 1974 (in author's collection); "The Bailes Brothers and Their West Virginia Home Folks," *NHN* (Jan.-Feb. 1948), p. 7; George D. Hay, *A Story of the Grand Ole Opry* (Nashville: Radio Station WSM, 1945), p. 62.

2. Susan Scott, "Little Jimmy Sang Way out of Coalfields," *Tennesseean* (Nashville), Nov. 26, 1973, p. 26. Ernest E. "Jimmy" Walker, personal interview, Point Pleasant, W. Va., Nov. 17, 1982.

3. Red O'Donnell, "Opry Hit the Hardest by Fatal Air Crash," *Nashville Banner*, Mar. 6, 1963, p. 1; *People's Defender* (West Union, Ohio), Mar. 7, 1963, p. 1.

4. Laura Eipper, "Wreck Kills Opry Star Red Sovine," *Tennesseean* (Nashville), Apr. 5, 1980, pp. 1, 6; "Red Sovine an MGM Star" (undated promo sheet in Country Music Foundation files, Nashville, Tenn.); John J. Bailes tape, Aug. 18, 1974; Woodrow Sovine, personal interview, McArthur, Ohio, July 4, 1973; Douglas B. Greene, taped interview with Woodrow "Red" Sovine, Nashville, Tenn., Nov. 3, 1975 (in Oral History Collection of Country Music Foundation Library).

5. Clarence C. Clere, personal interview, Hurricane, W. Va., July 21, 1981; Ernest E. Walker interview, Nov. 17, 1982; Marion R. Watson, "The Man with a Million Friends," *MBPR* (Feb.-Mar. 1947), pp. 5-9; Lynn Davis and Molly O'Day, personal interview, Huntington, W. Va., May 18, 1974.

6. Clarence C. Clere, personal interview, Hurricane, W. Va., June 11, 1982; Cecil Hartman, personal interview, Burlington, W. Va., Aug. 14, 1981; Walden Whytsell, personal interviews, Rio Grande, Ohio, Oct. 11, 1980; Oct. 8, 1982; Cecil Campbell, letter to author, Jan. 19, 1982.

7. Gentry, *History and Encyclopedia*, p. 431; see also Down Home Records, Country Catalog, 1982.

8. Daniel, "Wilma Lee Cooper," pp. 12-17.

9. John Grissim, *Country Music: White Man's Blues* (New York: Paperback Library, 1970), pp. 169-72; "Penny DeHaven," *Country Music World* (March-Apr. 1973), pp. 36-37; *Baltimore Sun*, Mar. 13, 1978; *Morgan Messenger* (Berkeley Springs, W. Va.), June 2, 1982; J.R. Monaghan, *Penny* (Brentwood, Tenn.: Morning Star Public Relations, 1982).

10. Larry Rhodes, "Charlie McCoy: Into Mountain Music," *BU* 15, no. 7 (Jan. 1981):15-16; Fred Dellar and Roy Thompson, *The Illustrated Encyclopedia of Country Music* (New York: Harmony Books, 1977), pp. 145-46; "Charlie McCoy," *Country Song Roundup Yearbook, 1983* (Derby, Conn.: Charlton Publications, 1983), pp. 53-55;

Don Rhodes, *Down Country Roads with Ramblin' Rhodes* (Hartwell, Ga.: North American Publications, 1982), pp. 39-40.

11. Mayfred Nutter, personal interview, Barnesville, Ohio, Sept. 23, 1982.

12. *Grand Ole Opry History-Picture Book* (Nashville: WSM, 1968), p. 25; *Grit*, Nov. 27, 1977; Laura Eipper, "Opry Quartet Welcomes Brand New Fourth Guy," *Tennesseean* (Nashville), May 30, 1980, p. 48; Walter Carter, "Fans and Auto Workers Push Four Guys Record," *Tennesseean* (Nashville), Jan. 22, 1982, p. 44.

13. Alan Cackett, "Mel Street," *Country Music People* (June 1975), p. 10; Stacy Harris, "Mel Street," *Inside Country Music* (Nov. 1982), pp. 58-59.

14. "Sandy Rucker Bio" (promotional sheet issued by Monument Records, Dec. 13, 1972, in Country Music Foundation files, Nashville, Tenn.); *Morgan Messenger* (Berkeley Springs, W. Va.), Aug. 4, 1982; *Jamboree in the Hills '81* (n.c.: n.p., 1981), p. 7.

15. Theodore H. White, *The Making of the President, 1960* (New York: Pocket Books, 1961), pp. 135-36; Comstock, *West Virginia Songbag*, pp. 551-52.

16. Comstock, *West Virginia Songbag*, p. 502; Red Foley, liner notes for Cecil Null, *Instrumental Country Hymns*, Decca DL 4934.

17. Harrell Bailey, *A History of the Liberty Mountaineers* (St. Albans, W. Va.: Harless Printing Co., 1979), pp. 2-3.

18. Daniel Pennel, personal interview, Fisher, W. Va., Aug. 15, 1981; WELD Country 69, "Daily Program Schedule" (brochure in author's collection).

19. John S. Newbraugh, letter to author, Mar. 2, Mar. 29, 1982.

20. Ibid., May 12, 1982.

21. Theresa Gregory, letter to author, Sept. 8, 1982; *Billboard*, May 9, 1982, p. 48; "Terry Gregory" (promotional sheet issued by Gallico Productions in author's collection); Don Rhodes, "Terry Gregory Bubbles with Optimism," *Augusta Chronicle* (Georgia), Nov. 15, 1981; Colette Bouchez, "Terry Gregory: I Believe," *Boston Herald American* (Celebrity Section), Apr. 18, 1982, p. 6; *Morgan Messenger* (Berkeley Springs, W. Va.), Apr. 14, 1982, p. 15.

22. *Martinsburg Journal*, Apr. 17, 1982; Charles K. Wolfe, "Fiddler in the Senate," *DB* 12, no. 4 (Dec. 1978):15-25; Roland Leiser, "Senator Robert C. Byrd: The Fiddling Politician," *Pickin'* (Sept. 1978), pp. 30-33.

9. Retrospect

1. Mary Jean Shurtz, *Favorite Radio Poems* (Woodsfield, Ohio: Monroe County Beacon, 1942); Mary Jean Shurtz and Chaw Mank, *Reminiscence and Other Poems* (Dexter, Mo.: Candor Press, 1947); Norma Clarke, personal interview, Newcomerstown, Ohio, Sept. 3, 1981.

Bibliographical Note

Since West Virginia country music and musicians are not the subjects of a great deal of readily available published material, and since the annotated citations are extensive, it seems that a formal bibliography would be somewhat redundant. I will therefore confine this section to a brief general discussion of source material. The reader who wishes more may examine the notes in detail.

Useful surveys of the state's historical development are Charles H. Ambler and Festus P. Sumner, *West Virginia, the Mountain State*, 2nd ed. (Englewood Cliffs, N.J.: Prentice-Hall, 1958); and John A. Williams, *West Virginia: A History* (New York: Norton, 1976). The early scholars who looked extensively at the Mountain State's folk music heritage included John Harrington Cox, *Folk Songs of the South* (Cambridge: Harvard Univ. Press, 1925); and Josiah Combs, *Folk-Songs du Midi des Etats-Unis* (Paris: Presses Universitaires de France, 1925); English edition, *Folk-Songs of the Southern United States* (University of Texas Press, 1967). Newer works are Patrick Gainer, *The West Virginia Centennial Book of One Hundred Songs, 1863-1963* (Morgantown: West Virginia Centennial Commission, 1963); *Folk Songs from the West Virginia Hills*, ed. Patrick Gainer (Grantsville, W. Va.: Seneca Books, ca. 1975); and Michael Bush, *Folk Songs of Central West Virginia*, 6 vols. (Ravenswood, W. Va.: Custom Printing, 1969ff). For a look at field recordings, see John A. Cuthbert, ed., *West Virginia Folk Music* (Morgantown: West Virginia Univ. Press, 1982). Two other song studies with considerable West Virginia content are Archie Green, *Only a Miner* (Urbana: Univ. of Illinois Press, 1972); and Norm Cohen, *Long Steel Rail: The Railroad in American Folksong* (Urbana: Univ. of Illinois Press, 1981).

The standard work on country music is Bill C. Malone, *Country Music U.S.A.* (Austin: Univ. of Texas Press, 1968); but Patrick Carr, ed., *The Illustrated History of Country Music* (Garden City, N.Y.: Doubleday, 1980) is also quite worthwhile, particularly the portions by Charles K. Wolfe. More popular in style but nonetheless worthy are Robert Shelton and Burt Goldblatt, *The Country Music Story* (Indianapolis: Bobbs-Merrill, 1966); and Douglas B. Green, *Country Roots* (New York: Hawthorn Books, 1975). Somewhat in a class of its own is the often perceptive, albeit sometimes sensationalist, Nick Tosches, *Country: The Biggest Music in America* (New York: Stein and Day, 1977). For bluegrass the best current treatment is Bob Artis, *Bluegrass* (New York: Hawthorn Books, 1975), although it may soon be supplanted by treatments by Bob Cantwell and Neil Rosenburg. As for country gospel, Lois S. Blackwell, *The Wings of the Dove: The Story of Gospel Music in America* (Norfolk, Va.: Donning, 1978) should shortly be supplanted by a multi-authored volume edited by Charles K. Wolfe. Jim Comstock, ed., *A West Virginia Songbag* (Richwood, W. Va.: Jim Comstock, 1974) is encyclopedic in approach but extremely uneven in quality. Charlie Poole's West Virginia associates are adequately treated in Kinney Rorrer, *Rambling Blues: The Life and Songs of Charlie Poole* (London: Old Time Music Books, 1982).

Since grassroots country music research is continually ongoing, the enthusiast needs to become familiar with periodicals. Especially important are *Bluegrass Unlimited, The Devil's Box, JEMF Quarterly, The Journal of Country Music*, and *Old Time Music*. Good pieces on West Virginia artists such as Doc Williams, Wilma Lee and Stoney Cooper, the Tweedy Brothers, Ellis Hall, and Jess Johnston have appeared in these journals, written by Barbara Kempf, Robert Cogswell, Charles K. Wolfe, Carl Fleischhauer, and Kinney Rorrer, respectively. In my own journal articles I have looked in detail at the careers of the Bailes Brothers, David Miller, the Lilly Brothers, and Buddy Starcher, among others. Material on contemporary artists can be found in *Country Music Magazine, Country Song Roundup*, and other such magazines frequently found on newstands, although they are more likely to contain articles of a "fanzine" nature than those listed above which are more research oriented. Valuable to researchers, although they are quite scarce and must be used with caution, are such defunct journals as *The Mountain Broadcast and Prairie Recorder* (1939-1947), *National Hillbilly News* (1945-1950), and *Musical Echoes* (ca. 1946-1948), all of which gave abundant attention to the West Virginia radio scene. Although not music-oriented, the West Virginia folklife journal *Goldenseal* has featured several articles on traditional and country music.

Radio station souvenir booklets and songbooks printed for artists vary in quality, but are on the whole useful although they are often hard to locate. The archive of the John Edwards Memorial Foundation, now at the University of North Carolina, Chapel Hill, has a good collection, and so too does the Country Music Foundation Library and Media Center, Nashville. Others are in the hands of private collectors. Wheeling's WWVA published booklets in 1936, 1946, 1950, 1951, 1953, 1954, 1955, 1965, 1973, and 1979 (and perhaps other years, too). The 1973 edition contains a popular history of the Jamboree by Virginia Alderman. Fairmont's WMMN had "Family Albums" in 1941 and 1948, and the West Virginia Network (WSAZ, WCHS, WPAR, WBLK) had one in 1940. Bluefield's WHIS apparently issued such publications although I lacked access to any copies. The *Bluefield Daily Telegraph*, however, had excellent coverage for the WHIS radio programs (due in part to their joint ownership), while such newspapers as the *Charleston Gazette, Charleston Daily Mail, Fairmont Times, Huntington Advertizer, Huntington Herald-Dispatch,* and *Wheeling Intelligencer* also had good local radio program listings for parts of the time period covered, although names of shows do not always reveal their nature.

Many former radio artists have retained quality photos, souvenirs, and documents pertaining to their careers and those of their contemporaries. Those whose collections proved helpful included the Bailes Brothers, John Bava, Clarence Clere, Lynn and Molly Davis, Charles Keaton, and Robert Shortridge. Bill Jaker of WNPB-TV Morgantown has a good collection of WMMN Fairmont memorabilia, including daily program logs for the 1936-1941 period. The Cliff Carlisle scrapbooks in the Country Music Foundation Library cover his West Virginia career. The Country Music Foundation also maintains a set of vertical files, most useful for data on artists of the last fifteen years. Newsclippings and a variety of promotional material comprise the bulk of their content.

Phonograph recordings and oral interviews must of necessity rank high among primary sources in a work of this nature. Recordings no longer available commercially can be difficult to obtain. The files of both the Country Music Foundation and the John Edwards Memorial Foundation as well as those of such private collectors as Joe Bussard, Norm Cohen, David Freeman, Pete Kuykendall, Frank Mare, John Morris, Robert Nobley, and Charles K. Wolfe supplemented my own efforts of the last fifteen years, as did those of artist-producers John Bava and Doc Williams.

Many of the oral interviews were taped. Especially notable ones included those of "Silver Yodelin' Bill" Jones on the early years of the WWVA Jamboree; Clarence "Slim" Clere, whose knowledge of country music in the Ashland, Huntington, and Charleston areas from the early 1930s (not to mention his experiences at WSB Atlanta,

1935-1938) is truly remarkable; Lee Moore, who touched base at every major West Virginia radio station; and Buddy Starcher, whose musical career and memory extend from pre-World War I square dances in isolated homesteads to the 1980s. From my initial interview with the late Bill Cox in his tiny shack on June 2, 1967, to a September 23, 1982, visit with Mayf Nutter in a Barnesville, Ohio, high school gym where the contemporary actor-vocalist described his spring tour of the People's Republic of China (we were sitting in total darkness due to a local power failure), all the interviews proved useful to the completion of the project.

Discographical Note

Since many of the recordings discussed in the text can no longer be purchased, only albums currently (or recently) available will be mentioned here. Among the early West Virginia artists, three have been subjects of featured albums: *Frank Hutchison: The Train That Carried My Girl from Town*, Rounder 1007; *The Kessinger Brothers*, County 536; and *Blind Alfred Reed: How Can a Poor Man Stand Such Times and Live?*, Rounder 1001. *The West Virginia Hills: Early Recordings from West Virginia*, Old Homestead CS 141, offers a sampling from the works of several pioneer figures including the McClung Brothers, David Miller, the Tweedy Brothers, Frank Welling, and John McGhee. *The North Carolina Ramblers*, Biograph 6005, spotlights Roy Harvey's contributions to a greater degree than the other fine reissues of this primarily Carolina-based group. A scattering of other West Virginia musicians appear on anthologies issued by Folkways, Old-Timey, Rounder, and especially County.

Several albums feature some of the best work of WWVA Jamboree figures who recorded extensively. Wilma Lee and Stoney Cooper may be heard to best advantage on *Early Recordings*, County CCS 103, which includes some of the best Columbia cuts from the 1949-1953 era, although some of their later efforts are still available. *Hawkshaw Hawkins: 16 Greatest Hits*, Starday SD 3013, is a less expertly edited sampling from King cuts of 1946-1953 and 1962, but manages to contain both "Sunny Side of the Mountain" and "Lonesome 7-7203." Lee Moore has seldom been adequately documented on disc but the import from Germany, *Wheeling's Coffee Drinking Night Hawk*, Cattle LP 44, probably is the best currently in print, while *Lee Moore Sings Radio Favorites*, Rural Rhythm 137, and *Everybody's Favorite*, Rural Rhythm 202, rank as easiest to obtain. Of several albums still in print by Doc Williams and his wife, *Doc Williams' Collector's Series No. 2*, Wheeling LPV 1542, *Chickie Williams Sings the Old Songs*, Wheeling WLP 4001, and *Doc 'n' Chickie Williams Together*, Wheeling WLP 2542, probably rank as most representative. A good anthology of Jamboree regulars from about 1970 is *WWVA Jamboree U.S.A.*, JUSA 101, which includes songs by such performers as Kenny Biggs, Jimmy Stephens, and Kenny Roberts. The German import *Skeeter Bonn: Star of the Wheeling Jamboree*, Castle CAS 8110, contains late 1950s recordings by one of the last Midwestern yodelers.

In the era since 1945, West Virginia artists who have had major impacts on the industry include the Bailes Brothers. Some of their work has been reissued as *Radio Favorites*, Old Homestead CS 109, which features duets by Johnnie and Walter from 1945 and 1947 sessions, while *The Bailes Brothers (Johnnie and Homer)*, Vols. I and II, Old Homestead CS 103 and CS 104, draw from 1949 radio shows at KWKH Shreveport, although about half of the second volume comes from 1947 recordings. Another good anthology, *The Four Bailes Brothers: 1947-1977*, Original OR 1001, includes material from both King and Loyal sessions, while *I've Got My One Way Ticket to the Sky*, Old Homestead OHS 70009, and *Reunion*, OHS 70023, contain newer sacred material, the latter featuring all four brothers and a sister.

Little Jimmy Dickens has had numerous albums over the years but of the three currently in print his *Greatest Hits*, Columbia LE 10106, has the most representative material. A similar statement can be made about *Red Sovine's 16 Greatest Hits*, Gusto SD 991. Unfortunately none of his earlier material from MGM or Decca is available except on the German import *Gone But Not Forgotten*, Castle CAS 8103. Two other imports, both from the Netherlands, *The "Cozy" Label*, White Label 8823, and *The "Island" Recordings*, White Label 8814, document the rise of rockabilly music in the Mountain State, sampling such performers as Keith Anderson, Dale Brooks, Bill Browning, and the later recordings of WMMN star Hank Stanford. Buddy Starcher's only in-print album is the German import *Country Love Songs*, Bear Family BFX 15017, which is from mid-1970s sessions but does include new versions of his better-known compositions and arrangements.

Numerous folk and bluegrass musicians from West Virginia have recorded but space permits only a sampling here. At least four albums from Clark Kessinger's later years remain in print, of which *The Legend of Clark Kessinger*, County 733, and *Sweet Bunch of Daisies*, County 747, are reissues from Kanawha and highest in quality. Among many other albums by West Virginia fiddlers, *Wilson Douglas*, Rounder 0047, *Woody Simmons*, Elderberry ER 002, and *Melvin Wine*, Poplar LP 1, seem most representative. Other notable traditional musicians are the multi-instrument playing *Frank George*, Kanawha 307, *Nimrod Workman*, Rounder 0076, and *Oscar and Eugene Wright*, Rounder 0089. Old-time banjo may be heard on *Elmer Bird's Greatest Licks*, Fret n Fiddle 956, and *Andrew F. Boarman*, June Appal 025 (which also has autoharp), while *Worley Gardner*, Oak Leaf OL 3-72, and Russell Fluharty, *West Virginia Heritage*, Page LP 601, play hammered dulcimer. *Shaking Down the Acorns*, Rounder 0018, and *A Study of a West Virginia Family's Tradition*, Library of Congress 65/66, document the field-recorded material by the Hammons Family of Pocahontas County. Of the many revival groups that feature old-time music, the best may well be Trapezoid, heard on *Three Forks of Cheat*, Rounder 0113; and *Now and Then*, Flying Fish FF239. Also able are the efforts of Hickory Wind on *At the Wednesday Night Waltz*, Adelphi AD 2002, and *Fresh Produce*, Flying Fish FF 018. Finally, the unrecorded Blind Ed Haley, a folk-fiddler parexcellence, was documented on some 1946 home-cut discs available on *Parkersburg Landing*, Rounder 1010, made long after he left his Logan County homeland for Ashland, Kentucky.

Some of the pioneer West Virginia bluegrass may be heard on *The Lilly Brothers and Don Stover: Early Recordings*, County 729, *The Lilly Brothers: Bluegrass Breakdown*, Rounder 01, *The Lilly Brothers: Country Songs*, Rounder 02, and *The Original Lonesome Pine Fiddlers: Early Bluegrass*, Old Homestead CS 127. Newer efforts in the more traditional vein include *The Lilly Brothers: What Will I Leave Behind*, County 742, *The Goins Brothers*, Rebel 1543, *The Goins Brothers at Their Best*, Old Homestead OH 90141, *Charlie Cline: Brushy Creek*, Old Homestead OH 90139, *The Butler Brothers: West Virginia Bluegrass*, Jalyn JLP 141; *Wilma Lee Cooper: A Daisy a Day*, Leather LBG 7705, and *Wilma Lee Cooper*, Rounder 0143. Progressive bluegrass by West Virginian Cliff Waldron includes *Right On*, Rebel 1496, and *Traveling Light*, Rebel 1500. More on the newgrass side are the Laurel Mountain Boys heard on *Long Black Beauty*, Old Homestead OH 90096, and *Carolina Sunshine*, Leather LBG 7710. Curley Ray Cline has several bluegrass fiddle albums, of which *Chicken Reel*, Rebel 1498, and *Boar Hog*, Old Homestead OH 90138, may be among the more appealing. High in musical quality is Ralph "Joe" Meadows, heard on *West Virginia Fiddler*, Old Homestead OH 90076, and *Super Fiddle*, Old Dominion, OD 498-13. Female folk-bluegrass vocalist Hazel Dickens may be heard to good advantage on *Hard Hitting Songs for Hard Hit People*, Rounder 0126.

Contemporary country stars sometimes find it increasingly difficult to get albums produced because of rising production costs.

Penny DeHaven, for instance has had sixteen chart songs but only one album, *Penny*, UAS 6821, but she also appears on the soundtrack *Broncho Billy*, Elektra, 5E 512. Terry Gregory is heard on *Just Like Me*, Handshake JW 37131, and *From the Heart*, Handshake FW 37907; the latter is the stronger effort overall but the former contains her biggest hit to date. Numerous Charlie McCoy albums remain on the market, with *The Nashville Hit Man*, Monument 6627, and *Greatest Hits*, Monument 7622, being representative. Billy Edd Wheeler's better material from the 1960s is out of print but *Wild Mountain Flower*, Flying Fish FF 085, showcases his composing and artistic abilities quite well. *Mayf Nutter: Goin' Skinny Dippin'*, GNP Crescendo GNPS 2104, is a fair sampling of that performer's music. A good collection of Mel Street material is available as *Mel Street's Greatest Hits*, Lake Shore LSM 511-K. Finally, perhaps the best-known of all West Virginia hillbilly musicians, although not just for his music, is represented on *U.S. Senator Robert Byrd: Mountain Fiddler*, County 769, which establishes him as a highly competent wielder of the bow with a true feel for his heritage.

Index

"Jackson," 157
Jackson, Alan, 192
Jackson, Aunt Molly, 156
Jackson, Denver, 162
Jackson, Harold (Shot), 111-12
Jackson, Milton, 102. *See also* Holden Brothers
Jackson, Stonewall, 176-77
Jackson County Barn Owls, 39
"Jailhouse Rag," 23
"Jailor's Daughter, The," 35
Jaker, Bill, 151
"Jamboree in the Hills," 71
Jamboree in the Hills, 71-72, 176, 187
Jamboree Records, 68
"Jamboree U.S.A." (radio show), 43-72, 148, 151, 175, 179, 187, 189, 192
James, Jimmy (Vincent Gamelli), 95
Jarvis, Reese, 37
Jeffers, George (Sleepy), 96, 111, 113, 118, 142-44, 147, 151, 157, 175, 192
Jeffers, Little Linda, 144
Jeffers, William M., Jr. (Slick), 96
Jeffers, William M., Sr. (Mack), 50, 53, 96
Jenkins, Andrew, 14
Jenkins, Gene, 60
Jenkins Family, 19
Jenks, Orville, 153
Jennings, Ordon L. (Gordon), 98-101, 124, 128, 136, 145-46
Jennings, Waylon, 103, 178
"Jesse James," 1
J.F.G. Coffee Boys, 101, 131
"Jim Walter Jubilee" (radio show), 146
Joe Woods' Harmony Band, 99
"John Hardy," 7, 9, 10, 14
"John Hardy Blues," 26
"John Henry," 7, 14, 24
John Henry Folk Festival, 160
"John L.'s Contract Time," 187
Johnnie and Jack, 117
"Johnny and Jane," 24
"Johnny Fair Syrup Time" (radio show), 171
Johnson, John F., 3, 12, 158
Johnson Mountain Boys, 167

Johnston, Jess, 26, 41-42
Jones, George, 69, 171, 192
Jones, Judie, 41, 101, 127
Jones, Julie, 41, 101, 127
Jones, Louis Marshall (Grandpa), 33, 46-47, 51, 71, 84, 95-96, 109, 124, 185, 187
Jones, Pap, 128
Jones, Raymond, 181
Jones, Rhoda, 50
Jones, Safe, 3
Jones, William W. (Silver Yodelin' Bill), 43-45, 53, 71, 161
Journal of American Folk-Lore, The, 9
Jubilee Boys, 92-93. *See also* Radio Dot
"Juke Box Play for Me," 65
"Juke Joint Johnny," 171
Justice, Dick, 37-38, 157
"Just Like Me," 181

"Kanawha March," 34
Kanawha Ramblers, 117
Kanawha Records, 156-57
Kanawha Singers, 41
Kanawha Valley Boys, 117
Kansas Clodhoppers, 48
"Kansas Roundup" (radio show), 106
"Katy Daley," 142
Kay, Francis, 102
"K.C. Blues," 24
KDKA, 43, 91, 149
Keaton, Charles (Big Foot), 74, 77, 84, 87, 96, 139-40, 151
Keeney, Lyle, 99
Keith, Leslie, 99-100, 117, 164
Kelly, Gene, 78
Kennedy, John L., 79
Kentucky Harmony, 13
Kentucky Hillbillies, 90
Kentucky Mountaineers, 74
Kentucky Pardners, 51. *See also* Monroe, Charlie
Kentucky Ridge Runners, 59. *See also* Belcher, Finley (Red)
Kentucky Twins (Mel and Stan Hankinson), 59
Kessinger, Clark, 33-34, 42, 83, 85, 116, 156
Kessinger, Luches, 33-35

"Wednesday Night Waltz," 34
Weeks, Steve, 3
WEIR, 177
WELC, 178
Welch Brothers, 158
WELD, 174, 180
Welling, Frank, 29-32, 38, 40, 42,
    74, 83, 86-88, 104, 116-17, 161,
    172, 184-85
Welling, Harvey, 30
Welling, Margie, 117
Welling, Thelma, 30, 74
Welling and McGhee, 30-32, 34
Welling and McGhee Trio, 30
Wellington, Sam, 177
Wellman, Curley, 77, 96, 139, 151
Wells, Fred, 92
Wells, Kitty, 117
"We Made Memories," 175
WEMM-FM, 173, 191
WEPM, 135
Wesbrooks, Cousin Wilbur, 66
Wesley, Charles, 13
West, Don, 159
West, Speedy, 173
Western Harp, 13
Western Pioneers, 139
Westfall, Ronnie, 166-67
"West Virginia," 147
West Virginia Boys, 166
West Virginia Coon Hunters, 28
"West Virginia Feud Song, A," 9
West Virginia Folk Festival, 154
West Virginia Folk-Lore Society,
    10-11
West Virginia Hillfolks, 133
"West Virginia Hills, The," 5-6, 32,
    41, 75
West Virginia Home Folks, 111
"West Virginia, I Love You," 167
West Virginia Melody Boys, 32, 39
West Virginia Mountain Boys, 90,
    124, 191
"West Virginia My Home," 167
West Virginia Network, 79, 83,
    103-4
West Virginia Night Owls, 27, 39
West Virginia Nite Hawks, 115
West Virginians, 127
"West Virginia Polka," 58
West Virginia Ramblers, 26, 74

West Virginia Revelers, 135
West Virginia Review, 109
West Virginia Snake Hunters, 29
West Virginia Trail Blazers, 29
West Virginia Travelers, 167
West Virginia University, 9-12,
    151, 155, 159
"We've Just Got to Have Them,
    That's All," 27
WFBR, 80
WFIL-TV, 56
WFMD, 135
WFSA, 170
WGNV, 117
WHAS, 49
WHDH, 75
Wheeler, Billy Edd, 157, 175
Wheeling Records, 61, 185
"When It's Lamplighting Time in
    the Valley," 41
"When the Roses Bloom Again for
    the Bootlegger," 25
"When the Ship Hit the Sand," 107
"When the Snowflakes Fall
    Again," 79
"When the Sun Sets in West
    Virginia," 167
"When They Found the Atomic
    Power," 57
"When You're Number Two," 178
Whetstone Run, 167
WHIS, 98-103, 105, 109, 117-18, 122,
    124, 126-28, 134, 144, 184, 186
Whispering Strings, 127-28
WHIS-TV, 144-45
White, Don (Walden Whytsell), 41-
    42, 174
White, Theodore, 179
Whiteacre Family, 158
White Oak Mountain Boys, 166
Whitt, Don, 146
Whitter, Henry, 19, 23
WHJC, 179
"Whoa Mule," 34
"Whole Dam Family, The," 36
"Whosoever Meaneth Me," 30
WHTN, 113-15,139,150
WHTN-TV, 142-43, 147
"Why Baby Why," 171
"Why Do You Bob Your Hair
    Girls?" 27